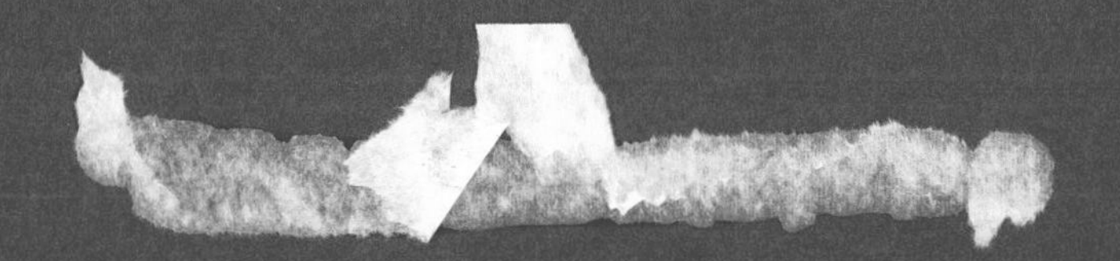

KT-418-808

30131 05729459 4
LONDON BOROUGH OF BARNET

WAKE UP

WAKE UP

Our eyes have been opened. We must never close them again.

PIERS MORGAN

HarperCollins*Publishers*

HarperCollins*Publishers*
1 London Bridge Street
London SE1 9GF

www.harpercollins.co.uk

First published by HarperCollins*Publishers* 2020

3 5 7 9 10 8 6 4 2

A catalogue record of this book is
available from the British Library

HB ISBN 978-0-00-839259-8
PB ISBN 978-0-00-839260-4

Printed and bound in Great Britain by
CPI Group (UK) Ltd, Croydon

MIX
Paper from
responsible sources
FSC™ C007454

This book is produced from independently certified FSC™ paper
to ensure responsible forest management.

For more information visit: www.harpercollins.co.uk/green

To John Ferriter.
'Be the person your dog thinks you are.'

CONTENTS

INTRODUCTION

The World's Gone Nuts

I don't know when it first hit me that the world had gone nuts.

It might have been when an American white woman named Rachel Dolezal self-identified as black on national television despite both her parents being white. That was nuts.

Or perhaps it was when Altrincham Grammar School for Girls in Manchester, England asked staff to refrain from calling female students 'girls' because it might offend transgender students – yet didn't change the gender-specific name of the school. That was nuts.

Maybe it was when there were strident calls from radical feminists – who, like all radicals, destroy support for their cause by taking everything to absurd extremes – for James Bond to be female. That was nuts.

Or was it when Google removed the egg from its salad emoji to make it 'more inclusive' to vegans? That was nuts.

It might have been when CeCe Telfer, a tall, powerfully built transgender woman, was named Female Athlete of the Year for 2019 by a sports news website after smashing women's college and state sprinting records – one year after competing far less successfully as a man. That was nuts.

Possibly, it was when students at the University of California, Berkeley demanded they be excused from exams because they 'didn't have enough privilege' to be able to handle them emotionally. That was nuts.

Or was it when other students at Oxford University in England banned clapping at student union events in case it triggered anxiety? That was nuts.

I pondered if it was when Marks & Spencer started selling gay sandwiches – the LGBT (lettuce, guacamole, bacon and tomato) to 'celebrate' Gay Pride season. Even my gay friends thought that was nuts.

Ultimately, I think the final straw for me came when Canadian Prime Minister Justin Trudeau called for the word 'mankind' to be outlawed because it was sexist. There, right there, was the purest, maddest example of the world going completely stark raving bonkers, and it came from one of the most powerful men, sorry 'persons', on Planet Earth. (Wait until Trudeau finds out the word 'man' appears in the word 'woman' ...)

So yes, the world had gone nuts. It had become a place where common sense was ignored, weakness celebrated, strength denigrated, failure replaced by 'participation prizes', accountability abandoned in the rush to blame others, dissenting views instantly crushed by a howling self-righteous mob and signalling one's dubious virtue was absolutely paramount. Why had the world gone this way? Who was causing this nonsense?

The answer is even more shocking than our inexorable descent into the abysmal PC-crazed abyss. For it's us liberals who are responsible. By 'us', I mean that I consider myself a liberal and it's my fellow liberals who have been driving this frantically illiberal assault on the very things we're supposed to stand for: freedom and tolerance.

This extraordinary state of affairs prompts the question, 'What *is* a liberal?' To which the answer is ... it's very hard to say anymore. Technically, the word 'liberal' is derived from the Latin words *liber* (meaning 'free', and also the root of 'liberty', meaning 'the quality or state of being free') and *liberalis* (meaning 'courteous, generous, gentlemanly').

The definitions of a liberal include 'one who is open-minded or not strict in the observance of orthodox, traditional or established forms or ways', a person who is 'willing to respect or accept behaviour or opinions different from one's own', 'favourable to or respectful of individual rights and freedoms', and 'concerned with broadening general knowledge and experience'.

Liberals believe that 'society should change gradually so that money, property and power are shared more equally'. Above all, liberals are supposed to be 'tolerant'. Yet here they are, screaming, shrieking, hollering and hectoring us all into a world of staggering intolerance and attempting to inhibit or silence our freedom of speech, particularly on our most pertinent societal issues.

HOW has this happened?

WHY has this happened?

WHAT will stop it?

When I first began writing this book in late 2019, I assumed it would lead to me being publicly 'cancelled' the moment it was published. I'd be shamed, vilified, mocked, abused, bullied and no-platformed. My book signings would be met with protests, possibly even threats of violence, and my media appearances to promote the book would be weirdly contentious. In fact, even the announcement I was writing a book on liberalism would be the catalyst for an immediate outpouring of 'liberal' rage on social media and accusations that I was just another middle-aged white conservative bad guy – many would refuse to believe I could possibly be a fellow liberal – trying to stop good people (like them) calling me out for my nasty, bigoted (in their eyes) opinions.

This, after all, had been happening to anyone who dared to challenge the woke world view. 'Woke' is a word that modern liberals proudly use to justify their illiberalism – only *they* are awake enough to see how the world should be, while the rest of us imbeciles are too sleepily stupid to understand.

As with so many things hijacked and abused by modern illiberal society, the term was first used with the very best of intentions in political ads supporting Abraham Lincoln during the 1860 presidential election. The 'Wide Awakes' movement was spawned by young Republicans to oppose the spread of slavery.

Being 'woke' burst into modern popular culture in a 1962 *New York Times* essay written by William Melvin Kelley entitled 'If You're Woke You Dig It', and in Erykah Badu's 2008 song 'Master Teacher' in which the soul singer repeats the phrase, 'I stay woke.'

It was supposed to indicate someone having a sharp political awareness of systemic social and racial injustices, which is an entirely admirable trait. But in recent years, being 'woke' has come to mean having an intransigent intolerance of myriad, often very trivial and pointless things, and the broadness of the 'woke' charge sheet is growingly absurdly long and often utterly ridiculous.

In the process, it's become a label attracting derision and mockery, gleefully used by right-wingers as a taunting tagline stick to beat liberals, and the essence of what being 'woke' originally stood for has been completely lost.

Rather than understand this, and re-calibrate what being 'woke' means, many liberals have instead become the very people their opponents mock them for – a bunch of constantly outraged illiberal lunatics who refuse to tolerate anyone or anything that doesn't fit their savagely prohibitive 'progressive' agenda.

INTRODUCTION

None of the faux outrage I anticipated over the publication of this book would bother me because I've spent years in the eye of the illiberal liberal storm. The woke crowd particularly loathed me because the informed ones know I'm actually a liberal. So, on paper, I'm one of them. I'm therefore the enemy within. For example, I consider myself to be a feminist, but whenever I say this, people – especially radical feminists – laugh with snorting, indignant derision. They think this must be a preposterous notion given how often and loudly I rail against absurd gender issues and the even more ridiculous antics of men-haters falsely claiming to be feminists. But I've loudly supported women's rights, as well as civil rights, gay rights and transgender rights (apart from the absurd new trend of limitless gender self-identification), and don't have a prejudiced bone in my body. Yet that hasn't stopped them regularly and furiously branding me racist, sexist, homophobic and transphobic.

There's no room for logic or reason in the world of illiberal liberalism. It's not what you believe that matters so much as how you express your beliefs, the precise language you use and a total unquestioning compliance with what *they* say is the way to behave. Of course, this is not just a problem for liberals. Extreme right-wingers can be just as self-righteous, obnoxious, intolerant, shaming and nasty.

Thanks to the explosion of social media fuelling echo chambers where people only expose themselves to singular thought processes that they already agree with, we have regressed as a world back thousands of years to the days when we existed in tribes that rarely met other tribes. In your own tribe, you dressed the same, spoke the same, behaved the same and had the same attitudes. Then slowly, you ventured outside of your tribe and encountered other tribes that dressed differently, spoke differently, behaved differently and had different attitudes. And both tribes responded to this startling discovery by deducing that the only way to handle it was to attack and kill the other tribe.

Twitter is the virtual version of that tribal warfare, especially when it comes to politics. You are pro-Trump or anti-Trump, but you can't be nuanced about Trump. In the same way that Britons can be passionately pro-Brexit or anti-Brexit, but they can't be neutral or fair-minded about it. The intolerant woke brigade are staunchly unwilling to hear opposing points of view, despite proudly proclaiming to be liberals.

Yet the baffling thing about these illiberal liberals is they are now behaving exactly like the people they profess to hate most. They've become the modern-day fascists, demanding we all lead our lives in a way that conforms strictly to their narrow world view. They're not interested in being tolerant or supporting freedom, and their inherent wokeness, paradoxically, causes societal division.

I have strong opinions about almost everything. And I actively dislike a lot of things that many might think are trivial and inconsequential, from papooses to vegan sausage rolls. But I don't want them banned, or to stop people being free to eat them or like them. I just want to exercise *my* freedom of speech to say I think they are abhorrent stains on society. And yes, I know that getting all worked up about a papoose or vegan sausage roll is in itself vaguely ridiculous, but I genuinely don't like either of them – and I should be allowed to say so without the entire world collapsing in a fit of collective hysterical pique. As a perfect illustration of my 'The World's Gone Nuts' mantra, my diatribe against papooses ended up as a two-minute segment on *NBC Nightly News*, America's most prestigious daily news broadcast.

That's where modern illiberal liberalism has dragged the world: everyone is free to have an opinion, right to the point where that opinion differs from the agreed 'acceptable' opinion dictated by self-righteous modern liberals who don't just think their opinion is right, they *know* it is. And woe betide anyone who dares to contradict them.

At this point, it's useful to go back in time to a more genuinely liberal world, and analyse why liberalism has been so badly traduced. John Locke, an English philosopher whose major works were written in the late seventeenth century, was dubbed the 'Father of Liberalism'. He is credited with developing the modern conceptions of identity and self through a continuity of consciousness. In simple terms, he believed we all start at birth with blank minds and develop knowledge by experience derived from sense perception. This is now known as 'empiricism'.

As Locke explained, 'Whatever I write, as soon as I discover it not to be true, my hand shall be the forwardest to throw it into the fire.' This shouldn't be a contentious statement, right? I mean, that is the very basis of education: we learn, we evolve.

Yet today, largely fuelled by the social media echo chambers, this rarely happens. Instead, we are driven to adopt increasingly strident opinions, often based on little scientific fact, and rather than being persuaded to change them when contradictory facts emerge, we double down on our own ill-informed opinion and we feel it even more strongly. This, surely, is the very antithesis of liberalism, is it not?

It is certainly the very antithesis of what Locke believed. His ideology was based on the premise that every opinion formed must be tested and challenged repeatedly, and that nothing is exempt from being disproven. He was also big on introspection, considering it vitally important to observe and carefully reflect on one's own emotions and behaviours, particularly when forming opinions.

Locke's overarching philosophy was that in a natural state, all people were equal and independent, and everyone had a basic right to defend 'life, health, liberty and possessions'. (Many scholars trace the phrase 'Life, Liberty and the pursuit of Happiness', in the American Declaration of Independence, to Locke's theory of rights.) But Locke didn't frame his liberalism in any political sense. That didn't start until long after he died in 1704. In fact, we know precisely when it did start.

There are many negative aspects to our new internet-powered world, but one of the great benefits is its ability to process historical data. Google has scanned millions of books published over centuries, and as a result the history of the word 'liberal', and the way it has been used, is clear to see. For many centuries, it held a strictly non-political tone and interpretation and was used to indicate generosity and tolerance. But from 1769, according to Google's Ngram Viewer – the online search engine that charts the historical frequency of phrase usage – everything changed. Suddenly, phrases like 'liberal plan', 'liberal views' and 'liberal principles' began appearing. *The Atlantic*, a leading American magazine, discovered this was largely down to two Scottish men, historian William Robertson and philosopher-economist Adam Smith, who both began repeatedly using the word 'liberal' in a political sense around that time.

Smith articulated what he perceived liberal principles to be: 'All systems either of preference or of restraint, therefore, being thus completely taken away, the obvious and simple system of natural liberty establishes itself of its own accord. Every man, as long as he does not violate the laws of justice, is left perfectly free to pursue his own interest his own way, and to bring both his industry and capital into competition with those of any other man, or order of men.'

In other words, liberalism is predicated on people being free to lead their lives how they wish, within the confines of the law. This seems a pretty good yardstick for my own understanding of what being a 'liberal' is all about.

The word 'liberal' took off towards the end of the century, spreading across Europe and then to the newly formed United States of America, and Google records the additional word 'liberalism' being used from around the 1820s. For a long time, Adam Smith's interpretation of it remained the accepted one. But today, liberalism has developed into almost the complete opposite of what he intended. It's come to represent a *lack* of freedom to pursue one's lawful life as one sees fit.

John Stuart Mill's *On Liberty*, published in 1859, has been cited as the closest thing to a founding tract for liberalism. In it, he explained why it is in the interest of society to give individuals the greatest possible right to speak and act as they wish, and to do so knowing we're all imperfect. Mill, like John Locke, believed that only by listening to those with whom we vehemently disagree, and testing our own strongly held ideas against equally strong counter-arguments, can we ever hope to reach the truth.

And if you consult Wikipedia today, it still defines 'liberalism' as, 'A political and moral philosophy based on liberty, consent of the governed and equality before the law. Liberals espouse a wide array of views depending on their understanding of these principles, but they generally support free market, free trade, limited government, individual rights (including civil rights and human rights), capitalism, democracy, secularism, gender equality, racial equality, internationalism, freedom of speech, freedom of the press and freedom of religion.'

In essence, liberalism can therefore be broadly defined in three ways: economic liberalism, meaning free competition and minimal government intervention in the economy; political liberalism, meaning the autonomy of the individual and standing up for the protection of political and civil liberties; and social liberalism, which promotes equality and protection for all minority groups. The combined power of these various facets of liberalism led the *Financial Times* to describe liberalism as 'the dominant Western ideology since the Second World War'.

Yet the rise of unabashed populists like Donald Trump and Boris Johnson, and events like Brexit, have led people to now conclude that liberalism is dying out. Indeed, Russian President Vladimir Putin went so far as to say liberalism has 'become obsolete'. He was supported by Hungarian Prime Minister Viktor Orbán, who said he wanted to create an 'illiberal state' because he believed authoritarian regimes like Russia and China worked better than liberal democracies.

One reason for the rise of populism as an 'antidote' to liberalism was the global financial crash of 2008. Michael Cox, a professor of international relations at the London School of Economics, told the BBC, 'Clearly, the liberal order we had until 2008 is in trouble.' He said that globalisation and the fact 'markets were allowed to determine everything' had brought about 'larger questions of identity and culture, with people feeling that their country is no longer their own'.

I would add the explosion of illiberal political correctness into the mix. If there's one thing guaranteed to drive people into the arms of a populist, it's the shrieking woke brigade telling them all day long what to think, say, eat, drink and laugh at. Yet those doing all the shrieking are actually a small minority. Twenty per cent of adults in the UK and USA use Twitter, and a recent survey in America found that, of those, 10 per cent post 80 per cent of the tweets. They tend to be the loudest and most aggressive, and therefore make the most noise and grab the most attention. They also tend to be very politically aware, and skew liberal.

This has created a weird two-worlds planet – those who are on Twitter and those who aren't. The former, especially the woke element of the 10 per cent doing 80 per cent of the tweeting, work themselves and like-minded tweeters into a relentless frenzy of self-righteousness that seeks to tell everyone how to live their lives, and shame, abuse and cancel them if they don't follow the exact rules laid down by the PC police. The latter, those not on Twitter, have no idea this is going on, and care even less, but when they're told, usually by mainstream media, that a bunch of mad-eyed PC cops wants to ban them from laughing at inappropriate jokes, they feel angry. Very, very angry. And that anger manifests itself in a vote for Trump or Brexit. The perverse irony of all this modern hysterical illiberalism is that it propels people who might otherwise consider themselves liberal into the arms of nationalists and authoritarians, who themselves like to exercise illiberal control over people.

Now as a liberal, I completely understand feeling angry at being told how to behave, particularly by people whose own behaviour and lifestyle appear so joyless and unappealing. I just want to get on with my life, enjoying what I enjoy doing within the parameters of the law, and exercising my right to free speech without some howling mob of purple-haired, ring-nosed, Trump-loathing, meat-hating, men-detesting lunatics ordering me to be like them instead or risk my life being ruined.

I wouldn't mind the woke crowd so much if they were prepared to engage me in proper civilised debate – but they're not. They don't see any need to debate anything because they're so utterly convinced that they are 100 per cent right about everything and hypocritically refuse to acknowledge the importance of discourse in a liberal society. If we all follow this path, democracy will surely die.

Politics is now so horribly toxic and divisive, it doesn't leave room for anyone not on the extremities, and least of all old-fashioned liberals who believe in free speech. And it's not just Vladimir Putin who thinks this marks the death of liberalism. Stephen Fry, speaking at the Festival for Dangerous Ideas in Sydney, said the same. 'A grand canyon has opened up in our world,' he said, 'and the cracks grow wider every day. As it widens, the armies on each side shriek more and more incontinently at their perceived enemies across the divide, their gestures and insults ever huger, cruder and louder. Classic liberalism and its postwar ideology of social democracy are dead. It's over, it's had its day. We've woken up to find ourselves uprooted and displaced. We are the ones cowering down in the ravine while the armies clash above. No one cares what we think.'

Fry was at pains to stress that although his own sympathies leaned more left than right, both sides in this ferocious culture war were to blame. 'Is that what is meant by the fine art of disagreement?' he asked. 'A plague on both their houses.' And he concluded with this advice: 'If someone is behaving like an arsehole, it isn't cancelled out by you behaving like an arsehole. Be better. Not better than they are. But better than you are. The shouting, the kicking, the name calling, spitting hatred, the dogmatic distrust, all have to stop.'

Of course, he's right. And I've been as guilty of this as anyone, frequently losing my rag on Twitter about everything from my beloved football team Arsenal to America's inexplicable love affair with guns. But one thing I've learned, the hard way, is the more you scream down those with whom you disagree, the less chance you have of winning an argument. This is not a lesson most people even want to hear, let alone heed.

Since Fry made his speech, things have got immeasurably worse. People are more entrenched, more hysterical, more abusive than ever before – and the worst offenders, by far, are the wokies and their intransigent illiberal liberalism. They scream and shout about the intolerance of others, the infringing of their rights, the excruciating difficulties of their day-to-day existence. They are constantly 'triggered' by things that offend and upset them. But the irony is that there are many reasons to believe this remains the best time ever to inhabit Planet Earth.

New York Times columnist Nick Kristof declared at the end of the last decade, 'If you're depressed by the state of the world, let me toss out an idea: In the long arc of human history, 2019 has been the best year ever.' As evidence, he cited record low levels of child deaths (whereas in 1950, 27 per cent of kids died by the age of 15, now that percentage is just 4 per cent) and record highs for adult literacy (90 per cent of adults are now literate). He also stated, 'Every single day in recent years, another 350,000 people got their first access to electricity, 200,000 more got piped water for the first time, and 650,000 went online for the first time.' Kristof concluded, 'When I was born in 1959, a majority of the world's population had always been illiterate and lived in extreme poverty. By the time I die, illiteracy and extreme poverty may be almost eliminated – and it's difficult to imagine a greater triumph for humanity on our watch.'

The good news doesn't stop there. People are living longer than ever before, thanks in part to more diseases being eradicated than at any time in history. Life expectancy worldwide is now 71 years, and in developed countries it's 80 years. That compares to an average of 30 for most of the 200,000 years of human existence, and that figure remained unchanged as we entered the twentieth century. Fewer wars are happening, and fewer people are dying from violent deaths.

Steven Pinker, the Canadian-American cognitive psychologist who has written a lot about why this is the greatest time to be alive, estimated that in prehistoric times, around 500 people out of every 100,000 were killed by other humans every year. Today, he estimates that annual figure to have fallen to just 6–8 people per 100,000, and even lower in developed countries. It's way safer in other ways too – with far smaller rates of accidental deaths from fire, water or falling off buildings thanks to better regulation and warning systems.

There's less poverty than ever – global extreme poverty has fallen to under 10 per cent of the world's population, when 200 years ago it was 90 per cent. We're better educated; over 90 per cent of the world aged between 15 and 23 can read and write, compared to 15 per cent for most of previous recorded history. And the percentage of girls who can do both has rocketed. Young people today have far higher IQs than their grandparents, and the global average score is rising at a rate of three points every new decade. Democracy has exploded. In 1850, only 7 per cent of countries were 'democratic', with their people living in freedom. Today, it's 70 per cent. We do fewer chores than ever (while in 1920, American families spent 11.5 hours per week on laundry, today it's just 90 minutes), and the amount of food available to people has soared.

In other words, this is a pretty damn good time to be a human being – safer, healthier, more prosperous, better fed and more peaceful than ever. Yet, for some inexplicable reason, many young people appear convinced this is the worst, scariest and most offensive time to ever exist, as their ludicrously over-the-top online antics prove. Staggeringly, they even make right-wingers look relatively tolerant.

So, I began 2020 sitting at my office desk, constructing a book based around a burning desire to try to persuade my fellow liberals to stop behaving like arseholes, even if they think everyone else is, and start behaving like liberals again.

To go back to being liberal. To re-learn the importance of freedom, particularly in relation to free speech. To regain a proper perspective on life. And to do so not as the devil so many wokies perceive me to be, but as potentially their saviour.

Then came coronavirus – and everything changed. The world got something it didn't want but perhaps, in a strange, perverse way, it needed – a global crisis of such magnitude that it made every one of us rethink the way we think about life. A tempest so torrid that it swept away so much that was dividing us and gave us that new, sharp perspective about what really matters that I felt was so lacking in much of society. Or it did for a while, anyway.

Locked down in our homes and unable to enjoy our normal freedoms, we re-established connections with family, friends, local communities and nature. Celebrity culture was shunned for a new appreciation of more deserving, non-famous stars – health and care workers. And wokery was temporarily banished because honestly nobody had the energy for it when really serious shit was going down.

Then, to my horror, it slowly came creeping back and eventually exploded in a summer of madness after the despicable killing of George Floyd in America, at the knee of a cop. The world took all leave of its senses, and illiberal liberalism rose up with even greater zealousness and ferocity than before the pandemic, tearing down – literally, in the case of statues – the very culture and history of great nations. It was like we'd learned absolutely nothing from such a life-changing event. I was reminded of the movie *Awakenings*, in which a group of zombie-like patients are brought back to their old, vibrant lives by a brilliant doctor and a wonder drug, only for the drug to then wear off and all the patients slump back to semi-comatose states again.

As the virus wreaked its havoc, I abandoned the original idea for this book, a thematic series of extended essays examining how woke culture had sent the world nuts. I've changed during this crisis, as I think we all have – for good and bad. It's made me re-evaluate a lot of things I thought, how I view the issues that had been sending everyone nuts, and how my own behaviour may have contributed to the problem. And, ironically, the same people who had spent the past few years lambasting me began to laud me, and those who had cheered me from the Twitter rooftops began to castigate me.

This was a weird evolution for me, but one that said a lot about how coronavirus has awakened the entire planet in what has been one of the most extraordinary, dramatic, scary and riveting episodes in modern history. As someone who has been a diarist for 25 years, I concluded that the best way to explain that change was in real time, as it happened.

This, then, is an account of how, thanks to a devastating pandemic, we've been given the wake-up moment of our lives, and why we cannot, *must* not, go back to sleep.

JANUARY

'Wuhan's as big as London ...'

WEDNESDAY 1 JANUARY 2020

The world seems relatively quiet this morning, though there's a disconcerting story coming out of China, where health authorities say they're investigating 27 cases of a new strain of viral pneumonia in the city of Wuhan in Central China which has left many of the people infected seriously ill.

There are rumours on Twitter that it may be another outbreak of SARS but Chinese officials are playing them down. 'The cause of the disease is not clear,' the official *People's Daily* newspaper said, citing unnamed hospital officials, continuing, 'We cannot confirm it is what's being spread online, that it is SARS virus. Other severe pneumonia is more likely.'

China doesn't have a good record for transparency in this area – it lied for weeks when SARS first erupted in 2003. And suggestions of something far nastier than just 'severe pneumonia' this time have been fuelled by the fact that Wuhan's massive Huanan Seafood Market – one of the country's many infamous 'wet markets' full of live animals – has today been shut down as a 'precaution'.

FRIDAY 3 JANUARY

It hasn't taken long for 2020 to live down to 2019's often bafflingly insane standards of 'woke' absurdity.

An employment tribunal judge today ruled that 'ethical veganism' qualifies as a philosophical belief protected under UK law. The successful claimant, a self-proclaimed 'ethical vegan' named Jordi Casamitjana, asserted he was fired by his own employer, animal welfare charity the League Against Cruel Sports, in April 2018 because he told colleagues their employer's pension fund was being invested in companies that experiment on animals.

The charity rejected the allegation, but the case really centred on whether 'ethical vegans', who follow strict vegan diets and oppose the use of animals for any purpose including laboratory testing, are entitled to the same legal rights and protections surrounding their 'belief' as, say, a person has for their religion, or other protected characteristics like their race, sex, pregnancy, maternity and sexuality. The answer, apparently, is yes. Judge Robin Postle said he was 'satisfied overwhelmingly' that ethical veganism meets the criteria of the Equality Act as a philosophical belief and not just an opinion. 'It is cogent, serious and important,' he concluded, 'and worthy of respect in democratic society.'

Of course, the news was greeted with raucous celebration by the more radical and preachy members of the vegan community, which has spent the past two days haranguing people like me into giving up meat for the dreaded 'Veganuary'. Finally, they've got what they want: legal validation for their war on carnivores. Kale-munching is no longer a lifestyle choice, it's a right. And as with all rights in the modern world, that brings with it an instant onslaught of self-righteousness and virtue-signalling. The latter, for the uninitiated, is 'the action or practice of expressing opinions or sentiments intended to demonstrate one's good character or the moral correctness of one's position on a particular issue'. In other words, doing or saying something to make oneself look virtuous. Since the advent of social media, this affliction has become a scourge of biblical proportions. Now, there's nothing wrong with virtue, it's just behaviour showing high moral standards. Nor is there anything wrong with signalling, that's just conveying information or instructions by means of a gesture, action or sound. The problem comes when you combine the two and start to signal your virtue; especially if you're signalling an entirely different virtue to the one that actually exists inside your soul.

I began to notice this curious phenomenon several years ago when a few famous friends of mine began tweeting (aka 'signalling') extraordinarily virtuous thoughts to their millions of followers that, let me be kind here, bore little relation to what they would spout to me over dinner. They do it to be liked – literally. They want to rack up 'likes' on social media, believing it to be a measure of their apparent popularity. To be most effective, the virtue-signalling needs to be expressed with extreme outrage, and preferably punctuated with profanity to show the world you REALLY F*CKING CARE!!!!

Veganism attracts the very worst kind of virtue-signallers.

I'll be honest, I find vegans annoying. Not the quiet ones who get on with their meat-free lives without bothering the rest of us, but the noisy, angry ones who demand we all do the same as them or automatically expose ourselves as disgusting monsters. And from my experience, most vegans are very, very noisy. As the joke goes, 'How do you know if someone's a vegan? Don't worry, they'll soon tell you.' Like all the best jokes, it carries with it a truism.

I like to eat meat. In fact, I like to gorge on beef, lamb, chicken, pork and, yes, even veal. I know exactly how it's all produced – vegans delight in constantly detailing the precise gory details lest we forget – and I still like eating meat. Just as many animals like eating other animals. I don't think there's anything a vegan can possibly say to me that will ever change my mind, although I am open, as with everything, to a reasonable discussion about it. The problem is that radical vegans, like all radical activists, don't want to be reasonable let alone have a discussion.

I honestly don't care if people want to be vegans. If they truly want to spend their life forgoing the joys of meat to dine on tasteless plants, that's their problem not mine. Or, rather, it's their life, not mine. But I do care when they decide to lecture me on how repulsive I am and try to push their eating habits onto me. Particularly when they try to play the holier-than-thou card, as they do so often.

As with all 'woke' activists, there is a woeful lack of tolerance from radical vegans. They want to shame, vilify, silence and convert meat-eaters, berating us into subservient compliance to their way of life. It's not enough that I respect their right to eat what they like; unless I follow their path then I am the enemy.

Whenever I publicly express my love of eating meat I am immediately greeted with a barrage of abuse on social media and demands for me to be 'cancelled'. This nasty uncompromising attitude was best typified by an incident in 2018 when a group of 20 vegans from a group called Direct Action Everywhere stormed the Brazilian-themed Touro Steakhouse in Brighton on the south coast of England (11 miles from the village of Newick where I grew up and still have a home), screaming and shouting, waving signs and placards, and playing loud sounds of cows being slaughtered. 'It's not meat, it's violence!' they hollered.

Unfortunately for the protestors, there was a large stag party of young men in the restaurant who retaliated by leaping to their feet and chanting, 'Stand up if you love red meat!' The activists didn't know what to do, so they just screamed their abuse even louder, as if somehow that would persuade a bunch of boozed-up carnivores to instantly renounce meat. Of course, that was never going to happen. In fact, all their antics achieved was to encourage the meat-eaters to want to eat even more meat. We see the same thing unfolding relentlessly online – abuse and shouting, with no intent to discuss, listen or learn.

This is why I suspect Mr Casamitjana's 'win' will turn out to be a loss for vegans in the long run, because people just don't like being told what to do, or think, or say, or eat – especially by angry activists shouting in their face. 'Woke' campaigners like this never understand that by adopting this kind of rigid, non-compromising approach to absolutely everything, they may win a battle or two but they won't win the war. They genuinely believe the more they harangue and hector, the more they will persuade, yet usually the complete opposite is true. And at the heart of all this enraged intransigence lies an absurd hypocrisy: it's not liberal, or even close to it. The whole principle of liberalism is predicated on a willingness to be tolerant of other people's views, not violently opposed to even considering them.

Yet even the most powerful companies in the world are rolling over to radical illiberal activism. Tech giant Google used to have a salad emoji on its search engine platform that contained the basics of most salads, including lettuce, tomato and a boiled egg. But this was deemed 'offensive' because the egg was not inclusive for vegans. So, the egg was removed. Jennifer Daniel, Google's 'user experience manager', proudly announced the change with this tweet: 'There's big talk about inclusion and diversity at Google so if you need any evidence of Google is making this priority, may I direct your attention to the [salad] emoji – we've removed the egg ... making this a more inclusive vegan salad.'

I was curious why Google felt the need to do this. Ms Daniel, when confronted with widespread scorn, said it was to fall in line with something called the Unicode Consortium which chooses and creates new emojis.

'Hello carnivores, vegans and everyone in between!' she tweeted again. 'Just want to clarify that the goal of the salad emoji redesign was to create an image more faithful to Unicode's description: "A bowl of healthy salad, containing lettuce, tomato and other salad items such as cucumber." Bon appetite [sic]!'

Aside from her poor French spelling, I noticed there was also no sign of cucumber in either the old or new salad emoji which seems very exclusionary to cucumbers and offensive to those who like eating them. Twitter was merciless on Google's vegan virtue-signalling.

'Excuse me,' said a Twitter user named Kuraha, 'I don't have legs, could you cut yours off, so I feel included? That's how it works, right?'

Others were concerned about people with allergies to tomatoes or lettuce: why didn't Google care about their feelings? For my part, I was bemused why my preferences were now deemed offensive. I like eating eggs. I've always liked eating eggs. Many scientists cite eggs as being very nutritious as part of a well-balanced diet, which is why billions of people have eaten eggs quite happily for centuries. Yet Google will no longer let me see eggs in a salad emoji because they're now 'offensive'? This is surely just as exclusionary as removing the eggs just to please vegans. Why are vegan rights more important than my carnivore rights? Who decided that? Do I have to go to court like Mr Casamitjana to fight for my right not to have my belief in eggs discriminated against in this way?

The British Egg Industry Council was similarly puzzled. 'We completely understand that vegans choose not to eat eggs, but in the UK egg sales are up by almost 5 per cent,' a spokesman said. 'Many people love them, so it seems a shame for the majority to be missing out due to concern for offending one group. Eggs are the perfect salad accompaniment – full of protein, vitamins and minerals.'

Inevitably, crafty commercial minds have realised that there is money to be made from all this nonsense. A year ago this week, Greggs, the British high street bakery chain, announced on Twitter, 'The wait is over ... #vegansausageroll.' I was incredulous. Who the hell had been waiting for a vegan sausage roll? And how can a sausage be vegan anyway? The very notion of a 'vegan sausage roll' makes no sense. Sausages are *meat* products. From the time they were first invented in 3100 BCE by the Sumerians in Mesopotamia – modern-day Iraq – they have always been made of meat. And anyway, why would vegans *want* to eat something named after a meat product if they hate meat so much?

As a meat-eater, I take exception to the use of meat labels in this way. The whole thing is a total sham, a con on the public designed to make people feel vegan-virtuous. The companies behind it are just virtue-signalling their spurious vegan credentials to make money from a small but noisy minority of their consumer base. I tweeted back at Greggs, 'Nobody was waiting for a vegan bloody sausage roll, you PC-ravaged clowns.'

'Oh, hello Piers, we've been expecting you,' they instantly replied, with a rapidity that suggested they had indeed been expecting me. Of course, all hell broke loose as the world's vegans rushed to abuse and shame me, playing right into Greggs' greedy little hands.

To sum up just how ridiculous this corporate virtue-signalling is, Wagamama has just announced its new dish: vegan tuna. 'Welcome to the bench our new vegan suika tuna,' the firm tweeted. 'Yep, you read that right. Vegan tuna. Now, that's next wave. But catch it while you can. Available exclusively for #veganuary only.'

Of course, there is no tuna in it. It's actually grilled watermelon.

SATURDAY 4 JANUARY

President Trump has taken out the second most powerful man in Iran, its military leader General Qasem Soleimani, who was blown up by a US drone strike on a convoy taking him to a meeting with the Iraqi prime minister in Baghdad.

This stunning move follows a series of recent Iran-inspired rocket attacks on US bases in Iraq, culminating in one a few days ago that killed an American contractor and injured US and Iraqi soldiers. Trump responded by ordering US strikes on Kataeb Hezbollah, the Iran proxy militia that carried out the rocket attacks, which prompted the group's furious supporters to break into the US embassy in Baghdad and set fire to the reception area.

For Trump and his military advisors, this situation was disturbingly reminiscent of the terrorist attack on the US consulate in Benghazi, Libya in 2012 when US Ambassador Christopher Stevens was killed. The president, who'd been heavily critical of his predecessor Barack Obama's inaction over that fiasco, knew that failure to act decisively now when confronted with a similar situation was not an option.

'Iran will be held fully responsible for lives lost, or damage incurred, at any of our facilities,' Trump tweeted. To which Iran's Supreme Leader Ayatollah Khamenei responded on

Twitter by taunting back at the US president, 'You can't do anything.'

There is something very surreal and unnerving about World War III being possibly started through the prism of a tweet exchange.

At the same time, the US reportedly received credible intelligence that Soleimani was actively plotting to kill more American military and diplomatic personnel in the Middle East. This represented a direct and immediate challenge to the security of the United States, but one that Iran arrogantly presumed America would do nothing about. They were wrong.

President Trump considered various military options presented to him and chose the killing of Soleimani to send Iran a firm message that yes, actually, the United States *could* and *would* do something to defend itself. Will Iran up the ante, or back down? Either way, this is the biggest test of Donald Trump's presidency and it will be fascinating to see how he handles a real crisis.

I've been friends with Trump for 13 years, since I competed in, and won, his inaugural season of *Celebrity Apprentice USA*. During the next few years, we exchanged frequent email correspondence, and he would call from time to time for a chat about life and the universe. I also acted as his boardroom advisor on numerous subsequent episodes of *The Apprentice* and interviewed him many times when I joined CNN. I've always liked Trump personally; the man I knew before he ran for president was funny, street-smart, flamboyant, gossipy and outrageously opinionated. He's also ferociously loyal – *if* you're loyal to him.

When I left CNN in 2014, returned to the UK and was no longer of any use to him, he rang me repeatedly to check how I was doing. During his 2016 election campaign, he gave me the only two British TV interviews he conducted as a presidential candidate, and since becoming president, he's given me the only three British TV interviews he's conducted as leader of the free world. He even invited me onto Air Force One to do one of them, which was an extraordinary experience. So, he treats his friends as well as he treats his enemies badly. Punch him in the face, metaphorically, and he'll delightedly keep punching back for the rest of time. Conflict is something Trump revels in.

It's not easy being friends with the president of the United States when he's as divisive as Trump. I've been pilloried in the media for it, abused mercilessly on Twitter, and even been subjected to verbal tirades in the street. But I've stayed friends with him because I like him, and he's been good to me, and because, contrary to popular myth, I've never let it stop me criticising him in print or on air when I feel the need to – often quite sharply, as I've done on issues like gun control, climate change, trophy hunting, his call for a Muslim ban, his 'grab 'em by the p*ssy' *Access Hollywood* tape, his 'fake news' attacks on the media and his ban on transgenders in the military. I've written over 100 columns about him for the *Daily Mail*'s US website and around half of them have been critical. I've also made it clear many times that I wouldn't personally vote for Trump, even if I could, as I'm not a Republican. But I think he's an extraordinary political character and find myself agreeing with as much of what he says and does as I disagree.

I see both good and bad in Trump, and right and wrong. In some ways, he is one of the least right-wing Republican presidents ever. For example, he was the first one to reference the LGBT community in his inauguration speech (which made his later transgender military ban all the more incomprehensible). His decision to kill Soleimani is a rarity in an otherwise militarily calm tenure in which Trump's gone out of his way to avoid the wars that most US leaders get sucked into, withdrawing most US troops from Iraq, Syria and Afghanistan, and forging peace with conventional US enemies like North Korea and Russia. He's presided over a very successful economy, achieved record low unemployment levels and launched what many see as an entirely justified trade war with China, a country that has been economically ransacking America for several decades. And yet a minute cannot pass without the 'woke' community being mortally offended by Trump. He seems to turn many liberals into permanent gibbering wrecks of blazing fury.

In fact, it was Trump's election which exposed one of the biggest problems at the core of wokedom: modern liberals, especially famous ones, are *very* sensitive. Not a minute of any day goes by without them being outraged by something. And that something is usually Donald Trump. The wild, foot-stomping, shrieking mania that greets the president's every utterance and movement is beyond anything I have ever witnessed in global politics.

Now, let me say this: much of the adverse reaction to Trump's presidency is perfectly understandable and acceptable. He's an inflammatory, deliberately provocative character who likes nothing better than winding up what he calls the 'sneering elites' into a slathering lather of blind rage.

So, I have no issue with people complaining or protesting about him, or with journalists holding his factual feet to the fire. But hysteria never won an argument, and I say that as someone who has occasionally got hysterical about stuff and never won those arguments.

MONDAY 6 JANUARY

I awoke at 1 am, still jetlagged, to watch Ricky Gervais host the Golden Globe Awards in Hollywood. The acid-tongued British comedian is one of the very few celebrities in the world who finds the whole idea of some kind of superior Planet Celebrity utterly ridiculous and revels in tearing to pieces the inherent pomposity and hypocrisy that lies at its heart.

As such, he is the perfect awards show host, because he doesn't give a rat's arse about offending the world's biggest stars sitting right in front of him like rabbits cowering in the middle of a motorway as a juggernaut lorry bears down on them with no intention of stopping even though the driver can see their terrified little eyes.

Gervais set out his stall a few days ago by saying: 'It [the Globes] is a room full of the biggest virtue-signallers and hypocrites in the world, so I've got to go after that.' And go after that he most definitely did. His opening monologue only lasted seven minutes and forty-two seconds. But that was long enough for him to burst the absurdly two-faced PC-crazed bubble that surrounds modern Hollywood. It was brutal, vicious ... and exactly what that crowd needed, even if their shocked, frozen (and not just from all the Botox) faces suggested they'd just stumbled into hell on earth. It was also what we all needed watching back at home.

Gervais point-blank refuses to bow to the modern-day anti-free-speech ultra-woke McCarthyism, ranting against it all day every day on Twitter with a mixture of incredulity, defiance and savagery. He doesn't care about all the flak he takes because his view is that comedy is comedy, jokes are jokes and thin-skinned little snowflakes who constantly throw their offended toys out of the pram should simply be ignored because their outrage doesn't – and shouldn't – trump his right to freedom of speech. And he doesn't care how rich, powerful or famous you are – everyone cops it.

That's why Ricky Gervais is the most successful comedian on the planet. From the moment Gervais appeared on stage and flashed that mischievous grin, it was clear he was going to be taking no prisoners. Though ironically, he started by targeting an actual recent prisoner. 'I came here in a limo tonight,' he quipped, 'and the licence plate was made by Felicity Huffman.' Huffman, a former Golden Globes-winning actress who is married to actor William H. Macy, was jailed in 2019 for her part in an infamous college exam cheating scandal after she admitted paying for a proctor to correct SAT questions answered incorrectly by her daughter.

'No, shush,' taunted Gervais as the audience reacted in dismay. 'It's her daughter I feel sorry for. That must be the most embarrassing thing that's ever happened to her ... and her dad was in *Wild Hogs*.'

Having immediately broken his solemn pre-show promise not to attack any individuals – a promise I knew he'd only made to throw everyone off their guard – Gervais sprayed a machine gun of mockery at big names in the audience, calling Joe Pesci 'Baby Yoda', ridiculing Martin Scorsese for his lack of height and ribbing Leonardo DiCaprio for his preference for youthful girlfriends.

'*Once Upon a Time in Hollywood*, nearly three hours long,' he smirked. 'Leonardo DiCaprio attended the premiere and by the end his date was too old for him.' As the camera panned to a clearly embarrassed DiCaprio, ruthless Gervais stuck the boot in further. 'Even Prince Andrew was, like, "Come on, Leo, mate. You're nearly fifty, son!"' (The prince had been accused of sexually assaulting young girls, which he denied.) By now, I was laughing so hard I went into a volatile coughing fit. But actors are relatively easy targets. It was when Gervais directed his fire at Hollywood itself that he excelled himself.

He accused the movie executives in the room of being 'terrified of Ronan Farrow' (the Pulitzer Prize-winning author whose investigative #MeToo journalism brought down Harvey Weinstein and a number of other powerful people) and branded them 'perverts', sneering, 'He's coming for ya!' Then he suggested Andrew's multi-millionaire paedophile and star-befriender pal Jeffrey Epstein killed himself, and as the audience booed (again), he scoffed, 'Shut up, I know he's your friend, but I don't care ... you had to make your own way here in your own plane, didn't you?'

He brilliantly mocked the town's dubiously self-interested reactive diversity initiatives. 'We were going to do an *In Memoriam* this year but when I saw the list of people who had died, it wasn't diverse enough. No, it was mostly white people and I thought, nah, not on my watch.' Gervais even hammered his own employers for the night, the Hollywood Foreign Press, as 'very, very racist' in reference to the lack of people of colour in many award categories, said 'most films are awful' – at an event supposedly celebrating film! – and railed against the new brand of corporate giants dominating Tinseltown.

'Apple roared into the TV game with *The Morning Show*,' he said, 'a superb drama about the importance of dignity and doing the right thing ... made by a company that runs sweatshops in China.' Ironically, Apple boss Tim Cook – who has denied the company uses sweatshops – looked rather sweaty himself when the cameras were on him in the audience.

Then Gervais rounded on the hypocritical stars again.

'You all say you're woke but the companies you work for – I mean, unbelievable. Apple, Amazon, Disney. If ISIS started a streaming service, you'd call your agent, wouldn't you?'

More gasps, but Gervais wasn't finished with them yet.

'So, if you do win an award tonight, don't use it as a platform to make a political speech. You're in no position to lecture the public about anything. You know nothing about the real world. Most of you spent less time in school than Greta Thunberg. So, if you win, come up, accept your little award, thank your agent and your God, and f*ck off, OK?!'

This wasn't how it was supposed to be. This was a Hollywood awards night, where stars are sycophantically praised not unceremoniously buried. This was intended as another chance to virtue-signal and remind the world how awful Trump is, not themselves! But Gervais knows that celebrities and comedians whacking Trump are two-a-penny. Far rarer is the star who shines a light on the stinking hypocrisy of Hollywood itself, the place that loves to take the high moral ground yet itself lurks in a sewer of immorality. It takes courage to do this in a town that can make or break entertainers' careers, real balls of glistening steel.

'Our next presenter starred in Netflix's *Bird Box*,' Gervais said towards the end, introducing Sandra Bullock. 'A movie where people survive by acting like they don't see a thing. Sort of like working for Harvey Weinstein.'

As the audience gasped and groaned again in more fake 'what, me?' horror – beautifully proving his point – before booing him, Gervais jeered back, '*You* did it, I didn't, you did it ...'

TUESDAY 7 JANUARY

The new year has begun for *Good Morning Britain* the way the old one ended, with Prime Minister Boris Johnson and his cabinet ministers refusing to come on the show. They're still sulking after our fearless correspondent Jonathan Swain chased Boris into a large fridge at a dairy farm on the eve of the election as we tried to get him to honour his repeated public promises to give us an interview.

They should heed the words of former Labour deputy leader Tom Watson, who writes in his new book, *Downsizing*, 'I knew for a fact that many Westminster politicians disliked appearing on *GMB*, fearing the programme's notoriously tough interviews. The combative Piers Morgan and the forensic Susanna Reid were indeed a formidable duo – I'd seen many a guest shrink as they received a breakfast-time grilling. But I'd always enjoyed the experience. I liked sparring with Piers, and I admired Susanna's incisive line of questioning.'

When I thanked him on Twitter for his comments, he replied, 'I honestly think Labour members should judge our leadership and deputy leadership candidates on their ability to handle tough interviews.' I couldn't agree more. What's baffling about the ban is that many politicians have told me in the past they get more feedback from constituents after they do *GMB* than any of the political shows, and particular praise if they give as good as they get.

I don't view these encounters with a cynical Jeremy Paxman 'why are these bastards lying to me?' mindset, but more a 'let's rough them up a bit and see what they're made of' attitude. The good ones will rise to the challenge and see their reputations enhanced, the bad ones will wilt under pressure and reveal themselves as not fit for ministerial purpose. But frankly, if they don't have the stomach for an argument on breakfast television, how on earth would they cope with handling a serious crisis?

WEDNESDAY 8 JANUARY

Iran has responded to the killing of Soleimani by launching missile strikes at US bases in Iraq. It's being seen as a 'proportionate response' and not a dramatic escalation. In other words, Iran has heeded President Trump's words of dire warning if they try anything foolish, and blinked.

I think Trump was absolutely right to take him out. Soleimani was the world's most dangerous terrorist. As such, he was no different ideologically from other terror leaders like Al Qaeda chief Osama bin Laden who Obama took out with SEAL Team 6 special forces in Pakistan, or ISIS leader Abu Bakr al-Baghdadi, who blew himself up with a suicide vest two months ago when US special forces, on Trump's orders, tracked him down in Syria's Idlib province. Like Bin Laden and Al-Baghdadi, Soleimani's life was devoted to killing people via terrorism, including many Americans. And like them, he was killed to stop him directing more terror acts.

Yet unlike Bin Laden, Soleimani's death has been met with howls of protests from the world's liberals. Within minutes of it being confirmed, out sprang the usual suspect, mouth-foaming, Trump-loathing celebrities who erupt in breathless rage every time he speaks, tweets or does anything, often with little knowledge of what has actually happened.

Actress and #MeToo activist Rose McGowan actually apologised to Iran. 'Dear Iran,' she tweeted, 'the USA has disrespected your country, your flag, your people. Fifty-two per cent of us humbly apologise. We want peace with your nation. We are being held hostage by a terrorist regime. We do not know how to escape. Please do not kill us.'

When this bizarre *mea culpa* prompted understandable outrage, she retorted, 'Of course Soleimani was an evil man who did evil things. But that at the moment is not the f*cking point.'

It's not? McGowan later backtracked, explaining, 'OK, so I freaked out because we may have impending war ... I do not want any more American soldiers killed, that's it.'

Of course, that is precisely why Trump had Soleimani killed. Ms McGowan wasn't the only one who sounded confused. Colin Kaepernick, the NFL quarterback famed for his kneeling protests against racial injustice during the US national anthem, accused Trump of having a racist motivation.

'There is nothing new about American terrorist attacks on Black and Brown people for the expansion of American imperialism,' he tweeted.

What?! Kaepernick either doesn't know, or chose to deliberately ignore, that for many years Iran has been committing terror attacks on black and brown people for the expansion of its own imperialist agenda in the Middle East. This action had nothing to do with racism. Nor do I believe, as some are suggesting, that it was designed to create a distraction from Trump's imminent impeachment trial in the US Senate, due to start next week, which seems to be helping not hindering him in the polls anyway.

No, I share the view of retired General David Petraeus, one of America's finest military minds, who said Soleimani's death was 'bigger than Bin Laden, bigger than Al-Baghdadi' and a 'very significant effort to re-establish deterrence'. Petraeus explained, 'Soleimani was the architect and operational commander of the Iranian effort to solidify the so-called Shia crescent stretching from Iran to Iraq, through Syria into southern Lebanon. He is responsible for providing explosives and arms and other munitions that killed well over 600 American soldiers and many more of our coalition partners, so his death is of enormous significance. Many people had rightly questioned whether America's deterrence had eroded somewhat because of the relatively insignificant responses to the earlier actions.'

I agree. President Trump called Iran's menacing, threatening, cocky, murderous bluff – to put them back in their box. *He* gave *them* the 'slap in the face' they deserved and warrants praise, not hypocritical liberal outrage, for taking such bold action. Far from making the world a more dangerous place, the world just got a lot safer without the presence of a loathsome terror leader like Qasem Soleimani.

It should be a moment to unite Americans, but it's not. And once again, woke outrage spews across social media, furthering division and threatening to inhibit any discussion on what is an incredibly important moment in US politics. Other Trump-bashing stars, from singer John Legend to actors John Cusack and Alyssa Milano, also felt compelled to tell the world how disgusting it was that Soleimani had been killed. Oh, they all agreed Soleimani was a very bad man who killed lots of people, but they also think he should have been kept alive – to do what exactly? Continue killing lots more people?

Epitomising this seemingly absurd contradictory attitude was Democrat presidential candidate Elizabeth Warren, whose initial response to the news was this: 'Soleimani was a murderer, responsible for the deaths of thousands, including hundreds of Americans.' One day later, Warren had a re-think and said that, in fact, the bad guy was President Trump, who had 'assassinated a senior foreign military official'. It's no coincidence that Warren's dramatic change in tone came after 24 hours of rage from fellow liberals horrified that she had told the truth about Soleimani's murderous record. But when repeatedly pressed yesterday by Meghan McCain on *The View* as to whether Soleimani was a terrorist, Warren finally said, 'Of course he was.'

So, let me get this straight: Soleimani was a mass-murdering terrorist responsible for killing thousands of people, including hundreds of Americans, but should be left alone because it might 'escalate the situation with Iran'? I don't remember the risk of escalating conflict being an issue with the killing of Bin Laden, who was also responsible for murdering thousands of people, including many Americans. No, when Obama ordered the execution of Bin Laden, liberals cheered him around the world. But Trump Derangement Syndrome, as the president's supporters call this kind of behaviour, dictates there must be a very different response when the current occupant of the White House kills a terror leader.

Trump can't win. Or, rather, he can win but his opponents will never give him any credit for winning. It's been like this ever since he was elected president, prompting many liberals to collapse into a form of spontaneous anaphylactic shock from which they still haven't recovered. These included a lot of entertainers, people from the worlds of film, television and music whose political opinions have never seemed so important – to themselves.

I'll never forget a video that went viral the week after Trump's stunning election victory featuring Yoko Ono's calm, measured response to the news. It lasted about 15 seconds and consisted of Yoko emitting a long, strangled, mournful, high-pitched scream like a malfunctioning kettle exploding. Her agonised reaction perfectly epitomised the ludicrously over-the-top global meltdown by the planet's celebrities to the result of a fair, open and democratic election. And it was only rivalled for insanity by an event organised a year on from Trump's win entitled 'Scream helplessly at the sky on the anniversary of the election' in which thousands of Trump-hating liberals in cities like Boston, New York and Philadelphia went outside, stared upwards and shouted their little heads off in rage. What could better illustrate the woke mindset than literally screaming because you don't get what you want?

This raging intolerance has manifested itself in a very dangerous manner, with direct inferences that Trump should be assassinated. Four sitting presidents – one in 12 of the 45 men who have held the office – have actually been murdered. I remain very concerned that Trump may become the fifth, such is the viciously violent vitriol aimed his way by those who should know better.

It was Madonna who started this disturbing trend by screaming at the Women's March the day after Trump's inauguration in January 2017 that she thought of 'blowing up the White House', although she quickly backtracked, claiming her remark had been taken out of context and that she had spoken in 'metaphor'. Following her outrageous outburst, which attracted global headlines, death threats were aimed at the new president on an unprecedented scale. Global artificial intelligence firm Dataminr reported that, in the next two weeks alone, more than 12,000 posts with the words 'assassinate Trump' were made on Twitter. The threats have carried on coming, many of them far more serious than a Twitter post, with the Secret Service working 24/7 to stop myriad plots to attack POTUS. Yet this hasn't stopped supposedly intelligent people from fanning the flames.

Comedian Kathy Griffin posted a photograph of herself clutching an image of Trump's severed, blood-splattered head. It was a just a joke, she wailed, when all hell broke loose. Really, Ms Griffin? It's 'funny' to hold a US president's severed head up to a camera at a time when ISIS barbarians were doing exactly that to fellow Americans?

'This is vile and wrong,' tweeted Chelsea Clinton in a very rare show of solidarity with Trump after Griffin's stunt. 'It is never funny to joke about killing a president.' There speaks someone who had to live for eight years as a young girl in the White House with the constant terrifying fear that someone might try to kill her father.

As outrage grew, and Trump and his family expressed horror over what she'd done, Griffin resorted to the natural preferred woke defence playbook of victimhood; she claimed she was being bullied by old, sexist and misogynist white men. Oh, and irony of ironies, *she* was now receiving death threats! She briefly apologised but later took back the apology.

In the short term, Griffin's career took a hit, but once she revved up the victim card, and went on the attack against Trump, she became a liberal heroine and is now even more famous and successful than she was before the severed head fiasco. Her behaviour exemplifies the horrible self-righteousness that pervades 'wokies'. They don't just think they're right – they *know* they're right. And they don't just think those who disagree are wrong, they *know* they're wrong. They also believe those who disagree with them are all dumb, bigoted morons who must be shamed, abused and preferably cancelled.

Trump brings out the worst in them all, just as he also brings out the worst in the US media, who exposed themselves during his presidential run, with a few notable exceptions, as a bunch of ratings- and circulation-hungry Dr Frankensteins that created and ravenously fuelled the monster of Trump the presidential candidate – before equally ravenously trying to kill him off when they suddenly realised to their horror he might actually win, and in a massive collective guilt trip ever since have spent his entire presidency trying to bring him down. In doing so, they have fallen into his trap. 'Good publicity is preferable to bad,' said Trump in his bestselling book *The Art of the Deal*, 'but from a bottom-line perspective, bad publicity is sometimes better than no publicity at all. Controversy, in short, sells.'

Trump's toxic relationship with the mainstream media in America now resembles a mutually abusive marriage. They can't live with each other with a constant undercurrent of visceral hostility, but nor can they live without each other. As a journalist for 35 years, I don't like Trump branding the media 'fake news', even if it's justified when a story turns out to be plain wrong. And I hate him calling the media 'the enemy of the people'. That's just downright dangerous. But the media, dominated by liberals, doesn't help itself with its obsessional 24/7 coverage of Trump over things like his supposed collusion with Russia to fix the 2016 election, which turned out to be a massive nothing-burger.

As with woke celebrities calling for the White House to be blown up, the constant self-serving hysteria helps him more than it hurts him. It also, more importantly, diminishes the significance of times when Trump does stuff that really does deserve massive critical attention.

Despite all the hysteria, or perhaps partly because of it, Trump now has the perfect platform for an incumbent US president to start re-election year. The US economy is purring along nicely, two of the world's worst terrorists have been taken out in the space of four months and the US is striving to end its involvement in cripplingly expensive wars. Unfortunately, the rigid nature of modern illiberal liberalism doesn't allow for him to get any credit for any of this. And if he wins again in November, they will only have themselves to blame. Jeremy, my army colonel brother and no fan of Trump, explained succinctly, 'It seems to me that there is a direct correlation between noisy liberal angst and silent popular voting.' The stats are on Trump's side: historically, 70 per cent of presidents who run again get re-elected. If they run on a soaring economy, that probability rises to over 90 per cent.

The way for liberals to beat Donald Trump is not by wishing him dead or screaming about him 24/7. It is by using everything in the American democratic system to defeat him by fair means not foul. That means at the ballot box. Though the president should be mindful of the warning from former British Prime Minister Harold Macmillan, who when asked what was the greatest challenge for a leader, was supposed to have replied, 'Events, dear boy, events.'

There are still ten months until the election and anything could happen.

THURSDAY 9 JANUARY

Bombshell news: Prince Harry and his wife Meghan have announced they are quitting the royal family.

In a statement released tonight on their glitzy new website, the Duke and Duchess of Sussex revealed they're relinquishing life as 'senior royals' with all the tedious duty that entails, and instead now want to be a 'progressive' force within 'this institution'. In other words, they want to be super-woke royals (with all the 'do as we say not as we do' hectoring hypocrisy they've already brought to that status) who get to keep all the trappings of royal life without any of the hard, boring bits.

In their lengthy list of pronouncements, Harry and Meghan say they will now be spending much of their time in North America, where they've just recently been lounging for six weeks' 'much-needed holiday' – a holiday from what, exactly? – at a multi-millionaire's waterside mansion in Canada. Oh, and they're going to seek to be 'financially independent'. It's only when you read the details of this 'independence' that you realise what it actually means is they want to live off Harry's dad's money, off Prince Charles and his Duchy of Cornwall.

They have also informed us they intend to continue living for free, when they grace the UK with their esteemed presence, at Frogmore Cottage, their palatial home in Windsor that was gifted to them by the Queen and which has been refurbished to their specifications at a cost to the taxpayer of millions of pounds. Oh, and they expect to continue having royal protection too – at further vast expense to the taxpayer – and all the other stuff that goes with that like VIP royal travel. We all know there's nothing these two fearless eco-warriors like more than stomping down their giant hypocritical carbon footprint one private jet at a time.

They also, hilariously, laid down their new rulebook for the media, saying they're getting rid of the traditional royal rota system and will instead be inviting special favoured journalists to attend their events and write nice positive things about them. I chuckled with disbelief as I read this. Even Putin wouldn't pull a stunt to control the press like that and it doesn't seem to fit very well with their woke world view. There is zero chance of the media following any 'rules' for covering these two, now they've swapped royal duty for money-grabbing celebrity stardom. If Meghan and Harry want to be the new Kardashians, that's fine, but they'll get treated like the new Kardashians. But, honestly, who the hell do they think they are?

I've seen some disgraceful royal antics in my time, but for pure arrogance, entitlement, greed, and wilful disrespect, nothing has ever quite matched this nonsense from the 'Duke and Duchess of Sussex'. I put inverted commas around those titles because I sincerely hope they won't exist much longer. Indeed, if I were Her Majesty the Queen, I would unceremoniously strip these deluded clowns of all their titles with immediate effect and despatch them back into civilian life.

Nobody tells the Queen what to do. She's the most powerful, respected person in Britain. And right now, she's facing a direct threat to everything she has worked so hard to maintain. Harry and Meghan's astonishingly brazen and selfish antics have left her no choice but to cut them loose and fire them both from the royal family. The Queen should get rid of these whining, ego-crazed leeches – before it's too late.

FRIDAY 10 JANUARY

I posted a new *Daily Mail* column attacking Harry and Meghan's statement, and it was met with people either furiously agreeing with me, or furiously disagreeing and accusing me of being 'obsessed' with Meghan because she'd ghosted me (for a brief period several years ago, I'd considered us to be friends), 'persecuting' her, 'damaging her mental health' and claiming, most absurdly, that I was only attacking her because she's black.

The *Guardian's* Carole Cadwalladr even branded me 'a bully in a country which has institutionalised bullying via popular press'. I found much of this reaction absurdly over-the-top. My criticism of Meghan has nothing to with her gender or skin colour. Nor is it 'bullying' to hold people to account if they're on the public purse.

As for the 'obsessed' charge, it's true that I've written and said a lot of stuff about Meghan and Harry, but that's because they're huge global celebrities who keep doing things that dominate the news cycle, and every time I write about them, the columns get massive traction, suggesting enormous public interest. I can't pretend the way she personally treated me – I was dropped like a stone the moment she met Harry, after 18 months of friendly communication originated by her, and a very cordial meeting, at her request, in my local pub when she pumped me for advice on how to handle the media – hasn't informed my view of her now, especially as I've seen her do the same to many others. It would surely influence anyone's thinking if someone they considered a friend suddenly ghosted them without explanation? As Maya Angelou once said, 'When someone shows you who they are, believe them the first time.'

MONDAY 13 JANUARY

The fallout from Harry and Meghan's royal resignation has grown unbelievably toxic. Like everything else these days, you must either love them or hate them, there can be no middle ground. And social media has turned into a vicious battlefield with me at the centre of much of it.

The narrative has firmly positioned Meghan and Harry as victims, and people like me as the heartless tormentors. The first problem I have with this tactic from these lazy 'woke' activists is that it represents a deliberate attempt to shut down freedom of the press, and discussion on important cultural and societal issues. But there's a wider concern: casually chucking around serious accusations of sexism or racism to stifle criticism is also designed to encourage the general public to take a binary, one-sided stance which risks creating further division in our increasingly divided society.

I've been watching this unedifying saga unfurl over the past few days with mounting fury. Predominantly, at the disgracefully disrespectful way the Sussexes are treating the Queen. But I'm also enraged by the specific growing narrative that the only reason Meghan's been so harshly criticised by the media is because we're all a bunch of racists living in a racist country. I just won't accept that.

From the moment Meghan came on the royal scene, and it was revealed she was from a mixed-race background, she was welcomed with warm, open, tolerant arms by a wonderfully multi-cultural and diverse modern Britain that was thrilled to finally see a non-white member of the royal family. She was showered with almost universal praise, especially when the engagement was announced. The media, in particular, was unanimous in its verdict that this was a great thing for the country. In fact, I haven't seen a press so united in joy for anything royal since Diana first became Charles's girlfriend.

This extraordinary tidal wave of goodwill continued through to the big wedding in May 2018 which, by common consent, was a triumph. As I wrote myself in the *Mail on Sunday* the following day, 'it mixed the best of traditional British pomp and majesty with large dollops of Markle Sparkle and the result was a bi-racial, Hollywood-fused union of very different cultures that worked magnificently well'. I added, 'It's hard to overstate the significance of this ceremony, beamed live around the world, to black people everywhere. To borrow the words of Dr King, this was a day when little black girls could watch TV and genuinely share little white girls' long-held dreams of one day marrying a Prince.'

These words, I would politely suggest, do not indicate the thoughts of a racist. Yet that is what I, and others working in the British media, have now been shamefully branded for daring to criticise Meghan for her – and Harry's – erratic and spectacularly ill-advised behaviour since the wedding.

I've been harsh in my criticism of the way they have treated and disowned Meghan's father Thomas after he foolishly but naively colluded with the paparazzi. But that's got nothing to do with her skin colour and everything to do with her tendency, as I discovered personally, to get rid of people in her life when they cease to be of use to her or become 'problematic'. My other criticisms have been centred around their hypocrisy: Meghan having a $500,000 celebrity-fuelled baby-shower party in New York, including a lift on George's Clooney jet, on the same day she and Harry tweeted a plea for people to think of the poor; the ridiculous lengths they went to hide basic details of their baby Archie's birth from the public that pays for much of their lavish lives; and the way they used Sir Elton John's private jet like a taxi service after repeatedly lecturing us all about the importance to watch our carbon footprint. None of this was racist, either overtly or subliminally. People might not agree with all or any of my criticisms, and perhaps the rhetoric I've occasionally used to reflect them has been a bit over the top, but they are all perfectly justified ones to make, which is why so many others have made them too.

Yet this hasn't stopped a Twitter-driven bandwagon developing that says all criticism of Ms Markle is racially motivated. In a disgraceful column for the *New York Times* headlined 'Black Britons Know Why Meghan Markle Wants Out – It's the Racism', author Afua Hirsch attacked the 'racist treatment of Meghan' and said, 'The British press has succeeded in its apparent project of hounding Meghan, Duchess of Sussex, out of Britain.' She cites, as examples of the supposed press racism, two things that appeared in the *Daily Mail.*

The first was a headline saying she was '(almost) straight outta Compton', one of the most gang-ravaged parts of America in south central Los Angeles, immortalised by rap group N.W.A. Now, I'll accept that headline was a bit misleading; Meghan actually comes from Crenshaw, a few miles from Compton, but also a place with a lot of gang-related crime. I don't believe this piece was used as a stick to racially insult her, but as simply an interesting observation about her undeniably very different upbringing to normal royal brides. Hirsch also lambasted a journalist, Boris Johnson's sister Rachel, for saying Meghan had 'exotic DNA'. I can understand that to some this carries connotation of 'othering', suggesting Meghan is somehow a lesser royal due to her background. And Rachel could certainly have used a less inflammatory phrase to make the point that Meghan is very different to any previous royal bride.

But, again, I would argue there was no intent to be offensive. I know Rachel well and she would never have intended it to be a racist jibe. Yet, according to Ms Hirsch, this is all hard damning evidence that the British press is inherently racist and has deliberately driven out Meghan because we can't stand the fact she's only half-white. What a load of inflammatory bilge. Hirsch should be ashamed of herself for spewing such hateful, race-baiting nonsense in one of American's most prominent newspapers. But she's not been alone.

Other mainstream news outlets like CNN and the *Washington Post* have published similar pieces intimating it's all about racism. Harry started all this when he attacked the media soon after their romance was made public, claiming non-existent 'racial undertones' in the tabloid newspapers. I saw none then and I have seen none since – because there have been none. This disingenuous nonsense is now being extended from a charge against the media to even bigger targets, with sinister threats of a 'tell-all' TV interview in which Meghan and Harry might apparently level sensational charges of racism at the door of other senior royals and their households.

More importantly, by crying 'RACISTS!' in the face of perfectly legitimate criticism, this petulant duo have made a mockery of true victims of racism. The reality is that Meghan and Harry have brought this ugly situation entirely on themselves and should somehow find the strength in their faux-victim-ravaged, virtue-signalling, self-obsessed souls to admit it has nothing to do with racism and everything to do with their fragile egos and a simmering feud with the Duke and Duchess of Cambridge, who will always be more important in the royal family as they will one day be King and Queen.

TUESDAY 14 JANUARY

There are so many strange double standards these days. Take 'sexism'.

Today, *GMB*'s excellent meteorologist Laura Tobin wore a very striking pair of skin-tight red trousers, so I jokingly complimented her for 'parading around in hot-pants'. We get on well and often exchange such light-hearted 'banter'. But I was immediately accused of being 'sexist' by several viewers on Twitter, so I read out their criticism and said, 'When a female presenter parades herself in skin-tight leather trousers to do the weather, you are going to get people going "wow".'

Laura, 38, clarified her outfit wasn't made of leather. They were, apparently, 'sustainable trousers'. 'They're certainly sustaining me,' I laughed. Of course, this prompted more furious tweets, which I also read out, including one that read, 'Well out of order, the sexist comment on Laura Tobin's trousers. A woman should be able to wear what she likes without it being sexualised.'

Susanna Reid, my long-time co-presenter, immediately sprang to her defence, branding me 'slightly creepy' and saying 'people don't want to be objectified at work'. When I pointed out that the women on our show often compliment their appearances on air and off, Susanna retorted, 'Complimenting each other is not the same as sexualising each other. You're saying "hot" as an alternative to "sexy".' I laughed, 'What's wrong with being sexy?' Laura was the least offended person. 'Thank you for noticing and giving me some airtime!' she declared.

But some viewers were having none of it. 'Piers Morgan showing that making women feel uncomfortable in the workplace for how they dress is still with us in 2020!' Another seethed, 'Piers just went into creepy perv mode over Laura's trousers. Very disturbing viewing.'

Various online newspaper stories erupted about me 'humiliating' Laura, until she eventually addressed them on Twitter, saying, 'Lots of reaction to my trousers today, I'm not humiliated by @piersmorgan. They're just a pair of trousers! I thought I was being stylish!'

This prompted a wave of people supporting me. 'It's called banter,' one viewer tweeted, 'having a laugh, like we used to be able to do years ago.' Another observed, 'I'm sure if Laura Tobin was humiliated, she's a strong enough person to have put Piers in his place and told him so.'

All of this just left me exhausted. One of the problems with the feminism debate these days is that some women want to have their hypocritical, sexist objectification cake and eat it too. When each new series of *Poldark* comes out, for example, the amount of drool spewed by Britain's women over lead actor Aidan Turner could fill an ocean, and his half-naked body fills the front pages. No man I know gives a damn about the way he's objectified, and I bet he doesn't either, but if we did the same to a female TV star now, radical feminists would rip us to shreds.

The double standards are laughable. Take, for example, US talk-show star Ellen DeGeneres, the darling of the woke community and a woman who drips unctuous sycophancy and virtue-signalling from every pore. Nobody has been more censorious about the behaviour of ghastly lecherous men than Ms DeGeneres, who identifies as a lesbian. Yet when she appeared at the People's Choice Awards in Los Angeles – accepting, of course, the award for 'Favourite Humanitarian'

– she said the following: 'You know, here's the thing, awards are great. But what really makes me happy is making other people happy. And tonight, I want to make you happy, so – I've brought a shirtless photo of Chris Hemsworth to share!' Gigantic images of the Australian actor stripped to the waist instantly beamed onto the big screens in the theatre, and to millions of viewers at home. Women in the audience screamed and howled with laughter as Mr Hemsworth smiled sheepishly and blushed. 'You're welcome!' cackled Ellen, as she left the stage delighted that her gag had gone down so well.

Sexism is a bad thing – let's all agree on that. But so is hypocrisy. Ms DeGeneres is a serial offender. In 2017, she wished Katy Perry happy birthday by posting a photo of herself leering at Perry's cleavage with the caption, 'Katy – it's time to bring out the big balloons!' Think I'd have got away with that? No, of course not.

It's time for women to either view male humour, and obvious harmless compliments such as mine about Laura Tobin's trousers, in the same way they view their own, or to be as indignant with themselves as they are with men when they feel the line gets crossed.

THURSDAY 16 JANUARY

James Bond will remain a man.

This shouldn't be a sentence I ever have to write, but sadly I do. The news was revealed by Barbara Broccoli, who has run the 007 movie franchise since the death of father Cubby, in an interview with *Variety*.

'James Bond can be of any colour,' she said, 'but he is male. I'm not particularly interested in taking a male character and having a woman play it. I think women are far more interesting than that.'

Thank God for that. I've waged a lengthy campaign to save Bond from the clutches of radical feminists, who take the very laudable cause of feminism and apply a totally uncompromising intolerance to anyone who strays from their rigid belief of what is acceptable. And these radical feminists have proven far more dangerous to Bond's existence than Jaws, Blofeld or Oddjob. After all, as a white heterosexual man who kills people, seduces random women, brazenly chats up female co-workers, drinks, gambles, smokes cigars and cracks inappropriate jokes, Bond represents the very antithesis of everything the PC-crazed snowflake world stands for, so must of course be eliminated from public life.

Broccoli spoke out after rumours began to run riot that Bond would be turned into a woman. The warning signs came with alarming regularity via leaks from the set of the latest Bond movie, *No Time to Die*. First, it was reported that the script began with James now retired and temporarily replaced as 007 by a black woman, played by Lashana Lynch. Then it emerged that producers had determined James must now 'navigate the #MeToo movement', which apparently involves him becoming a hyper-sensitive, emotionally aware wokie who cries in front of women rather than beds them. Yet is that really the kind of Bond that women want?

The campaign to neuter the most masculine icon in movie history reached an entirely predictable nadir with a call for him to become female. Astonishingly, it was actively encouraged by former Bond stars. 'Get out of the way, guys!' demanded feminist-by-proxy Pierce Brosnan, who played 007 four times, 'and put a woman up there! I think it would be exhilarating, it would be exciting!' Curiously, I don't remember Mr Brosnan suggesting this when *he* was 007.

This is not about equality. I don't object to women playing Bond because they somehow lack the requisite skills to do so.

I'm sure there are many female spies operating right now who are just as adept at killing people, seducing members of the opposite sex, chatting up co-workers, drinking, gambling, smoking and cracking inappropriate jokes.

No, I object to it because James Bond is a man, was always intended to be a man by Bond writer Ian Fleming – and should therefore remain a man. As Broccoli said, you can make Bond a black man – I'd love to see Idris Elba take over from Daniel Craig – or a man of any other ethnicity for that matter, but you can't make him a woman. If Pierce Brosnan needs someone other than me to explain why this is a dumb idea, then he should ask Rosamund Pike, who co-starred with him in *Die Another Day*.

'James Bond is a character that Ian Fleming created,' she said, 'and the character is a man. It's a very masculine creation. Why should a woman get sort of sloppy seconds? Why should she have been a man and now it has to be played by a woman? Why not be a kick-ass female agent in her own right?'

Exactly. By all means create your own super-spies, ladies, but for Christ's sake, leave our guy alone. Bond, like him or loathe him, is a male, straight, womanising loner who likes killing bad guys and prefers wearing tuxedos to dresses. That's just who he is. And that's why he's been so beloved for so many decades and retained such a powerful place in British culture. As Sean Connery once put it, 'Bond is important: this invincible superman that every man would like to copy, that every woman would like to conquer, this dream we all have of survival.'

As with all these stupid 'woke' campaigns, very few people outside the radical liberal bubble actually want it to happen. On *GMB*, we ran a poll asking if Bond should be a woman and 86 per cent of viewers (in a very large response) said no. So, this is yet another example of the troubling modern phenomenon of politically correct subservience to the outraged whim of a small minority against the wishes of the vast majority. I suspect there were even more women than men voting against it, because for many women, and I hate to break this to you my darling feministas, James Bond represents gloriously macho fantasy escapism.

Unfortunately, the war on Bond is part of a wider war on masculinity. I say this as a man who's actually proud of being a man, and who also likes being masculine. I realise this is a horrendous thing to say, and I can only offer my insincere apologies to all the radical feminists now exploding with rage. If there's one thing they loathe even more than the M-word, it's the longer M-word. But why? Masculinity simply means 'having qualities or appearances traditionally associated with men'. That's it, nothing more sinister.

It dates back to the Latin word *masculus* meaning 'male, worthy of a man' and has been widely used in the English language since the middle of the fourteenth century. By the 1620s, it was further taken to mean 'manly, virile, powerful'.

So, for nearly 400 years, it was assumed to be a positive word, one that represented the very best of men. Not anymore.

Thanks to women of radical feminist persuasion who've gleefully hijacked the #MeToo and #TimesUp campaigns to serve their own man-hating purposes, masculinity has become the most controversial, detestable word in the English lexicon. And it's now impossible to be 'masculine' without also being accused of 'toxic masculinity'. The best conversation I've had about all this was with the singer Annie Lennox, who said it was 'important to bring men with you' on the feminist journey. 'But,' she cautioned, 'the debate has to be less hostile to men for that to happen.' Sadly, the opposite has happened and there is now constant outright hostility towards men and masculinity.

One of the more disturbing reports came from the American Psychological Association, which released a set of guidelines 'to help psychologists work with men and boys' in which aspects of traditional masculinity were condemned as 'harmful'. Specifically, it stated that male traits like 'stoicism', 'competitiveness', 'achievement', 'eschewal of the appearance of weakness', 'adventure' and 'risk' should be discarded in favour of finding potentially positive aspects in traits like 'courage' and 'leadership'. It basically implied that a lot of the common ideologies surrounding masculinity can lead to problems elsewhere in the social sphere.

As David French, a writer for the *National Review*, put it in a withering response to the report, 'The assault on traditional masculinity – while liberating to men who don't fit traditional norms – is itself harmful to the millions of young men who seek to be physically and mentally tough, to rise to challenges, and demonstrate leadership under pressure. The assault on traditional masculinity is an assault on their very natures. Are boys disproportionately adventurous? Are they risk-takers? Do they feel a need to be strong? Do they often by default reject stereotypically "feminine" characteristics? Yes, yes, yes and yes.'

One of the very worst things about radical feminism is the scourge of pathetic male virtue-signallers that urge them on. As an obvious (or so I thought) tongue-in-cheek joke on International Men's Day two years ago, I tweeted, 'Happy #InternationalMensDay! Stay strong lads, we're not illegal – yet.'

Most people reacted in the way I would react if someone else had tweeted that – by laughing. Others weren't so amused, bombarding me with hateful abuse about my supposed 'toxic masculinity'. A man named Box Brown, who has a verified Twitter account and claims to be a *New York Times*-bestselling cartoonist, replied simply, 'Die.' How laughably hypocritical; this angry little clown races to attack what he presumably perceives to be my aggressive maleness – yet does so by saying he wants me dead.

While I may have joked about International Men's Day, of course I understand and appreciate there is a very serious side to it too. The stats tell the grim story: 76 per cent of suicides are by men, 85 per cent of homeless people are men, 70 per cent of homicide victims are men, men serve 64 per cent longer in prison and are 3.4 times more likely to be imprisoned than women when both committed the same crime. And wars are still fought by male-dominated armed forces. So, it's not all a patriarchal bed of roses being a man.

There is also no doubt women have historically been treated unfairly in terms of equality, and that many women continue to be treated unfairly. I also fully accept that women have been subjected to far more harassment, sexual abuse and domestic violence than men. That is where the #MeToo and #TimesUp movements have performed a valuable public service in highlighting and exposing genuinely bad, unacceptable and in some cases criminal behaviour. In fact, I don't know any of my male friends who wouldn't agree with that.

However, what I refuse to accept is that all masculinity is therefore now automatically a bad thing, or that being a man is suddenly something to be ashamed about. Nor do I believe that most women actually want the kind of emasculated, papoose-clad, weeping, permanently apologising doormats that radical feminists are trying to make us become. And once again, a very important and legitimate movement – feminism – has been hijacked and its momentum redirected towards something as trivial and misguided as a war on masculinity, or on a beloved pop culture figure like Bond.

Let me therefore offer some friendly advice from a man who loves women. We don't want to be told we can't appreciate a female star's beauty because it's offensive to feminists, then see feminists like Ellen DeGeneres openly objectifying famous men's bodies at awards shows – to no complaint. We don't want to be informed that James Bond has to stop hitting on women because it's now deemed politically incorrect, especially as none of the women he ever hits on seem to be anything but ecstatically thrilled about it. We don't want to be disapprovingly frowned at for opening doors for women, or standing up for them on trains or when they walk into a room, or paying the bill for dinner if we want to.

Chivalry remains a good, not oppressive thing. We want to pride ourselves on being a protective modern-day hunter and provider, in whatever capacity that manifests itself to the benefit of a woman or family – without promptly being labelled a 'dinosaur' or 'caveman'. Some of us – in fact, most of us, I suspect – like to preserve the right not to be seen blubbing in public every five minutes just to prove we're in touch with our emotional side. In short, we'd just like to still enjoy being men, if that's OK? Just as we'd like women to enjoy being women.

Those seeking to ignore this advice do so at their peril. For 30 years, Gillette's commercials had unashamedly celebrated men and masculinity. They used the tagline 'The best a man can get' to persuade people like me to part with large sums of money for their expensive shaving blades and foam. We watched them and felt good about being male. Not just because they made us aspire to be a winner and successful achiever, but because they also encouraged us to be a good father, son, husband and friend. As a result of this consistently upbeat and positive marketing style, Gillette grew into the most successful razor firm in history, generating annual sales of $6 billion a year. I was one of its most loyal customers, buying Gillette products for over three decades. I didn't do so because their stuff is significantly better than their main competitors. (I've tried them all, and they're not especially.) I did so because I liked Gillette's brand and what I thought it stood for. Then, suddenly and inexplicably, in another depressing act of corporate virtue-signalling, Gillette decided to turn on men, and specifically 'toxic masculinity'.

In January 2019, the company released a new commercial, a short film entitled 'Believe', with the new tagline, 'The best men can be'. Gone was the celebration of masculinity. In its place came an ugly, vindictive two-minute homage to everything that's bad about masculinity. The film asked, 'Is this the best a man can get?' before flashing up images alluding to sexual harassment, sexist behaviour, the #MeToo movement and bullying – interspersed with a patronising series of educational visual entreaties about what men should do in various unpleasant situations. The subliminal message was clear: men, *all* men, are bad, shameful people who need to be directed in how to be better people. It was truly one of the most pathetic, virtue-signalling things I've ever endured watching.

Gillette said the purpose of the new campaign was to urge men to hold each other 'accountable' for bad behaviour. Right, because the one thing that's not happening right now in the world is men being held accountable for bad behaviour! I don't seek to diminish the importance of the #MeToo campaign, which has shone an important and long-overdue light on completely unacceptable sexual harassment, bullying and abuse. But why should all men be tarred with the same monstrous brush in the way this Gillette campaign sets out to do? It is the assumption that we are automatically culpable – that we have done something wrong by just existing as men

– which I find so offensive. Particularly as, if a commercial was made with the same inference about women being collectively awful until they proved otherwise, outrage would soon ensue.

There was only one thing Gillette really wanted to achieve with this new campaign, and that was to emasculate the very men it had spent 30 years persuading to be masculine. As one male customer's Twitter response, which quickly went viral, said, 'Just used a Gillette razor blade to cut off my testicles. No more toxic masculinity for me. Thanks Gillette!'

He was not alone in his fury. The YouTube version of the ad was watched many millions of times but attracted ten times as many 'dislikes' as 'likes', fast turning 'Believe' into one of the least popular commercials in US history. Gillette – which believes so much in women's rights that at the time of this commercial it had just two women on its board of nine directors – thought it was being clever by tapping into the radical feminist assault on men and masculinity. In fact, it was being unutterably dumb.

In a massive global two-fingered response, Gillette's male product sales collapsed in the space of just a few months, causing a staggering $8 BILLION write-down in the company's value and a humiliating U-turn back to macho commercials starring burly firemen who risk their lives. Gillette learned the hard way that most men don't actually want to be snivelling, apologetic little snowflakes.

Somewhere in this whole masculinity debate, common sense got lost. I don't know any woman who really wants her man to be anything but masculine, as the word was intended. Yet now they're being encouraged by companies like Gillette to find the whole concept of masculinity repellent and to think that being 'masculine' means to damagingly suppress emotions, maintain a fake impression of macho hardness, and to use violence as a means to illustrate physical power and gender superiority. What a load of bollocks.

FRIDAY 17 JANUARY

The actor Laurence Fox is at the centre of a firestorm after appearing on the *Question Time* panel last night and getting into a fierce debate with a mixed-race audience member who called press coverage of Meghan Markle 'racist'.

'Let's be really clear about what this is, and call it by its name,' said Rachel Boyle. 'It's racism and she's been torn to pieces.'

'It's not racism,' replied Fox.

'It absolutely is,' Boyle insisted.

'We're the most tolerant, lovely country in Europe,' Fox said. 'It's so easy to throw the charge of racism at everybody ... and it's really starting to get boring now.'

'What worries me about your comment is you are a white privileged male,' said Boyle, a comment that prompted widespread groans and boos from other audience members.

'Oh God,' sighed Fox, 'I can't help what I am, I was born like this, it's an immutable characteristic. So, to call me a white privileged male is to be racist. *You're* being racist.'

Fox then said racism should be called out when it is 'seen, when it's obvious and when it's there' and that 'throwing racism around' was dangerous.

There's been a furious reaction to the clash, led by Femi Oluwole, a prominent pro-European activist, who tweeted, 'So when Laurence Fox calls it racist to point out that he's a white privileged male, when he's trying to downplay racism, even though, as a white privileged male, he has even less of an experience of the adversity racism causes than I do as a black privileged male. Apparently, we should only call out racism when it's seen and obvious ... So subtle racism behind closed doors ... Absolutely fine. Cheers Laurence Fox!'

This struck me as an absurd overreaction and a direct threat to his freedom of speech. Fox was right to say the Meghan media coverage hasn't been driven by racism. He was also right to say that he has no control over his skin colour, and for someone to use that as a stick to suppress his view of racism is in itself racist and denies him the right to express a freely held opinion.

That's not to say there aren't racists in Britain – of course there are. Sadly, we saw all too many of them rear their ugly heads in a horrible manner during the Brexit campaign. But that doesn't make Britain a racist country – recent polls do suggest we're one of the least racist and most tolerant countries in Europe – nor does it mean media criticism of a high-profile black person is necessarily driven by racism. And if the woke brigade use Twitter to cancel and silence anyone and anything they deem to be racist, even when it's patently not the case, they are furthering divisions and making things worse, not better.

Laurence Fox has been hounded mercilessly since *Question Time* aired, in the most disgusting and vicious way. All because he refused to accept the media coverage of Meghan Markle has been racist. He may not have personally experienced the kind of racism a black person endures, but that surely doesn't disqualify him from discussing it. Just as Annie Lennox said about feminism, for true racial equality to succeed it will need white people to come on the journey too, and for that to happen open discussion and debate are absolutely critical. That's what a proper liberal would call for, isn't it?

Even more worryingly, there have now been calls to 'cancel' Fox's acting career. And incredibly, they've come loudest from minority representatives of the actors' union Equity, which fired off a series of accusations on Twitter against Fox, saying he wanted to 'berate and bully women of colour attempting to discuss issues of race and gender discrimination', was 'playing to the gallery, a populist tirade, with women of colour being used as cannon fodder' and 'occupied a highly advantaged position' while trying to 'damn any recognition of that privilege as the very racism he claims is exaggerated when people of colour try to discuss it'. This is such a sinister attack on free speech. And where does the logic of it leave us? Can nobody now have an opinion on anything we haven't personally experienced?

'Cancel culture', as it's become known, is one of the very worst things about modern society, and it's driven by the same woke liberals who profess to stand for tolerance. They would do well to listen to Barack Obama, who is celebrated by liberals worldwide but finds cancel culture ridiculous and harmful. Speaking in Chicago at his own Obama Foundation Summit in 2019, he warned, 'This idea of purity and that you're never compromised and you're always politically woke – you should get over that quickly. The world is messy. There are ambiguities. People who do really good stuff have flaws. People who you are fighting might love their kids. One danger I see with young people, particularly on college campuses ... there is this sense sometimes of the way of me making change is to be as judgmental as possible about other people and that's enough. Like, if I tweet or hashtag about how you didn't do something right, or used the wrong verb, then I can sit back and feel pretty good about myself. That's not activism. That's not bringing about change. If all you're doing is casting stones, you're probably not going to get that far.'

SATURDAY 18 JANUARY

The Queen has sensationally ordered Harry and Meghan to drop their HRH titles and repay the £2.4 million of public cash spent on Frogmore Cottage, as part of their 'severance deal' with the royal family. Harry will even have to give up all his military titles. It's being billed as an 'amicable settlement' but it's very clear there's nothing remotely amicable about it. This is a bitter divorce, and like King Edward VIII, Harry's giving everything up for his wife – a woman who seems to specialise in dropping people.

'Only surprised it took her so long to get Harry to ditch his family, the monarchy, the military and his country,' I tweeted. 'What a piece of work.' Feminists reacted with fury. TV presenter Beverley Turner said the phrase 'piece of work' is 'almost uniquely aimed at women ... its [sic] dehumanising and belittling.'

'Oh Beverley, cool your "SEXISM!" jets. A "piece of work" is non-gender-specific,' I replied. 'People say it about me ... often for very good reason.'

One of the many irritations of radical activists is their fervent desire to banish perfectly anodyne words because they've been weaponised. These PC language cops don't just want to control how we think but also how we speak. By playing the victim to common-usage words, women are surely being the opposite of empowered. It just makes them look weak, and slightly pathetic. I've been called far worse than any of this, for a very long time, and often found it hugely empowering. It also, again, takes the focus away from very real feminist issues like the ongoing gender pay gap, which was 17.3 per cent in the UK in 2019. By ranting away about trivial nonsense like banning words, at the expense of meaningful structural change in the way women get paid, feminists shoot themselves in their stilettos.

TUESDAY 21 JANUARY

A fascinating debate erupted today over the word 'woke'. It began when *Guardian* journalist Steve Rose claimed it had been weaponised by the right, like the phrase 'politically correct' before it, so it's now come to be interpreted as the opposite of what it was originally intended to mean.

'Technically,' he wrote, 'going by the Merriam-Webster dictionary's definition, woke means "aware of and actively attentive to important facts and issues (especially issues of racial and social justice)" but today we are more likely to see it being used as a stick with which to beat people who aspire to such values, often wielded by those who don't recognise how un-woke they are, or are proud of the fact.' He added, 'Criticising "woke culture" has become a way of claiming victim status for yourself rather than acknowledging that more deserving others hold that status. It has gone from a virtue signal to a dog whistle. The language has been successfully co-opted – but as long as the underlying injustices remain, new words will emerge to describe them.'

Rose is right about what's happened to the word 'woke' but not about the culprits. It's the wokies who have wrecked their own word by being so absurdly illiberal to the point where even many liberals like me find them laughable.

Freddie Gray in the *Spectator* responded to Rose by saying the word 'woke' has degenerated into 'a meaningless term of abuse'. He argued, 'The whole idea of being woke – suddenly alert – to racial or social injustice is not real, and never was,' and went on to say, 'and therefore the movement against it is similarly fake. Right-wingers have the same concept and call it "redpilling"; in both cases, it means a sort of lobotomised enlightenment for people who only enjoy feeling aggrieved. Scratch the surface – go beneath the endless viral spats between trolls on social media – and you realise that nobody means what they are saying. Nobody is actually redpilled. And nobody, come to that, is woke.'

Gray was right that these labels on both sides of the political divide have become tribal partisan badges more than a reflection of genuinely held beliefs. He was also spot on about what drives wokery, which in many instances is just blind allegiance to issues regardless of any real intellectual rigour, and a desire to be liked.

'Many of my friends spend hours virtue-signalling (another word that is fast approaching redundancy) on Facebook or Twitter or Instagram,' he said. 'But if I ever ask them about it, they'll explain that they only shared the sanctimonious meme because everyone in their office did, or they just thought that is what you have to do. [...] At some point the mask becomes the man, as in the story of the Happy Hypocrite. We are what we emote. If we spend our lives hectoring and censoring each other online, that will eventually bleed into everyday life. But it's useful sometimes to remember, as we all gorge on offence culture every day, that most people don't mean it, and nobody is really woke.'

I don't think that last point is true. There are many people fighting for racial and social justice who are principled, decent human beings that are knowledgeable about the issues and prepared to engage people in democratic debate about how best to fix the problems.

THURSDAY 23 JANUARY

China has now identified the mystery pneumonia-like disease in Wuhan as a new SARS-like coronavirus. It has already killed 17 people and is causing so much concern that the entire city of 11 million people has been shut down to try to contain it.

The World Health Organization, having tweeted on 14 January that there was no evidence of 'human-to-human transmission' with the virus, now says that *is* happening and has recommended avoidance of large gatherings, isolating infected people and extensive hand washing as the best way to combat its spread. It all sounds rather worrying, but in a statement to the House of Commons, Health Secretary Matt Hancock reassured MPs that it presents little danger to the UK. He said Chief Medical Officer Professor Chris Whitty has advised that the risk to the UK population is 'low' and that 'while there is an increased likelihood that cases may arise in this country, we are well prepared and well equipped to deal with them'.

Hancock added that the UK 'is one of the first countries in the world to have developed an accurate test for this coronavirus and Public Health England has confirmed to me that it can scale up this test so we are in a position to deal with cases in this country if necessary'. And he declared, 'The public can be assured that the whole of the UK is always well-prepared for these types of outbreaks.'

In response, on behalf of the Opposition, Shadow Minister for Public Health Sharon Hodgson said, 'There is a chance that a global pandemic can be avoided if governments across the world take the right measures in a timely fashion.'

SUNDAY 26 JANUARY

The government has continued refusing to put up any ministers for interview on *GMB*. It's all been very petty, but I assumed the ban would be lifted now there appears to be a rather serious global health crisis developing with the coronavirus from China.

'Tell the government we expect them to put up the Health or Home Secretary tomorrow,' I emailed the *GMB* production team this afternoon. 'It is their duty to appear and talk about this.'

'We don't have anybody to put to you for tomorrow,' came the response from Number 10, with the patronising additional aside, 'Thanks for checking in.'

I was so angry I tweeted, 'As #coronavirus threatens to hit Britain, we asked the British government to put up a cabinet minister to speak about it & reassure *GMB* viewers. They said "nobody is available". Shameful dereliction of duty.' I copied in Boris Johnson for good measure.

MONDAY 27 JANUARY

Most of the show was dominated by the awful news of US basketball legend Kobe Bryant's death in a helicopter crash, and a new interview with Thomas Markle in which he emphatically denied the press had been racist to his daughter. We also interviewed a British ex-pat, Ian Thompson, who is locked down in Wuhan and painted a disturbing, almost apocalyptic picture.

'It's extremely strange,' he said, 'and very scary too. The streets are completely empty, there's no one walking around, and everyone's been told to stay in their houses. There's no transportation anywhere, and all the restaurants, bars and most shops are closed down. Local stores are open at the moment which are being supplied by special trucks coming in. The amount you can get is quite limited because everyone's rushing and panic buying.'

Susanna and I were both shocked by what he told us. 'Wuhan's as big as London,' she said during the next commercial break. 'Can you imagine that happening here?'

THURSDAY 30 JANUARY

The WHO today declared the coronavirus – now named Covid-19 (short for Corona Virus Disease 2019) – a 'global public health emergency'. An hour later, my youngest son Bertie posted a photo to our father and sons WhatsApp group of a man in a full white hazmat suit walking outside his halls at Bristol University.

'What's this?' I asked, assuming it was some kind of student joke meme playing off the news.

'One of the students has gone down with flu-like symptoms and been taken to hospital,' he replied. 'It's scary, there were people in these suits all over the place. There was an ambulance too. If it's coronavirus, we're being sent home.'

'This thing is no joke,' my eldest son Spencer replied. 'Look how fast it's spreading and watch the movie *Contagion*.'

I looked at the photo again. It does resemble something out of *Contagion* – a film about a deadly virus pandemic that ravages the world. But this is obviously very real, and increasingly unsettling.

FRIDAY 31 JANUARY

Awoke this morning to breaking news that two people in England have tested positive for the disease. I wonder if one of them was that Bristol student? Is Bertie now at risk?

The troubling development rounds off a remarkably busy month for news, with horrendous bushfires in Australia, General Soleimani's killing, Trump's impeachment trial in the US Senate, Harry and Meghan quitting the royal family, and Kobe Bryant's shocking death.

All of these events generated massive media attention, and furious debate – especially on social media – about hot-button issues like climate change, race, privilege, gender and nationalism. Today heralded the denouement of perhaps the most seismic and contentious story of all, with Britain's formal withdrawal from the European Union – or Brexit as it has become known.

As someone who voted Remain but believed passionately that once my side lost the vote we had to accept the result, I've been dismayed to watch fellow Remainers spend the past three and a half years shrieking in fury and refusing to admit defeat. It's been an unedifying, ugly, visceral spectacle and what's made it particularly distasteful is that so many of these 'Remoaners', as they've been dubbed, identify themselves as liberals.

Yet their pathetic response to losing a free, democratic referendum has been the complete opposite of everything liberalism once stood for, including fairness, reason and adherence to basic principles of democracy. I became so infuriated with the sore-loser squealing that I even voted for Boris 'Let's Get Brexit Done!' Johnson's Conservative Party at the general election last month because he was the only leader promising to honour the vote of the people. Of course, this made me an even bigger target for the howling liberal woke brigade.

Today, as Brexit becomes a legal reality, the cacophony of incessant liberal whining fills the air like a toxic stench. It's been an issue that's ripped Britain in two, dividing families and friends, turning mainstream and social media into seething cesspits, and leaving everyone drained, fractious and indignant. Even a specially minted commemorative 50 pence Brexit coin inscribed with the seemingly non-contentious words 'Peace, prosperity and friendship with all nations' ignited a poisonous row between deranged Remoaners and rabid Brexiters. It's so depressing to see such utterly uncompromising attitudes, on both sides, over even something as trivial as a coin. Democracy is going to wither away unless something changes.

As with those other extraordinarily polarising subjects, Donald Trump and Meghan/Harry, Brexit is not something you're allowed to be neutral about. It's imperative to take a firm, unyielding position and stick to it, even if facts emerge that contradict things you believed.

Yet on Brexit and Trump, I've found myself in a curiously middle-of-the-road place – voting against the former but wanting it delivered to safeguard democracy, and being a good personal friend of the latter who wouldn't vote for him but wants to cover his presidency in a fair, non-partisan, critical-where-he-deserves-it manner. None of this has gone down well with the Brexit or Trump tribes. Nuance or impartiality just doesn't cut it anymore in political debate.

As for Meghan and Harry, I admit to viewing the pair of them as disingenuous, virtue-signalling, hypocritical, selfish, narcissistic brats. Has some of my criticism of them been too aggressive? Probably. Has it been unfair? On occasion, perhaps. So, am I part of the tribal problem?

Yes, I guess I am. I have a dog-with-a-bone personality that can be a force for good, or perhaps not so good, depending on what bone I am gnawing on – from campaigning against the Iraq War when I was Editor of the *Daily Mirror* and waging a lengthy battle for better gun control in America when I worked at CNN, to trying to oust former Arsenal manager Arsène Wenger, or just feeling very irritated by vegan sausage rolls. The only common denominator is that once the bone's in my mouth, I find it very hard to stop gnawing, sometimes to my own detriment.

At 11 pm tonight, as Brexit became official, I felt nothing but a weary sense of relief and hope, perhaps forlornly, that we could all finally stop shouting at each other and find some common purpose.

FEBRUARY

Pantomime Villain

SATURDAY 1 FEBRUARY

The word 'thick' has been trending in the UK on Twitter ever since we formally left the EU last night. It's because Remoaners have been tweeting the word so much about Brexiters, implying that all 17.4 million people who voted to leave are so stupid they didn't know what they were doing.

What's amazing to me is how liberals keep losing elections and referendums (from Brexit to Trump) despite being – in many minds – so much smarter than their opponents. As I tweeted, 'If you're all so f*cking smart, how did you get beaten by a bunch of thickos?'

Tribal warfare is contaminating society and it's making us forget what really matters in life. Families, friends and communities are all being fractured and poisoned with the angry, bitter, hyper-partisan hostilities fuelled by social media. Tennis star Novak Djokovic, after winning the Australian Open today, made a moving courtside speech in which he spoke about the bushfires and the death of his friend Kobe Bryant. 'It's a reminder to all of us that we should stick together more than ever. Be with our families, stay close to the people that love you and care about you. It's important to be conscious and humble about things that are happening around you.'

Fine words, yet the world's never seemed less capable of actually doing this. We're too busy screaming abuse at each other to see how bad it's getting and the damage it's doing. And when we're not doing that, we're engaging in a daily global competition to see who can say the most preposterously virtue-signalling thing.

This week alone, hugely rich American socialite Nicky Hilton proudly declared she was saving the planet by catching the subway and wearing a vintage Chanel bag to a party 'in the name of sustainability and in the pursuit of carbon footprint offset'; and Democratic presidential candidate Elizabeth Warren told a hustings crowd that she would ensure a 'young trans person' would interview her future secretary of education and she would only hire this future secretary of education if the young trans person approves.

Do they realise how ridiculous this kind of thing sounds to anyone outside the woke bubble? Wokery drives people-pleasing celebrities to lose all sense of perspective, and 'progressive' politicians to lose all sense of what really matters to most people about issues like education.

As I've been saying repeatedly on *GMB* (the show's brilliant director Erron Gordon now has a specific button in his control room to press with me speaking in an exaggerated American accent whenever I feel the urge): THE WORLD'S GONE NUTS.

SUNDAY 2 FEBRUARY

Health Secretary Matt Hancock tweeted today that lots of people have asked him what we can all do to stop the spread of coronavirus. 'The answer is simple,' he said, 'and the same as for the flu – use tissues to catch coughs and sneezes, wash your hands.' Is this virus the same as the flu, though? From what the WHO is saying, it appears far more virulent and deadly than normal flu.

'One thing YOU should do as Health Secretary,' I replied, 'is come on @GMB tomorrow to reassure our viewers about this global health crisis.' He declined, which does seem utterly extraordinary given how serious this might be and an insult to our viewers (we have nine million across the week) who need and deserve to be informed.

Regardless of what the government thinks of *GMB*, we make a lot of noise and news, as the *Observer* confirmed with a seven-page in-depth feature on us today entitled 'IS GOOD MORNING BRITAIN THE WAKE-UP CALL WE DESERVE?' The writer, Tim Adams, watched the show every day in January, calling it his personal 'Morganuary'.

'I've done my best to avoid watching *Good Morning Britain*,' he explained, 'because who in their right mind wants to start the day with Morgan at their breakfast table? But the fact is, there is no escape. You don't need to be among the million viewers who tune in to *Good Morning Britain* to feel its daily presence in your life. Anyone with an eye on this country's media, whether print, social, broadcast, will have absorbed Morgan's more strident opinions – about vegan sausage rolls or Donald Trump or gender identity – by osmosis. [...] It can seem that no reporting of a world event is complete without input from Morgan.'

Adams added, '"Culture war" seems a grandiose term for what *Good Morning Britain* does. But the effect is to add to that pervasive impression that public life is a zero-sum game in which for me to win, you have to lose. [...] Morgan's main opponent in this war is consensus. Increasingly of course, that means he casts himself as the defender of "common sense" and plain speaking in straw-man arguments about whether "clapping should be replaced with 'jazz hands' to make it more inclusive"; or in rants about plus-sized models, gender-neutral clothing or men carrying babies in papooses.'

He then quotes me from a previous interview as saying, 'My persona in public is a slight pantomime villain. I constantly fuel this because it's fun, it's entertaining, it's provocative, it gets everybody going, it encourages debate. All the things I like.'

Adams doesn't like it as much as me, sniping, 'Watching Morgan at breakfast over a period of time, and despite all the self-mockery, that old tabloid nastiness is never too far from the surface. Though by all accounts an affable and charming colleague and friend, in his professional life, even at 7 am, he retains the right to a bully's instinct for taking advantage of vulnerability. That instinct, which he exploits more effectively than any other journalist in our tribal times, drives attention where he wants it: towards him. He knows how to feed that playground impulse that made you want to run towards a scrap when the cry of "Fight!" went up.'

I found the piece a slightly disconcerting read. There's a fine line between being forcefully provocative or challenging, and bullying, a word more people are using about me now, and I can't deny he's right that sometimes I cross it. I don't want to be a bully – the guy known for punching down not up. And in calling out the absurd things about which woke liberals become outraged, I don't want to further distract people from the important stuff in life by waging a perpetual culture war over irrelevant, inconsequential things.

MONDAY 3 FEBRUARY

Last night's BAFTA Awards turned into a self-loathing parade in the wake of every acting nomination, male and female, going to white actors. As he accepted his award for Best Actor, Joaquin Phoenix raged, 'I think that we send a very clear message to people of colour that you're not welcome here, I think that's the message that we're sending to people that have contributed so much to our medium, and our industry, in ways that we benefit from. This is not a self-righteous condemnation, because I'm ashamed to say that I'm part of the problem. I have not done everything in my power to ensure that the sets I work on are inclusive, but I think that it's more than just having sets that are multicultural. I think that we have to really do the hard work to truly understand systemic racism. I think that it is the obligation of the people that have created and perpetuate and benefit from a system of oppression to be the ones that dismantle it.'

Of course, the best way Mr Phoenix could have expressed his outrage would have been to refuse to fly across the Atlantic to accept it. Not least because of his well-documented desire to save the planet. He's not wrong about the diversity issue though.

Prince William, President of BAFTA, urged the industry to make changes, telling the audience, 'Yet in 2020 and not for the first time in the last few years we find ourselves talking again about the need to do more to ensure diversity in the sector and in the awards process. That simply cannot be right in this day and age.'

No, but how does it get fixed?

I asked this question of Andi Peters, the black TV presenter who now makes a lucrative living by producing and fronting all our competitions on *GMB* and other ITV shows. 'Where is the diversity?' I asked him on air today. 'What is going wrong?'

Andi thought for a moment, then replied, 'I think fundamentally there aren't enough people of colour working in our industry. That's a fact.' Then Andi looked around and said, 'Am I, or am I not, the only person of colour standing in this studio right now?' He walked a few feet to double check who was operating the cameras. 'Yes. I am. So there just aren't enough people working in this industry to then be nominated based on their talent.'

GMB does have black people who work in the production crews, but none were working today. There must have been around 15 people in the studio, and all but one were white. I hadn't even noticed, but Andi had.

'If I am a role model to anyone who is watching,' he continued, 'I want to say, "You can do it." I may not have my own show in a primetime slot, but I have been on telly for 30 years. I remember I was being black on television when there was only me, Trevor McDonald and Lenny Henry.'

I was so admiring of his balls for speaking out like this, and what he said made me really think hard. This is what black people mean when they say white people can never understand racism like they do, because we don't see it the way they see it. I didn't notice the studio was all-white because it didn't seem strange to me. But Andi had noticed it immediately, and it was the perfect illustration of why BAFTA is struggling so much to achieve the diversity it says it craves.

True racial equality will only come when white people accept that we generally have more advantages in life than black people – and do something about it. It's not enough to just say how awful we think racism is. I do think people cry 'racism' when it doesn't exist, and I don't believe media coverage of Meghan Markle has been racist, for example, but Andi showed with brutal simplicity why racial inequality doesn't always manifest itself in obvious ways. This is the kind of thing we should be addressing hard as a society, not woke nonsense of the kind that came later in the show when we debated an announcement by animal rights group PETA (People for the Ethical Treatment of Animals) that they want to ban the word 'pet' because it is 'derogatory'.

'Animal protection organisations such as PETA prefer the term "companion animal",' it declared, 'as it more accurately describes the ideal relationship between humans and animals.' It also wants to replace a series of other well-known phrases with less offensive terms that don't, as they see it, 'perpetuate violence against animals' and 'normalise abuse'.

So, for 'Kill two birds with one stone' PETA now wants us to use the words 'Feed two birds with one scone'.

For 'Let the cat out of the bag' use 'Spill the beans'.

For 'Take the bull by the horns' use 'Take the flower by the thorns'.

For 'Be a guinea pig' use 'Be a test tube'.

For 'Hold your horses' use 'Hold the phone'.

For 'Open a can of worms' use 'Open Pandora's box'.

For 'Bring home the bacon' use 'Bring home the bagels'.

For 'Put all your eggs in one basket' use 'Put all your berries in one bowl'.

For 'Cry over spilled milk' use 'Cry over burnt toast'.

For 'Packed in like sardines' use 'Packed in like pickles'.

For 'On a wild goose chase' use 'Out chasing rainbows'.

For 'Ants in your pants' use 'Pepper in your pants'.

And for 'Walk on eggshells' use 'Walk on broken glass'.

As I read this list, published on PETA's website, I felt a mixture of hilarity and deep, deep irritation. This is one of those utterly insane and totally ineffective examples of 'activism' that will obviously have the complete opposite effect to the one those campaigning hope to achieve. All it will do is annoy everyone and make us even more determined to continue using the word 'pet' for our pets. And who the hell are these people to lecture the rest of us on how we speak? It's getting to the stage where almost any word or phrase can be deemed offensive to someone, somewhere, and if we constantly bow to the outrage then freedom of speech will be destroyed.

THURSDAY 6 FEBRUARY

'Coronavirus 3rd case in UK – man in Brighton,' Rupert, my youngest brother, posted on the family WhatsApp chat group.

'We're all doomed,' said Spencer.

'More people are dying of the average flu,' said one of my nieces, Phoebe.

'You are well protected here,' said Mum, 'it's the countries with weaker health systems who will suffer most if it spreads.'

'Not really,' said Spencer, 'because there's no cure. So, if you get it, it's purely a case of whether your immune system is up to the task.'

'There is no cure for many viruses,' said Mum. 'We all have good immune systems to fight them off.'

I'm sure we're not the only family having this kind of conversation. People are beginning to talk more and more about this virus, some worrying about it more than others. I don't know what to think about it yet. SARS scared the hell out of everyone but ended up killing fewer than 800 people worldwide. If this is a similar coronavirus, as seems to be the case, then it may be something that can also be contained quite quickly.

SUNDAY 9 FEBRUARY

There is a splendid, if depressing, irony that the more celebrity wokies howl their outrage about something, the more they cement societal division and endanger the very tolerance they profess to crave. Awards shows have become their preaching pulpit, with the Academy Awards the ultimate virtue-signalling platform.

For many years now, the Oscars has sunk ever deeper into an abyss of politically correct claptrap. It used to be a dazzlingly glamorous celebration of the very best of Hollywood, a four-hour piece of joyous escapism hosted by comedy greats like Bob Hope and Billy Crystal. But it's become an increasingly tedious platform for actors to preach to us about their views on life. And since Kevin Hart was axed from presenting last year's Oscars at the last minute over decade-old homophobic 'joke' tweets for which he had already apologised, no prospective host can now pass the impossibly high ethical bar required by the Twitter thought police, so it's host-less.

This year's event was a particularly excruciating affair, from the very first seconds when Brad Pitt got all political about Trump's impeachment ('They told me I only have 45 seconds up here, which is more than the Senate gave John Bolton this week') to the end when self-righteous vegan Joaquin Phoenix ordered us all to stop drinking milk. 'We feel entitled to artificially inseminate a cow,' he said, tears welling up, 'and when she gives birth, we steal her baby, even though her cries of anguish are unmistakable. And then we take her milk that's intended for her calf and we put it in our coffee and our cereal.'

I actually burst out laughing when he said this. Not because I'm a callous bastard who doesn't care about the plight of calves. But because of all the things for an actor to lecture the world about, the oppression of cows for their milk is perhaps the most ridiculous.

Joaquin, like many celebrity do-gooders, seems very conflicted when it comes to his own personal sacrifices for our greater good. For example, he flies in fuel-guzzling private planes to climate-change marches where he then browbeats us about our carbon footprint. To assuage his hypocritical guilt, though, he's been very keen to point out he's worn the same Stella McCartney tuxedo throughout this year's awards season to minimise waste and help save the planet, which will hugely impress the vast majority of movie-goers who can only afford one tuxedo in their entire lives, if they can afford one at all.

There's been the same kind of laughably deluded nonsense at the awards show dinners, where organisers have proudly served up 'plant-based' menus to show off their worthy environmental credentials. At last month's Golden Globes, stars were served 'vibrant chilled golden beet soup', 'king oyster mushroom scallops risotto' and a 'vegan opera dome dessert'. 'See, we're saving the planet!' was the proud collective message, spoken by multi-millionaire thespians who'd flown to Los Angeles in their private jets and been driven to the Beverly Hilton hotel in stretch limousines.

The hypocrisy ran deep during tonight's ceremony. Documentary maker Julia Reichert, who won an Oscar for the Obama-endorsed movie *American Factory*, made a Marxist call to action for 'workers of the world to unite' against income inequality and was loudly cheered by the highly privileged and elitist mega-rich crowd, clad in $100,000 dresses and dripping in equally expensive jewellery, all seemingly oblivious to their own grotesque contribution to this very inequality. Jane Fonda epitomised this double-standard by tweeting, 'At Oscars wearing Pomellato jewellery because it only uses responsible, ethically harvested gold and sustainable diamonds.' As Jonathan Pie, a fictitious online news reporter created by comedian Tom Walker, retorted, 'I don't think you could be more detached from reality if you laced your morning corn flakes with ethically-sourced LSD.'

The 'preach one thing, do another' theme continued with Natalie Portman, who wore a cape with the names of all the female directors who weren't nominated for an Oscar. A fine gesture, yet as someone on Twitter soon pointed out, Portman's own production company Handsomecharlie Films has only ever hired one female director to make any of its films – and that was Portman herself.

The theme of hard-done-by women dominated proceedings. 'All women are superheroes,' bellowed Sigourney Weaver, indignantly. But they're not. With all due respect to my opposite gender, some women are awful. Just as some men, and I realise this will shock and dismay radical feminists, are good people. The Oscars propagated this hyperbolic pro-women guff all night to mask the fact it still doesn't practise what it preaches and had a male-only director nominee list despite many very good female directors doing excellent work in the past year, including Greta Gerwig (*Little Women*), Lulu Wang (*The Farewell*), Marielle Heller (*A Beautiful Day in the Neighborhood*), Lorene Scafaria (*Hustlers*) and Alma Har'el (*Honey Boy*). In the Oscars' 92-year history, only five women have made it onto the Best Director shortlist, and only one – Kathryn Bigelow – has ever won, for *The Hurt Locker*. Like BAFTA, the Academy bangs on about diversity yet had a virtually all-white nominee list in every acting category.

So, to atone for the lack of diversity, it ordered a procession of 'diverse' performers like Janelle Monáe to proclaim, 'We celebrate all the women who directed phenomenal films!' and 'I'm proud to be standing here as a black, queer artist!' It smacked of desperation, of an organisation full of old white male dinosaurs on its voting membership who I bet couldn't care less about delivering on diversity but don't want to be accused of being sexist or racist.

Sadly, that's why I'm slightly cynical about why *Parasite* – which is undeniably a very good film – won Best Picture. The Academy can now point to a non-English-speaking film winning the top award, and several dozen jubilant Koreans wildly celebrating on stage as the show ended, and say, 'There you go, DIVERSITY!' But at least it threw up the one truly bright light of the night – *Parasite*'s brilliantly charismatic director Bong Joon-ho who declared, 'I'm bloody ready to drink all night!' By the end of the wokest-ever Oscars, I shared his sentiment.

WEDNESDAY 12 FEBRUARY

An interesting development on a story I've been following for a while: the families of three American female high school runners in Connecticut have filed a federal lawsuit seeking to block transgender athletes from participating in girls' sport.

Selina Soule, Alanna Smith and Chelsea Mitchell are represented by conservative non-profit organisation Alliance Defending Freedom, which argues that allowing athletes with a male anatomy to compete has deprived their clients of track titles and scholarship opportunities.

'Forcing them to compete against boys isn't fair, shatters their dreams, and destroys their athletic opportunities,' their attorney said in a statement. 'Having separate boys' and girls' sports has always been based on biological differences, not what people believe about their gender, because those differences matter for fair competition. And forcing girls to be spectators in their own sports is completely at odds with Title IX, a federal law designed to create equal opportunities for women in education and athletics. Connecticut's policy violates that law and reverses nearly 50 years of advances for women.'

The lawsuit centres around two transgender sprinters, Terry Miller and Andraya Yearwood, who were born to male biological bodies but now identify as female. They have won a combined 15 girls' state indoor or outdoor championships since 2017 and the three plaintiffs have competed directly against them, almost always losing to Miller and usually trailing Yearwood.

'Mentally and physically, we know the outcome before the race even starts,' said Alanna Smith. 'That biological unfairness doesn't go away because of what someone believes about gender identity. All girls deserve the chance to compete on a level playing field.' Selina Soule said, 'I fully support and am happy for these athletes for being true to themselves. They should have the right to express themselves in school, but athletics have always had extra rules to keep the competition fair.'

The transgender athletes are both tall, powerful and muscular and described as being 'in the process of transitioning' but they deny this gives them an unfair advantage. 'I have faced discrimination in every aspect of my life and I no longer want to remain silent,' said Miller. 'I am a girl and I am a runner. I participate in athletics just like my peers to excel, find community, and meaning in my life. It is both unfair and painful that my victories have to be attacked and my hard work ignored.' Yearwood agreed. 'I will never stop being me!' she said. 'I hope the next generation of trans youth doesn't have to fight the fights that I have. I hope they can be celebrated when they succeed, not demonised. For the next generation, I run for you!'

She has previously argued that mere physical advantages may not guarantee victory. 'One high jumper could be taller and have longer legs than another,' said Yearwood in 2019, 'but the other could have perfect form and then do better. One sprinter could have parents who spend so much money on personal training for their child, which in turn, would cause that child to run faster.'

In America, transgender athletes can compete without restrictions in Connecticut, which is one of 17 states that currently permits this. It is harder for transgender athletes to compete in school in eight other states, as controls are in place that mean they have to participate under the gender on their birth certificates, unless they've had sex reassignment procedures or hormone therapies.

All of this raises hugely important questions about the whole trans debate that has raged furiously for the past few years. What's being lost in the laudable process of the battle in trans rights for fairness and equality to be recognised ... is fairness and equality.

Men and women are different physiological creatures, and a person's sex is an immutable characteristic the vast majority of the time. That's why they have always competed separately in events like the Olympics. If men and women were to compete with each other, it would destroy women's sport forever. In fact, I doubt a woman would win a single gold medal. Not because women are less important or mentally inferior to men, but because when you put the strongest, most powerful and fastest men up against their female equivalents, the men will invariably win. I have no desire to stop the male-bodied female transgender athletes playing sport or competing – that would be unfair – but allowing them to compete against women born with female biological bodies is also unfair.

Serena Williams is the greatest female tennis player to ever lift a racquet. She's dominated her sport in such a spectacular manner that it's made her one of the richest, most successful sports stars in America, earning $30 million a year from prize money and endorsements. One of the major contributors to her triumphant career has been her extraordinary physique: Serena's a tall, powerful woman. She's 5 ft 9 in, weighs 155 lb and can bench press 225 lb, though interestingly she once said she doesn't do much weight training because her muscles are natural and need little work. Yet even that would give her no chance against a top or even average male professional player.

Aged ten years old, Serena beat male US star Andy Roddick 6–1 in a single set when they were both junior players in Florida. But if they had played each other again when he became the men's world no. 1, Roddick wouldn't just have won, he'd have annihilated her. Serena would have been lucky to pick up even a single game. And it would likely be exactly the same outcome if she now played any of the 1,000 best male tennis players in the world – John McEnroe has said he thinks Serena would rank 700th in men's tennis, but other experts said he was being very generous. This has got nothing to do with her incredible talent, and everything to do with her physiology. Male tennis players are just bigger, stronger, faster than her, and Serena is one of the biggest, strongest, fastest female tennis players in history. So, it's not 'sexist' or 'bigoted' to say the top 1,000 men would beat Serena Williams – it's just a cold, hard, statistical fact.

Now imagine a scenario where a 25-year-old male player ranked, say, no. 300 in the world, and earning around $100,000 a year, suddenly decides he wants to identify as female – either for entirely genuine reasons or for duplicitous, fraudulent, cynically commercial reasons of the kind that have made many athletes cheat – and now wishes to compete against women. That player, if he underwent hormonal treatment to reduce his testosterone levels to the required levels (under current rules, he would not be obliged to make any surgical transition), could spend the next three or four years playing as a woman on the women's tour. He, now '*she*', would instantly be the best female tennis player that's ever lived.

'She' would destroy Serena Williams, and every other woman player. 'She' would win every major tournament, break every women's tennis record and win tens, potentially hundreds of millions of dollars in the process. And 'she' would kill women's tennis forever. Oh, and if 'she' then wished to, 'she' could retire, and announce 'he' was now identifying as male again. This was the potentially ruinous scenario tennis legend Martina Navratilova articulated in a newspaper opinion column that promptly made her the most hated LGBTQ woman in America. 'A man can decide to be female,' she wrote in the *Sunday Times*, 'take hormones if required by whatever sporting organisation is concerned, win everything in sight and perhaps earn a fortune, and then reverse his decision and go back to making babies if he so desires. It's insane and it's cheating.' Yes, it is. And to those who scoff at the notion that sportspeople might go to that kind of length to cheat, I scoff back: some sportspeople, as the likes of Lance Armstrong sadly reminded us, will go to *any* lengths to cheat if there is big money to be made.

Within hours of her common-sense column appearing, Navratilova was dropped as an ambassador for Athlete Ally, a US-based organisation that campaigns for LGBTQ sportspeople. They said her comments 'perpetuate dangerous myths'. She was viciously vilified on social media and accused of being 'transphobic'. Yet Navratilova, who herself faced huge amounts of abuse when she courageously came out as gay in

1981, has been one of the loudest and most loyal 'allies' to the LGBTQ community for decades. She even hired Renée Richards, the first transgender tennis star, as her coach. That, though, counted for nothing. For daring to challenge the undeniable inequality created by transgender women participating in women's sport, she had to be brutally attacked and silenced.

As the furore grew, a harassed Navratilova posted a new response, apologising for using the word 'cheating' but reiterating her concerns. 'I am not trying to exclude trans people from living a fully, healthy life,' she said. 'All I am trying to do is make sure that girls and women who were born female are competing on as level a playing field as possible within their sport.' She was widely supported by other athletes, including former British Olympic swimmer Sharron Davies, who said transgender women should not be permitted to compete in female competitions.

'There is a fundamental difference between the binary sex you are born with and the gender you may identify as,' Davies said. 'To protect women's sport, those with a male sex advantage should not be able to compete in women's sport. Every single woman athlete I've spoken to, and I have spoken to many, all of my friends in international sports, understand and feel the same way as me. It's not a transphobic thing. We have no issue with people who are transgender.'

Predictably, Davies was also promptly accused of being a 'transphobe' and 'sharing hate speech' by transgender cyclist Rachel McKinnon, who became UCI Masters Track World Champion despite having a vastly superior size advantage (she is 6 ft and weighs 200 lb) over female rivals. It's the go-to weapon to silence anyone these days and threaten one's right to freedom of speech – just call them a bigot even when they respectfully suggest something is self-evidently unfair.

I watched all this with open-mouthed astonishment. First, at the fact we were even having this debate when Martina Navratilova was so obviously right. Second, that anyone like her who dares to say the bleeding obvious is immediately and shamefully subjected to the most appalling bullying in a bid to silence an opinion the notoriously aggressive transgender lobby doesn't want to hear. And third, that the vitriol and silencing present a real threat to our right to freedom of speech – a right that is never more crucial and in more need of upholding than when it comes to issues like this.

Amid all the debate-suppressing fury, though, the facts speak for themselves. As more and more transgender women compete in women's sport, so their performances grow more and more dominant. In Brazil, Tiffany Abreu became the first transgender player in the top-flight women's volleyball league in 2017, after a lengthy career as a male competitor. Her record performances since have enraged some female players. In an open letter to the IOC, Ana Henkel, who represented Brazil at four Olympics in volleyball and beach volleyball, said, 'This rushed decision to include biological men, born and built with testosterone, with their height, their strength and aerobic capacity of men, is beyond the sphere of tolerance. It represses, embarrasses, humiliates and excludes women.'

The irony of this debate is that the transgender community has rightly fought for years to win equality and fairness. It's a battle I have always supported. Yet now they are fighting equally ferociously for the right to have an unfair and unequal advantage over women in sport who were born biologically female.

It's not 'transphobic' to believe transgender women have an unfair edge in women's sport that is purely down to their biological male bodies. It's just a fact. And as the US conservative pundit Ben Shapiro once observed, 'Facts don't care about your feelings.'

THURSDAY 13 FEBRUARY

Harry and Meghan have flown in a private jet, from the $11 million mansion in Vancouver they've been living in for the past few weeks as guests of a mysterious billionaire benefactor, to Florida for an event hosted by JP Morgan Chase & Co, America's largest bank and the seventh largest in the world with total assets of $2.6 trillion. And they were reportedly being paid between $500,000 and $1 million for their appearance, including a speech by Harry. What did he speak about? Mental health, obviously. But that raises a real problem for me.

There's a big difference between talking about mental health to raise public awareness of grief-related mental health issues and doing it privately for a big fat fee to a bunch of super-rich bankers, business tycoons, politicians and celebrities. Also, by commercially exploiting his privileged position in the royal household like this, isn't Harry behaving in exactly the same way he professes to despise in his media pronouncements? And for a pair of self-proclaimed eco-warriors, what exactly has been their host JP Morgan's contribution to saving the planet? The bank was recently revealed, by the Rainforest Action Network, to have invested $195 billion in fossil fuel companies in the past three years alone. They were by far the worst offenders on the banking list of shame, with Wells Fargo a distant second at $151 billion.

When I posted a link to yet another column about them saying all this, a singer named Roses Gabor tweeted back to me, 'Honestly, I don't know how you're not bored and tired.' It was a fair observation. 'Actually, I am bored and tired with Harry and Meghan,' I replied. 'They're exhausting, but they keep doing stuff that's newsworthy, usually for the wrong reasons, and my job is to write about the news.' And there, right there, is the chicken and egg conundrum. *Are* they still newsworthy? *Do* they deserve all the relentless attention the media, including me, gives them?

'Dad, why do you care so much about Meghan and Harry?' my middle son Stanley asked over dinner.

'I don't really,' I replied, but even as I said that I knew it sounded absurd given how much I bang on about them.

'Well, if you don't care, stop making it look like you do!' Stan retorted. He's got a point. Aren't there more important issues for me to be focusing on and getting angry about?

SATURDAY 15 FEBRUARY

I was sitting outside having breakfast when a WhatsApp message pinged from Stan in his bedroom.

'Caroline Flack found dead.'

I grabbed my phone and saw the breaking news, about my 40-year-old TV presenter friend, exploding like a bomb on Twitter. What the hell's happened?

It quickly emerged that she took her own life at her London flat after being briefly left alone by a friend who'd been staying with her. I felt sick to the pit of my stomach. This is what I had feared might happen for the past few weeks.

Caroline was a whip-smart, warm, funny, complicated and incredibly likeable bundle of energy with a tempestuous tabloid-headline-grabbing love life and a penchant for hard partying. But her world fell apart in mid-December when she was charged with assaulting her boyfriend, tennis player Lewis Burton, during an early-hours row at her Islington flat that left him bleeding from injuries allegedly caused by something she threw at him. Caroline was reported to have told police 'I did it' and then to have warned she would kill herself.

I was due to see her at my annual Christmas party in my local Kensington pub on 19 December, but on the day I received another text: 'Don't think I'll make it tonight. I can't even leave the hotel, let alone go home. This has been the worst time of my life. And for what? Throwing a phone in anger. It's so hard for one person to take this all on.'

'Understood,' I replied. 'It's all a massive overreaction, and it will pass. So sorry you're going through hell, but having been through a few tough times myself, I can assure you that you'll get through it. At the end of the day, it's just bloody telly and nobody died.'

'Thanks Piers, appreciate the support, have a lovely evening.'

On 23 December, Caroline pleaded not guilty and was bailed until trial on 4 March on condition she didn't contact her boyfriend, despite Burton saying he didn't support the prosecution and that 'he is not the victim'.

I watched her leave court looking haunted, exhausted and terrified, and felt so sorry for her. But social media was having none of it and she was summarily convicted in the court of public opinion and subjected to a sustained campaign of appalling vitriol. Knowing how avidly she reads stuff on social media, I can only imagine how it must have been eating away at her soul. I stayed in touch with her and tried to keep her spirits up by defending her on Twitter and on TV. But it was obvious she was going through utter hell.

According to some reports, Caroline was told just a few hours before she took her life that she would definitely face trial. Burton yesterday posted an Instagram post to her featuring a photo of them together and the caption, 'Happy Valentines, Love you.' I don't want to guess why Caroline thought she couldn't go on, but it's not hard to imagine the combination of these two things might have tipped her over the edge of despair.

She'd lost the job she loved, wasn't allowed to see or talk to the man she loved and was now facing the very public humiliation of what would undoubtedly have been a very sensationalised court case. Despite widespread support from her family and many concerned friends, it obviously all got too much for her. And that's just an absolute tragedy.

'Oh my God, this is horrendous,' I tweeted. 'Caroline was a fun, bright & sparky person whose whole world collapsed recently, both professionally & personally. She told me it had been the worst time of her life and was clearly struggling to cope with losing everything she held dear. This is such sad, awful news.'

The reaction to me saying this was fast, furious and vicious. The court of public opinion instantly delivered another verdict: I was to blame for Caroline's suicide. Yes, me, someone who had tried to help her privately and publicly through her darkest time, and who had never written or said a bad word about her in my life. It's absolutely true that she endured a barrage of tremendously negative media and social media attention since her arrest, and I know from what she told me that it was all having a very damaging effect on her mental wellbeing. I also accept that as a former tabloid editor, I published many negative stories about other celebrities caught up in similar scrapes, so don't have entirely clean hands in this regard.

But Caroline was a friend of mine and I had nothing to do with her death, so the ferocious outpouring of abuse suggesting I did is as wrong as it is hurtful.

'Piers Morgan, who spends most of his days vilifying women, can f*ck the f*ck off and then, when he's f*cked off, can f*ck off a bit more,' said a former lawyer named Emma Kennedy who seems to spew similar abuse on Twitter to everyone she dislikes, all day every day.

'Spare us your shock Piers,' said some random tweeter, 'you are one of the many dickheads that cause SO much pain, learn from this and BE F*CKING KIND.'

'F*ck off you two faced twat,' spat the author Irvine Welsh.

Even Alastair Campbell, the man who spun an illegal war that killed a million people, tried to take the moral high ground, telling me, 'Suggest you have a day off.'

The foul-mouthed savagery of the 'YOU F*CKING KILLED HER YOU C*NT' vitriol spewing into my Twitter feed stung more than the usual troll abuse. I feel desperately saddened by her death and utterly enraged at now being blamed for it. And what a sick irony that the very same keyboard warriors accusing people like me of hounding Caroline to her death are the people who incessantly post abuse to celebrities and people in the media – and who are right now busily hounding those same people online. This is social media at its worst – a vicious mob intent on 'cancelling' anyone and anything it could think of to blame for something it was upset about.

SUNDAY 16 FEBRUARY

Awoke at 4 am again after a fitful night's sleep and made the mistake of immediately turning on Twitter to see a further bombardment of abuse aimed at me for 'killing Caroline'.

Normally, abuse from troll idiots flies off me like water off the proverbial duck's back. I genuinely don't give a monkey's cuss what they think of me, and frankly if you embrace the jungle of Twitter as enthusiastically and aggressively as I do, then a strong reaction is to be expected. But this time, it is getting to me. It's so particularly vile and personal, and based on utter lies. I feel peculiarly raw and fried – shocked and upset by Caroline's death, and sickened at being blamed for it.

British actress Jameela Jamil, mental-health and body-image activist and self-proclaimed 'feminist-in-progress', has led the blame-game charge, tweeting, 'It was only a matter of time before the media and the prolonged social media dogpile, hers lasted for MONTHS, pushed someone completely over the edge. Rest in Peace Caroline Flack. This is f*cking horrendous.'

Jamil also called for the government to launch an urgent inquiry into 'the British press and their practices' following the 'maltreatment of those in the public eye including Caroline Flack and Harry and Meghan Markle, to name a few. The headlines, harassment and trial by media has to end and they must be held accountable.'

As I read this, I had a sudden memory of an Instagram direct message exchange Caroline and I had about Jamil a few months ago – and found it on my phone. It was from 22 October last year, after Jamil attacked Caroline's new (now cancelled) plastic-surgery-themed Channel 4 show *The Surjury* without having even seen it, accusing her of being involved in something that would 'prey on people's insecurities'.

This led to so many of Jamil's one million followers bombarding Caroline with abuse that Caroline messaged me to say, 'I'm struggling with Jameela, the hate she aims at me ...'

Yet here is the same Jameela Jamil now leading a campaign to make the media accountable for Caroline's death. The brazen hypocrisy is staggering. And repulsive. I toyed with posting my conversation with Caroline, to expose Jamil and shut her up, but decided against it. Why incite even more rage and abuse?

TUESDAY 18 FEBRUARY

A senior Labour politician Dawn Butler, the shadow women and equalities secretary, appeared on *GMB* today (in my absence – she always refuses to come on if I am there because she finds me too offensive) to defend the party's position on radical gender identity and announced, 'A child is born without sex, a child is formed without sex in the beginning.' This was one of the most extraordinary things I've ever heard come out of a politician's mouth, and the bar for that accolade is exceedingly low.

In a later attempt to clarify her words, Butler said, 'The thing is, when you are born, you're told by the doctor, "Congratulations, it's a boy" or "Congratulations, it's a girl." But I was trying to make the point that, you know, it's also not a given. There's lots of people that identify as non-binary.'

Butler, in her *GMB* interview, was also asked if people are 'transphobic' if they believe there is a biological difference between men who say they are women even if they haven't had surgery, and women born to female biological bodies.

'If you're saying that a trans woman isn't a woman,' she said, 'then there are issues around that. Talking about penises and vaginas doesn't help the conversation because then you're saying that a trans woman isn't a woman.'

This whole wild exchange exposed how the gender debate has got completely out of control and become one of the most divisive and polarising of our time. It boils down to this: the natural liberal instinct is to strongly defend transgender rights, but also to strongly defend women's rights. The conflict comes when the former trumps the latter or, for me, when all societal norms have to be abandoned at the frenzied altar of political correctness.

For example, what possible good does it do anyone when a girls' school bans pupils from being called girls? In a letter to parents in early 2018, Stephanie Gill – head teacher of Altrincham Grammar School for Girls in Manchester, England – said the term 'girls' would no longer be used when addressing the school's 1,350 students, to break 'ingrained habits in the way pupils are spoken to and spoken about'. Ms Gill explained the motivation for the ban was to stop transgender students being 'misgendered'.

'We have moved to using gender-neutral language in all our communications with students and parents,' she wrote. 'We know that for many transgender students being misgendered can be very hurtful.' So, the word 'girls' would be replaced by 'students' and a girls' school, which only accepts girls, was now banning the use of the word 'girls' in case it offended somebody. I assumed this move would necessitate an automatic change to the school's name, but I was wrong; Altrincham Grammar School for Girls is still called Altrincham Grammar School for Girls. It's just that nobody is allowed to use the word 'girls'.

Once again, the PC language cops' lack of consistency is glaring and grating.

Chris McGovern, of the Campaign for Real Education – and coincidentally, a former teacher of mine in Lewes, Sussex – described the move as 'complete folly' and explained the inherent problem. 'Children who have issues over their gender identity can be treated with respect without the English language being altered to accommodate them. Instead, this kind of move risks leading to more bullying of transgender pupils who may be wrongly blamed for this move.' Exactly.

But there are wider issues here too. Why does Ms Gill not respect the wishes of the vast majority of her students who wish to continue being called 'girls'? Why is *their* identity deemed less worthy of respect than a transgender student's? Why have *their* rights been trampled on? This move by one head teacher exposed the worst virtue-signalling trait of 'wokery' – the desperate need to be seen to 'do the right thing' and make oneself look wholesomely virtuous, even if it means crushing the very life out of basic common sense in the process. It also exposed the basic problem with the ongoing high-octane gender debate: what's the point of it? And aren't there more important issues?

Like so much in life, things were all so much easier a century ago, when gender was a little-used word and it was just assumed everyone was either male or female, based on their designated sex at birth. Henry Watson Fowler, an English schoolmaster and expert on the English language – he wrote *A Dictionary of Modern English Usage* and was once described as a 'lexicographical genius' by *The Times* – stated in 1926 that 'Gender ... is a grammatical term only. To talk of persons ... of the masculine or feminine gender, meaning of the male or female sex, is either a jocularity (permissible or not according to context) or a blunder.'

Despite this, people still conflate the two, believing gender and sex are the same thing, which is why in ordinary speech sex and gender are often used interchangeably. Indeed, in certain countries like Germany or Finland, there are no separate words for them. But they're not the same thing at all.

A person's sex is defined biologically: humans are born with 46 chromosomes in 23 pairs. The X and Y chromosomes determine a person's sex. Most women are 46XX and most men are 46XY. Babies are thus categorised at birth as male or female depending on their genitals. However, it's not quite as simple as that. In a few births per thousand, some individuals will be born with a single sex chromosome (45X and 45Y) and some with three or more sex chromosomes (47XXX, 47XYY or 47XXY, etc.). So, for some people, the feeling of belonging to the wrong sex is not a choice but based on real science. Hence the rise in the past hundred years of 'sex re-assignment surgery' for people to transition from one sex to the other. And there are some people who are born with biological sex characteristics that complicate sex assignment, so they are known as 'intersex'.

Gender, though, has nothing to do with biological sex. In essence, it's a state of mind; a social construct based around behaviour, expression, perception and identity. And as the rush to self-identify gender has intensified, so has the level of contorted confusion surrounding it. Nobody, frankly, seems to have a clue what 'gender' now really means or how many 'genders' actually exist. Even supposed experts lack any certainty about where the line is drawn, or whether there should be any line at all.

The Royal College of General Practitioners – one of Britain's most respected medical bodies that governs the work practice of family doctors and primary care physicians – recognises just six types of gender: male, female, gender-neutral, non-binary, gender-fluid and gender-queer. Yet Stonewall, which advises the UK government and employers on gender issues, lists 17. And on social media platforms, the number grows ever bigger. Tumblr, for example, says there are 112 genders. One of these is 'Astralgender', which is apparently 'a gender that feels connected to space'. Another is 'Astergender', which is a gender that 'feels bright and celestial'. Facebook got up to 71 genders but was then deluged with so many complaints about not being 'inclusionary' enough that several years ago it announced there were now just three types of gender: male, female and anything else you like. Little wonder that some want gender killed off altogether.

The *Guardian* newspaper, Britain's most 'woke' media entity, invited its journalists in 2019 to attend a writing work-shop ('wokeshop'?) entitled '(A) Wake for Gender'. Presented by a self-proclaimed 'artist and educator' named Soofiya, the sessions were described as 'an imaginary funeral for "Gender"'.

Invitees were encouraged to explore their feelings from 'relief' to 'grief' at Gender's death, and to join other members of the audience to 'mourn, celebrate, observe and collectively write a legacy for what "Gender" leaves behind, creating a ritual to mark its passing while imagining our futures without it'.

So, are we witnessing the death of gender? Sadly, I would say yes. Or, rather, we are witnessing the death of any conventional notion of gender, as the more extreme arm of the transgender lobby bullies the world into not just being tolerant to transgender people, which is a thoroughly admirable aspiration that I fully endorse, but into also denouncing and cancelling all accepted societal gender norms and smashing women's rights too if necessary.

The hypocrisy and inconsistency surrounding the gender debate was laid bare to me when the BBC, Britain's publicly funded broadcaster, released an educational video, made by its BBC Teach department, that informed children between the ages of nine and twelve there are now 'over 100, if not more, gender identities' and that this fact is 'really exciting'. Is it? Or is telling young impressionable children they can identify as pretty much whatever they like in fact deluded, disingenuous and downright dangerous? And if anyone really *can* identify as anything they like, what harm does that do to transgender people who've actually gone through the full physical and emotional trauma of transitioning from male to female, or female to male, a process that can take years?

Naturally, when I expressed my concerns about the BBC's gender stance on *Good Morning Britain*, I was promptly accused of being a hateful transphobic bigot and a petition was started to have me fired. This is a familiar response mechanism for wokies – if someone dares to challenge their opinion, that person must be publicly and viciously shamed, vilified and cancelled. However, as an old-school liberal, I was prepared to debate the issue with someone who supported the BBC. That person was gay activist journalist Ben Butterworth, who said he signed the petition to have me fired 'because you don't seem to want to learn'. This is another familiar refrain from wokies – they're here to educate us lesser mortal imbeciles about the way we should think.

The response to this debate was fast and furious, the most extreme fury coming from the very same gender warriors who demand that we should respect *all* forms of self-identity – no questions asked. Of course, what they really mean by this apparently liberal, tolerant view is that self-identification is absolutely fine so long as you self-identify in a way that meets their approval. Otherwise, you must be silenced.

I fully understand and respect that some people genuinely feel they were born to the wrong biological sex. I interviewed Caitlyn Jenner for my *Life Stories* show and came away massively impressed by her extraordinary courage and determination in transitioning from all-American male Olympic gold medal hero Bruce Jenner to a woman. This is not the sort of thing that anyone does lightly, and those who do it should be given complete respect and offered the same rights as everyone else. If, on reaching adulthood, someone like Caitlyn Jenner comes to the informed, mature and unchanging conclusion that they were born into the wrong sex, then I will be the first to offer respect and encouragement for them to transition and fight for them to have equal rights.

But I find it unconscionable to insist that kids as young as five should be enabled to change their gender or even begin the transformation of their sex. Anyone who's had children knows they go through all kinds of confusing emotional turmoil before, during and after puberty. How can they possibly be sure what sex or gender they really want to be when they're not even old enough to understand the terms?

There has been considerable concern surrounding the Tavistock and Portman NHS Foundation Trust, which offers gender identity services for children under 18, with some patients as young as three or four years old. The Trust has had a record number of referrals and now sees 3,200 per cent more patients than it did 10 years ago – with the increase for girls up by 5,337 per cent.

In a statement the Tavistock and Portman NHS Foundation Trust says it 'stands by' the 2019 review of the NHS Gender Identity Development Service (GIDS) and is 'confident that it fairly addressed the issues raised', adding 'safeguarding is of the utmost importance to the Trust'.

Yet at the same time, many young transgender people have been seeking help to 'detransition' back to their original sex.

A disturbing Sky News report in October 2019 featured a 28-year-old woman named Charlie Evans who had set up a charity after detransitioning back to a female after ten years as a male. She claimed that hundreds of other transgender people contacted her after she went public to say they want to do the same.

'I'm in communication with 19- and 20-year-olds who have had full gender reassignment surgery who wish they hadn't,' she said, 'and their dysphoria hasn't been relieved, they don't feel better for it.' Now, from my point of view there is no doubt that for many people, transitioning works and they are much happier as a result. But there is increasing evidence that a lot of young people race into it and then regret it – as they do with many things in life. Yet for the more radical arm of the trans lobby, even using the word detransition is 'transphobic'.

This new gender battle has been hijacked in a self-destructive way by extremists who are as damaging to the cause as radical feminists are to feminism. They don't just demand equality but a new form of inequality too – one in which women's rights are diminished, not enhanced. For example, some schools now allow boys who self-identify as girls to use the female bathrooms. Has anyone given any real thought to how this might create huge unease, confusion and discomfort for young girls already deeply anxious about their changing body shapes? Are their rights deemed to be as worthy of respect as those of the self-identifying transgender pupils? At the very least, there should surely be proper debate about it, without everyone expressing concern being branded 'transphobic'.

The problem gets even more acute when we consider sexual offenders in prison, as exemplified by one notorious case in 2018. As a man, Stephen Wood had previously been convicted of indecent assault and indecent exposure, and gross indecency involving children. It emerged when he was imprisoned again for attacking a neighbour with a steak knife that Wood had also raped two other women. But he then announced he was now identifying as a woman, Karen White, and despite undergoing no physical changes, 'she' was transferred to a women's prison where 'she' promptly sexually assaulted two women in three months before being transferred back to a male prison.

Prosecutor Christopher Dunn told the court, 'She is allegedly a transgender female. The prosecution say allegedly because there's smatterings of evidence that the defendant's approach to transitioning has been less than committed ... so the defendant can use a transgender persona to put herself in contact with vulnerable persons she can then abuse.'

Frances Crook, chief executive of the Howard League for Penal Reform, told the *Sunday Times* that prison managers were having to make decisions on prisoners claiming to be transgender 'in a toxic political environment'. She said, 'I am asking them to err on the side of caution as there is emerging evidence that certain men are jumping on the bandwagon to access and harm very vulnerable women in prison.' It's alarming to see self-identity open to all manner of abuse like this.

There are so many other unresolved problems with this surging transgender activism. Things might be easier for the trans activist movement if they didn't try so hard to police the language used about them.

They can call themselves any pronouns they like. But to react furiously if others accidentally 'misgender' them, and demand they be 'cancelled', does nothing to foster support and stifles people's willingness to engage and debate in transgender issues.

British actor Ian McShane, who filmed with non-binary actor Asia Kate Dillon, summed up the obvious problem. 'I worked with a girl on *John Wick: Chapter 3*,' he told the *Independent*. 'I shouldn't say "girl" because she prefers "them", but she's a lovely girl. She's a terrific actor, too, but before we started, I told her that I was sorry if I sometimes said "she" but it's hard to say "them" when there's only one of you.' Of course, McShane was immediately branded transphobic, yet he surely spoke for the vast majority of people who find much of the transgender debate, and the ridiculous language surrounding it, completely mystifying. Again, I simply urge common sense and a sensible, mutually tolerant way to deal with what is a sensitive issue.

THURSDAY 20 FEBRUARY

A woman named Kayleigh Dray has let rip at me in *Stylist* magazine following the news that I've been shortlisted for Columnist of the Year at the British Press Awards.

'It's difficult to ignore Piers Morgan, however hard we may try,' she writes. 'He's got a platform on live TV, he's all over Twitter and he has his own newspaper column. And now that same column – which, in the last two months alone, has taken aim at Meghan Markle, Prince Harry, J-Lo, Shakira, "deluded liberals" and "Hollywood's virtue-signalling hypocrites" – has been nominated as Columnist of the Year. Which is good for Morgan, I guess, but very bad for society as a whole. The year is 2020, and the theme of our new decade (at least ostensibly) is this: be kinder.' Ms Dray insisted she believes in the importance of reading views she doesn't agree with, but added, 'While the internet should be a place for people to share ideas and communicate with one another, trolls like Morgan have created a climate that causes more pain. One that makes it unsafe to lead with vulnerability or stand out. One that pushes us to hate one another, to lash out at one another, to scream our opinions in capital letters across the internet. And his "opinions" – so carefully chosen to divide us into two camps, to inspire and profit from outrage – are dangerous, too. [...] Morgan's column [...] enables him to speak to people in their homes over breakfast. Those who hate him and his opinions flick to that page because they want to know what outrageous thing he's said. And those who do agree with him, meanwhile, latch onto his examples of "woke" liberals, "rabid feminists" and "emasculated" men as proof of all that is wrong with the 21st century. Nobody wins ... except Morgan himself, of course. So, it's time to do what we should have done a long time ago. Don't lash out, or hurl insults at him, or bully him. And, for Christ's sake, don't bloody nominate him as columnist of the year (why are we rewarding his bullying antics?). Instead, ignore his column, ignore his tweets, ignore his ridiculous comments on *GMB*. It's hard, I know (I find it almost impossible not to rise to the bait), but by refusing to engage with him, we make this business of trolling far less lucrative. Because, just as a fire goes out when we stop feeding it oxygen, so trolls run out of steam when we stop giving them attention.'

Of course, there's an amusing irony in *Stylist* devoting so much attention to me while telling people to stop paying attention to me, and in the writer speaking about me in the same aggressively personal way she professes to dislike in me speaking about others. But once again, I feel slightly uneasy about this ongoing theme that I'm some kind of troll bully spewing mindless, aggressive opinions for clickbait. I don't see myself like that and would argue that many of my so-called 'targets' are very prolific in dishing it out themselves, especially at me. But I'm increasingly aware that others do.

And while I find it utterly ridiculous that people like Jameela Jamil and Meghan Markle are being cited as 'victims' given the way they have conducted themselves, it's increasing clear that I can't beat them in this game of hypocritical, attention-seeking, virtue-signalling, self-pitying nonsense. I can only add to the noise, the toxicity and their sense of victimhood. And where does all of this venomous tribal arguing lead to anyway? As Caroline Flack has so tragically shown us, it can end in absolute tragedy.

FRIDAY 21 FEBRUARY

President Trump today tweeted his support for a new Bollywood gay love story movie, *Shubh Mangal Zyada Saavdhan* (Extra Careful of Marriage), which follows a gay couple as they struggle to win over disapproving parents. Even as I write these words, I can't quite believe them. But then much of what Trump says or does is inexplicable, inconsistent or downright weird. It's part of his unique character, good, bad and ugly.

What made it all the more unexpected is that he was responding to a tweet from left-wing British gay rights campaigner Peter Tatchell. Tatchell tweeted an article in *Pink News*, the gay newspaper website, about the film with the words, 'Win over older people, following the decriminalisation of homosexuality.' He was referring to India's ruling in late 2018 that gay sex is no longer a crime.

'Great!' retweeted Trump.

'Wow,' I replied. 'President Trump tweeting supportively to Peter Tatchell about a ground-breaking gay Bollywood rom-com is not what I expected to see on Twitter today. Great to see.'

Tatchell, clearly stunned to receive support from a man who represents pretty much everything he opposes in public life, responded to me, 'I hope this is the beginning of President Trump's genuine embrace of LGBT rights and not just a PR stunt.' Who knows with Trump? But I've always taken the view that where the president does something good, liberals should acknowledge it and praise him. If they calmed down a bit, so might he.

Most, I have to say, don't agree with me.

SUNDAY 23 FEBRUARY

Jameela Jamil has continued to spew abuse at the media for causing Caroline's death, and her hypocrisy continues to disgust me. Today, I finally snapped and tweeted what Caroline had told me about her.

'Jameela Jamil is having a lot to say about online harassment,' I said. 'So in the interests of balance, here is a message Caroline Flack sent me last October after the same Jameela

Jamil led an online pile-on against her regarding a new TV show she was doing.' I included a screen-grab of Caroline's anguished plea: 'I'm struggling with Jameela ... The hate she aims at me.'

Twitter erupted, with people either abusing me for publishing it, or abusing Jamil for her hypocrisy. As I watched the debate raging ferociously, I felt an increasing discomfort. Is this where we've got to? Everyone screaming horrible abuse at everyone else over the tragic suicide of a young woman driven to despair by all the online abuse *she* had received? Society – decent, kind, civilised society – is broken, and social media's the main reason for it.

The phrase 'Be Kind' has been trending all week since Caroline died, as a tribute to her own words in December before her world fell apart: 'In a world where you can be anything, be kind.' Yet here we are, after the person who wrote that has killed herself, and the one thing nobody is being is kind.

MONDAY 24 FEBRUARY

Harvey Weinstein was convicted today of rape and will almost certainly spend the rest of his life behind bars. His astonishing downfall is thus complete. It's been extraordinary to watch someone I knew well for many years, and who was one of the most powerful and successful forces in Hollywood, crash and burn in such appalling ignominy and disgrace. In many ways, Weinstein represented the very worst excesses of a business full of loathsome predators and sharks.

The last time I saw him was in January 2017, ten months before he was exposed, when we had lunch to discuss a US gun violence documentary I'd been working on. He was his usual bombastic, high-energy, super-confident self. However, when we spoke briefly on the phone after the scandal broke he sounded a very different, downcast and desperate man. He was hiding in an Arizona clinic, had been fired from his own company, dumped by his wife Georgina, disowned by Hollywood, including his own brother and business partner Bob, and was facing criminal prosecution.

Now he's been found guilty, and there's no defence for the sickening way Harvey Weinstein treated so many women. Yet there's a lot of hypocrisy surrounding the way Hollywood has now turned its back on him. I remember being at his very exclusive pre-Oscars dinner a few years ago and seeing A-listers like Meryl Streep, Bono, Oprah Winfrey, Robert De Niro, Jamie Foxx, Taylor Swift and Harry Styles fawning all over him. At the end of the night, Harvey took the microphone and said, 'There are only two things you have to answer to in life – God and Meryl Streep. Thank you and goodnight.' Everyone roared. Meryl held her heart and blew him a kiss. In that moment, Harvey Weinstein was King of Hollywood.

Now he's the Devil, a man whose face adorned the cover of *TIME* magazine with the headline 'PRODUCER. PREDATOR. PARIAH.', and who has been exposed as a ruthless, selfish, bullying, misogynist prone to harassing, abusing and raping women and trading sexual favours for movie roles.

I applaud the courageous women who came forward to lift the lid off Weinstein's decades of depravity when he was still in a position of great power to make or break careers. But this scandal goes much further and is much murkier than just Harvey Weinstein. It goes right to the heart of Hollywood's moral hypocrisy. There's always been a shockingly complacent attitude to morality in Tinseltown, where the bar for acceptable behaviour seems entirely conditional on a star's success and ability to make others successful. The outrage over Weinstein is flying most furiously from those who seem to apply an extraordinarily malleable ethical standard.

Take his great friend Meryl, for example. Streep, eventually, after four days of silence, described the revelations as 'disgraceful' and said they 'appalled those of us whose work he championed'. Then she insisted, 'One thing can be clarified. Not everybody knew. I didn't know about these offenses. I did not know about his settlements with actresses and colleagues. I did not know about his having meetings in his hotel room, his bathroom, or other inappropriate, coercive acts.' She ended by saying, 'The behaviour is inexcusable, but the abuse of power familiar. Each brave word that is raised, heard and credited by our watchdog media will ultimately change the game.'

Fine words, but how exactly do they sit with Streep's public displays of support for another notorious Hollywood sex abuser, Roman Polanski? In 2003, Polanski won Best Director at the Oscars for *The Pianist*. When Harrison Ford announced his name, the audience – comprising all the great and good of the movie business – burst into prolonged loud clapping and cheering. Leading the applause was Meryl Streep, who sprang to her feet to give Polanski a standing ovation. Yet why was Polanski not himself able to receive the award in person? The answer is because he's a child rapist who fled justice.

In March 1977, Polanksi was arrested and charged in Los Angeles with five offences against Samantha Gailey (now Geimer), a 13-year-old girl: rape by use of drugs, perversion, sodomy, lewd and lascivious act upon a child under 14, and furnishing a controlled substance to a minor. Polanski, then 43, did a deal with prosecutors in which he pleaded guilty to a charge of engaging in unlawful sexual intercourse with a minor. He thought he would get off with probation, but then heard rumours he would more likely face lengthy imprisonment – so Polanski fled the country to France, hours before he was due to be sentenced. He has never returned and has since avoided visiting any countries that may extradite him back to the USA.

Now, you might think that moralistic Hollywood would have revolted against this sickening fugitive child rapist. This is the same Hollywood, after all, that led the global outrage against Donald Trump when a tape emerged of him talking in a lewd, disgraceful manner about how his celebrity status enabled him to grab women 'by the p*ssy'.

Meryl Streep was almost as shocked and offended by Trump's behaviour as she now says she is by her once great friend Weinstein's. Within days, she appeared in a video called 'Not Okay' that challenged Trump's characterisation of his comments as 'locker room talk'. The video began with powerful evocative testimonials from women and teenagers who had experienced groping and sexual harassment, intercut with the *Access Hollywood* video featuring Trump's lewd boasts. It ended with a series of famous women, including Whoopi Goldberg, Maggie Gyllenhaal and Amy Schumer, giving their own response. 'Not okay,' said Meryl Streep, shaking her head.

It was a strong public statement from Hollywood's most successful female star that sexual harassment from rich, powerful men was unacceptable. At the Golden Globes in January 2017, Streep said of Trump, 'This instinct to humiliate, when it's modelled by someone in the public platform by someone powerful, it filters down into everybody's life, because it kind of gives permission to other people to do the same thing. Disrespect invites disrespect. Violence incites violence. When the powerful use their position to bully others, we all lose.' A month later, she attacked the now president again. 'Evil prospers when good men do nothing … ain't that the truth.'

Yes, it is, Meryl. But it thus begs the question: why, then, did you give a standing ovation to Roman Polanski, knowing what he did? And why, when asked about him at a press conference, did you say, 'Roman Polanski? I'm very sorry that he's in jail.'

The truth is that Harvey Weinstein was able to get away with what he did for so long because Hollywood didn't really give a damn about powerful men abusing young women. That's why Hollywood people cheered Polanski and still financed and starred in his movies for decades after he fled justice.

It's also why I have a problem with the conflicting opinions of actresses like Scarlett Johansson, who once publicly humiliated James Franco. 'I want my pin back!' she screamed from the podium at a Women's March in Los Angeles, after Franco, who sported a 'TimesUp' pin on his tuxedo at the Golden Globes, was accused of sexual misconduct by five women. 'My mind baffles,' steamed Scarlett. 'How could a person publicly stand by an organisation that helps to provide support for victims of sexual assault while privately preying on people who have no power?'

Johansson convicted Franco in the court of public opinion. Franco strenuously denied the allegations and has not been arrested or charged with any related criminal offence. But such trifling details cut no ice with Ms Johansson as she destroyed him in front of a huge crowd and millions more watching on TV around the world. 'How is it OK for someone in a position of power to use that power to take advantage of someone in a lesser position?' she seethed. 'Just because you can, does that ever make it OK?'

Ms Johansson was rather less censorious at the 2014 César Film Awards in Paris, when she found herself on stage at the same time as Roman Polanski. Pictures from that night show that she went over to him, placed her hand affectionately on his shoulder, smiled broadly and whispered something that made him smile too. An odd reaction, you might think, from a woman outraged by powerful men preying on vulnerable women, towards a convicted child rapist who fled America to avoid being held accountable for his appalling crime.

I've never met James Franco and have no idea what kind of man he is away from the cameras. Similarly, I've no idea if his accusers are credible or not. I don't subscribe to the 'MY truth' is automatically 'THE truth' subtext of the otherwise laudable #MeToo campaign, not least because in Britain there have been numerous rape cases against young men that have collapsed recently after suppressed evidence emerged proving their female accusers had lied. The truth, in matters as serious as rape and sexual assault, should be established by due legal process after all evidence has been considered. Otherwise what are we – a kangaroo court with trial by Twitter? But when the woke elite like Meryl Streep and Scarlett Johansson display such rank hypocrisy and double standards, they diminish the integrity of otherwise very credible causes like the #MeToo and #TimesUp movements.

TUESDAY 25 FEBRUARY

ITV is running a mental health awareness campaign and well-known mental health campaigner Matt Haig is trying to use it to get me fired. 'I know ITV are committed to mental health,' he tweeted. 'They have done campaigns about it, which is genuinely admirable. But I think they should also act when one of their most high profile presenters clearly targets and harasses women who have been open about their mental health issues.' A couple of hours later he tweeted, '"Stand up to bullies" isn't just a phrase. It is clear who the bullies are.

They should not be rewarded for their bullying. And people who employ them to bully are no better than the bullies themselves. Stop funding hate. Stop appealing to the worst of people.' This from a guy who regularly spews vitriol at me on Twitter, leading to vicious pile-ons from his many followers, without a care for *my* mental health.

To sum up just how insane this is all getting, Yorkshire Tea's Twitter account has urged people to 'try to be kind' because it was viciously trolled after Chancellor Rishi Sunak posted a pre-budget photo of himself with a big bag of the tea. It prompted a series of angry messages from Twitter users saying they were going to boycott the brand.

'Well, that's the kiss of f*cking death to that brand now,' raged one.

'You can tell a lot about a company by the people that endorse it,' spat another. 'Parasitic hedge funds.'

'Why are you promoting this fool?' queried a third. 'Never buying Yorkshire Tea again.'

And one even said, 'I can't wait for 500,000 Labour Party members to boycott Yorkshire Tea.'

Incredibly, there were also furious abusive calls to Yorkshire Tea's offices. In response, the Harrogate-based company's Twitter account said, 'So it's been a rough weekend. On Friday, the Chancellor shared a photo of our tea. Politicians do that sometimes (Jeremy Corbyn did it in 2017). We weren't asked or involved – and we said so the same day. Lots of people got angry with us all the same. We've spent the last three days answering furious accusations and boycott calls. For some, our tea just being drunk by someone they don't like means it's forever tainted, and they've made sure we know it. It's easier to be on the receiving end of this as a brand than as an individual. There's more emotional distance and I've had a team to support me when it got a bit much. But for anyone about to vent their rage online, even to a company – please remember there's a human on the other end of it and try to be kind.'

I read all this with sinking despair. How has it come to this? What the hell is happening to our country when a tea brand comes under such repulsive attack through no fault of its own? It sadly reaffirms my fear that we've lost all sense of proportion and perspective.

Tonight, *Channel 4 News* had a very unsettling interview with John Ashton, a British doctor and former public health official, in which he said the coronavirus is now a pandemic, and we need to 'think the unthinkable' on containing the virus. What does 'unthinkable' mean?

I tweeted, 'I'd rather we all overreacted about coronavirus than underreacted. The threat seems very real & entering a very dangerous phase. Remember the 7 Ps: Prior Planning & Preparation Prevents Piss-Poor Performance.'

'Stop scare-mongering,' came an instant response. 'It's just the bloody flu.'

Many replies agreed with this sentiment. There's still an extraordinary amount of complacency about it in Britain. Most people seem to think it will all just blow over, but pandemics, if that is what this is, don't just blow over.

THURSDAY 27 FEBRUARY

Stock markets continue to crater as coronavirus sweeps the world, and the blame game has already started with a familiar target identified. Gail Collins from the *New York Times* penned a column today headlined, 'Let's Call It Trumpvirus – if you're feeling awful, you know who to blame.' This perfectly epitomises the liberal media response to everything – just blame Trump.

The problem with this kind of mindset is not just that it's unfair and inaccurate – he's not to blame for many things, including the onset of this virus – but it also foments the rabid tribalism surrounding political debate. Liberals all cheer it on and convince themselves that Trump really is to blame for absolutely everything. Meanwhile, Trump's base uses this kind of nonsense to rally even harder behind their guy.

The victim in all this is reasonable debate of the kind that used to happen, where different opinions would be publicly expressed, points of consensus would be met, and everyone could go for a drink afterwards. Now the only liquid the warring sides want to share with each other is sulphuric acid.

I tweeted, 'You can't blame an American president for a health crisis that started in China. But you CAN blame Trump if he fails to properly deal with the coronavirus threat now it's hit America. I hope he does a good job but will be the first to criticise if he doesn't.'

The bestselling horror author Stephen King, who spews regular bile about Trump, replied, 'Point taken. The question now is how he'll handle this crisis. Plus, you must admit the man has had no problem taking CREDIT for the market, so he has to shoulder at least some of the blame.'

This is such bullshit. Trump, for all his previous, often exaggerated but also often entirely justified, boasts about the success of the US economy cannot possibly be blamed for the economy now collapsing due to a global pandemic that began in another country. However, he most definitely can be blamed if his actions to combat the virus now cause additional unnecessary harm to the American people.

FRIDAY 28 FEBRUARY

The first British death from coronavirus has been recorded, on a cruise ship in Japan, and the virus now appears to be swarming across the world at a scary pace. Yet the prime minister still doesn't seem to be taking this seriously and isn't even bothering to host a COBRA meeting until Monday.

'So Boris Johnson's not having a COBRA meeting re Coronavirus until next week,' I tweeted, '& his big advice to everyone in the meantime is "wash your hands!" How comforting. Enjoy your weekend, Prime Minister.'

I'm not a public health expert, but I was running the *Daily Mirror* when the foot-and-mouth epidemic struck the UK in 2001, and both Tony Blair and Gordon Brown told me afterwards that their biggest regret in handling the crisis was not reacting harder to the threat, and faster. I hope we're not making the same mistake now.

MARCH

Womxn? Bullshixt

SUNDAY 1 MARCH

The ridiculous government ban on ministers coming on *GMB* remains in force, so when I saw Matt Hancock appearing on Andrew Marr's BBC One show this morning, I tweeted him some forceful words of encouragement. 'Will you be coming on *GMB* tomorrow to inform our viewers of the latest situation, or will you be snubbing us as the entire cabinet has done since the election? Our viewers pay your salary, you have a duty in times of crisis to address their concerns. Snub us & you snub them.'

We were later informed he would indeed be snubbing us, and our viewers, so I told the *GMB* team to book his Labour shadow counterpart Jon Ashworth instead. Naturally, Ashworth agreed faster than a greyhound flies out of a trap. I announced this on Twitter: 'We'll have him [Ashworth] on every day he wants to appear during the coronavirus crisis, as Fridge-Hider Boris Johnson & his cowardly cabinet continue to snub our viewers.' Ashworth was thrilled. 'If you're offering,' he tweeted back, 'I'm more than happy to come on every day, let's book it in!'

Based on 25 years of dealing with governments since I first became editor of the *News of the World* in 1994, my guess is that this little exchange will finally force Hancock's hand. It's one thing to boycott a show, it's quite another to see your rival taking up all the airtime you have surrendered, especially during a crisis. It's pathetically gutless and a dereliction of ministerial duty to be accountable to the electorate. It's also breathtakingly hypocritical.

Aside from the fact Boris Johnson used to be a journalist who banged on ad nauseam about the vital importance of democracy and freedom of speech, the man behind the ban is Number 10's Director of Communications Lee Cain, who previously worked for the *Daily Mirror*, where he used to dress up as a giant yellow chicken and harangue Conservative politicians in the street for avoiding TV debates.

MONDAY 2 MARCH

In the USA, Senator Amy Klobuchar has quit the Democratic presidential candidate race – which means the remaining candidates are Elizabeth Warren, aged 70, Bernie Sanders, 78, Michael Bloomberg, 78, and Joe Biden, 77. The party of diversity will now likely choose a candidate from three old white guys to take on a 73-year-old white guy. It's one thing to talk the talk on liberal values, it's another to actually walk it. If wokies spent less time shrieking about Donald Trump and more time focusing on their own liberal backyard, they might have found a more inspiring, diverse and less hypocritical line-up.

TUESDAY 3 MARCH

NHS England today declared coronavirus a 'Level 4 incident' – its highest level of emergency. Britain hasn't yet suffered a death on her own soil from the disease, but we've now had 30 reported cases, and we've all seen what carnage it's already caused in many other countries. Covid-19, the most dangerous threat to public health since the Spanish flu pandemic 100 years ago, is here and wreaking its havoc.

Matt Hancock, who as I predicted, finally agreed to be interviewed on *GMB* after we handed airtime to his opposite number, appeared down the line from Westminster. 'These circumstances are very concerning,' he said, 'and we have a clear plan for how the country can get through this as well as possible. We're still in the phase where we're trying to contain this disease, working internationally, and trying to stop it from becoming widespread right across the country as it has in some other places. But we're also setting out today the sorts of measures we might have to take if it becomes more widespread. We're not saying these are things we will definitely do, and lots of them are things I'm reluctant to do, but we will do them if the scientists tell us they will help to keep people safe.'

'Health Secretary,' I replied, 'the truth is it's going to be when, not if, isn't it? SARS in its entire duration infected just over 8,000 people and killed 770 or so. We're already at 89,000 coronavirus infections and over 3,000 deaths. We know the rate of transmission is massively faster than anything we've seen or that I can remember. So surely it is now time for the government to accept this and to start getting ahead of this by taking dramatic action. What surprises me is there's a lot of talk about what we might do, but what we're not doing is what the Chinese did, which is go into effective lockdown. Why are we not doing that, and what will it take for the government to take us into similar territory?'

'We'll follow the scientific advice on what works,' Hancock replied.

He then said people should carry on flying, schools should stay open and mass gatherings should continue, including big football matches, which he said 'would not be appropriate' to cancel. None of this makes any sense to me. Why is it OK for large groups of people to be mingling together if this is such a virulently transmissible virus?

'Should people be shaking hands?' I asked.

'I've taken the medical advice on that and the medical advice is that the impact of shaking hands is actually very small. What matters is that you wash your hands more regularly than usual and, as the prime minister said, sing "Happy Birthday" while you're doing it.'

Again, I was baffled. This answer was totally at odds with current WHO advice, which states that people should 'avoid shaking hands' to protect themselves and others from Covid-19, and warns, 'Respiratory viruses can be passed by shaking hands and touching your eyes, nose and/or mouth.'

Shaking hands as a lethal virus spreads is obviously not a good idea. Common sense seems to have been abandoned. I ended by asking Hancock the most burning question. 'Given the rate of expansion of coronavirus now into 80 countries, whereas SARS only got into 29 countries, and given the rate of transmission, what are the chances of this developing into a global pandemic?'

'We do think that is a very serious possibility,' he said. 'But we haven't given up on containing it yet.' What I don't understand is how we intend to contain it, if our only weapon appears to be handwashing.

London Mayor Sadiq Khan appeared later in the programme and declared, 'There is no risk in using the tube or buses or other forms of public transport.'

I was incredulous.

'How do you know that, Mr Mayor?' I retorted. 'No disrespect, but how on earth can you say that in a city of 12 million people there is no risk given that we now know it's here and it's beginning to spread here and we know that in other countries the spread has been ferocious, places like Italy and Iran. How can you say as Mayor of London there is no risk to people using public transport?'

'Because I rely upon the advice I receive from Public Health England and the Chief Medical Officer,' he replied, 'and the advice is you're not going to catch it if you wash your hands regularly and if you use public transport ... on the tube on a daily basis there are five million journeys, on our buses six million journeys. The evidence we have so far is it's possible to contain it.' As with Hancock's responses, this sounded extraordinarily complacent.

'You seem remarkably relaxed about big numbers of people being in close proximity to big numbers of other people,' I persisted, 'when in Italy they've now cancelled big football matches ... and when the evidence from other places is that once this thing starts in a country it moves very fast.'

'It's really important we take the advice we're given,' he replied. 'We've had no fatalities in our country, and I would say to *GMB* viewers to have confidence in our experts.'

'Are you shaking people's hands?' I asked.

'I'm not,' Khan replied.

What?! My incredulity returned. 'You say there's no risk to people using public transport in confined areas around lots of people,' I snapped, 'yet here's you, the London Mayor, saying you're no longer shaking people's hands because you've taken a view that there is a risk.'

'The advice is that it's perfectly safe to use the tube and public transport,' the mayoral parrot replied. Again, where does common sense come into it?

Boris Johnson later hosted the daily government coronavirus news briefing and warned we need to prepare against 'a possible, very significant expansion of coronavirus in the UK population'. Asked if *he* was still shaking hands, he boasted, 'I can tell you I'm shaking hands continuously! I was at a hospital the other night where I think there were actually a few coronavirus patients and I shook hands with everybody, you'll be pleased to know, and I continue to shake hands, and it's very important that people should make up their own minds but our judgement is that washing your hands is the crucial thing.'

It was an extraordinary spectacle. Why would anyone, let alone the leader of a country, encourage people to shake as many hands as possible given the WHO has said the coronavirus is easily transmitted in that way? Why would Boris think we'd all be *pleased to know* this?

Three more things happened today that made me think the shit with coronavirus just got very real. First, the head of the WHO, Tedros Adhanom Ghebreyesus, warned after massive spikes in coronavirus infection in the worst-hit countries like South Korea, Italy, Iran and Japan, 'We are in unchartered territory.' He also revealed the death rate for it has risen to 3.4 per cent compared with less than 1 per cent for regular seasonal flu.

Second, America's Federal Reserve took the drastic emergency move to slash the interest rate by half a percentage point to limit damage to the economy from the virus. To put this into perspective, the US central bank hasn't done anything like this since Lehman Brothers collapsed in 2008 to trigger the global financial crisis. And nobody's convinced that slashing interest rates now will make much difference to combating a disease. 'It's like placing a Band-Aid on an arm to cure a headache,' said Bernard Baumohl, chief global economist at *The Economist*. Indeed, after a brief rally, the cut prompted a further crash in the stock markets, which have already been suffering their worst run since 2008.

Third, the Queen – the very epitome of 'Keep Calm and Carry On' common sense – wore long, heavy-duty white gloves to present members of the public with honours at Buckingham Palace, the first time she is believed to have ever done this for an investiture.

Oh, and if all this wasn't disconcerting enough, the French health minister called for a ban on the nation's favourite practice, kissing. None of this seems like an overreaction to me.

In the USA, President Trump is desperately keen to keep a lid on a health crisis that could yet pose a decisive threat to his chances of winning the 2020 election in November. 'Coronavirus is very much under control in the USA,' he tweeted, the day after the Centers for Disease Control and Protection (CDC) said the spread of the virus was inevitable. The CDC's prediction sent the media into overdrive, which prompted Mick Mulvaney, acting White House chief of staff, to say it was overreacting about coronavirus because 'they think this is going to be what brings down the president'. But ironically, it will be *under*reaction to coronavirus by the Trump administration that could bring down the president.

If tough decisions need to be taken to contain the virus, then take them now. Nobody with half a brain will blame leaders like Donald Trump and Boris Johnson for doing too much too soon to combat what is clearly a very serious global threat to human life. But people rarely forgive their leaders for doing too little, too late. I'm not a normal panicker but I think coronavirus is going to be much more serious than people realise. And the war against it won't be helped by either timidity or wokery.

The WHO has issued a new advisory saying: 'DO – talk about people "acquiring" or "contracting" #Covid-19 ... DON'T – talk about people "transmitting Covid-19", "infecting others" or "spreading the virus" as it implies intentional transmission & assigns blame.' What an absurd load of virtue-signalling guff.

This really doesn't seem a good time to be going all politically correct on the language used to describe how you catch the virus. Surely, the stronger the wording, the more impact it will have and the more lives it will save. And conversely, the weaker the wording, the less impact it will have, and the fewer lives it will save. This bullshit advisory will simply annoy people and make them less likely to follow the guidance. So, in an absurd attempt to appease the wokies and PC language cops, the WHO – whose whole purpose is to save lives – may now cost lives.

WEDNESDAY 4 MARCH

Amid the growing global alarm over coronavirus, actress Busy Philipps announced on Twitter, 'I will never stop talking about my abortion or my periods or my experiences in childbirth, my episiotomies, my yeast infections, or my ovulation that lines up w/ the moon!'

Dear God, if there's only one good thing that comes out of this crisis, can it be that celebrities stop telling us about their yeast infections?

THURSDAY 5 MARCH

There's been the first Covid-19 death on UK soil and the WHO's Tedros Adhanom Ghebreyesus has warned: 'We're concerned that in some countries the level of political commitment & the actions that demonstrate that commitment don't match the level of the threat we all face. This is NOT a drill, NOT the time to give up, NOT a time for excuses. This is a time for pulling out all the stops.'

It's staggering to me that people, let alone world leaders, need to be told this given what's happening in Italy, which today reported 769 new cases and 41 new deaths (bringing its death total to 148). It's turning into total carnage there, yet Italy has one of the world's best health-care systems.

Matt Hancock appeared on *Question Time* tonight and got a ridiculously easy time, so much so that he tweeted afterwards what 'a pleasure' it had been. He should have had much tougher interrogation, particularly given his continued insistence that mass gatherings are fine and don't need to be cancelled.

'Public gatherings aren't a problem?' I tweeted, incredulously. 'Really? Then why is half the world moving to stop them?'

It would be nice to think we could enjoy a cessation of nauseating wokery until this is all over, but sadly not. Across the pond, Elizabeth Warren has pulled out of the race to be Democratic nominee, and of course blamed sexism. 'One of the hardest parts of this is all those pinky promises and all those little girls who are going to have to wait four more years,' she moaned. 'That's going to be hard.'

What self-pitying tripe, straight out of the Hillary 'I won the popular vote!' Clinton playbook. The truth is neither Clinton nor Warren ran good enough campaigns to beat the men they ran against. Playing the sexism card is pathetic and completely unjustified, and why should 'little girls' only want to vote for women anyway? Warren's statement suggests women can't win a US election at the moment, when there is no evidence to support that theory. They just need to be better candidates. Cynics said the same about a black person becoming president, then Obama came along to prove them all wrong by running a brilliant campaign.

This 'pinky promises' nonsense does women such a disservice.

FRIDAY 6 MARCH

Former Home Secretary Amber Rudd has been no-platformed by students half an hour before she was due to speak at Oxford University's UN Women Oxford UK Society today about her experiences of being a minister for women and equalities.

Rudd, who stepped down as an MP in December, had her invitation pulled because of her previous involvement in the Windrush scandal. She was forced to resign as home secretary in April 2018, after it emerged that a large number of black legal immigrants had been illegally detained, denied legal rights, and in 83 cases deported from Britain, many of them people who had arrived before 1973 from Caribbean countries as members of the 'Windrush generation' – named after the *Empire Windrush* boat that brought one of the first groups of West Indian migrants to the UK in 1948.

It was a disgraceful episode, and Rudd was right to take responsibility and fall on her ministerial sword. But it should not disbar her from ever speaking to students about women's rights. Rudd condemned her treatment by the students as 'badly judged and rude' and urged them to 'stop hiding and start engaging'.

I'd have gone a lot further than that if they tried to pull this stunt on me. Surely, the whole point of university is to have your own opinions challenged, and to challenge other people's opinions – not ban anyone whose opinions you don't like? Why have our students become such a bunch of spineless snowflakes?

Universities used to be a place where contrary opinions were not just encouraged but considered essential to a student's education. Somewhere that liberalism – discourse – was embraced and championed, and where freedom of speech was celebrated. Life on campus was once full of rigorous lively debate and speakers of all types were invited to come and give their opinions, the more controversial the better. Now, the only permitted opinions in universities around the world are those that the woke brigade have deemed permissible. If you deviate from these in any way, then you run the risk of being shamed, abused, no-platformed and, crucially, silenced.

This nonsense is a problem we've inherited from the USA, where no-platforming has been out of control for years – stifling free speech in the process – in an increasingly insidious way. One of America's most no-platformed targets is firebrand conservative media pundit Ann Coulter, who is regularly the subject of abusive and violent scenes when she attends universities and colleges to speak.

Ms Coulter and I don't see eye-to-eye about many things. I once spent 30 minutes shouting at her on CNN when she tried to defend calling President Obama a 'retard'. Coulter can be obtuse, contradictory, offensive and incredibly irritating, and I usually completely disagree with everything she is saying. But I always enjoy our battles because she's also very smart, highly entertaining and, like me, loves a good argument. More importantly, she also makes me think hard about my own opinions on big issues – challenging me to see another viewpoint. After all, there are tens of millions of Americans who think exactly like she does, which is why Coulter's books invariably power to no. 1 in the *New York Times* bestseller list. And ultimately, this is how a proper democratic society should work: people with strongly held disparate views coming together to thrash them out in a public forum and hopefully reach points of consensus that benefit society. Unfortunately, that's not how many liberals now see democracy.

I thus found it particularly dispiriting when Coulter was banned from speaking at the University of California, Berkeley because the bosses claimed it would prompt violent protests. 'Unfortunately,' Berkeley said in a letter to its student College Republicans group, '[campus police] decided that, given currently active security threats, it is not possible to assure the event could be held successfully.' In other words, they choked to pressure from activists threatening violence to suppress democracy. Rather than stand up for freedom of speech, they bowed to mob rule.

What's astonishing about this is that Berkeley was the very home of the Free Speech Movement of the 1960s. In 1964, Berkeley student Mario Savio made a speech about the vital importance of free and open discussion at the college. He urged the university to encourage students to debate all ideas, both mainstream and radical. Savio's struggle was eventually successful, but only after he and his supporters endured suspension, arrest, fines and jail time. Yet Berkeley now seems to have decided it should be the home of killing off free speech, not promoting it. I find this appalling but not surprising.

The sad truth about modern liberals is that many of them don't believe in free speech at all. They only believe in it if people agree with them. They don't see their own opinions as opinions, they see them as 'truth', and if they don't like what they're hearing, they scream and shout, punch and kick, petrol bomb and stab, and furiously demand the offender be silenced and banned.

Ironically, Barack Obama, a woke hero, knows how dangerous it is. 'It's not just sometimes folks who are mad that colleges are too liberal that have a problem,' he said at a town hall meeting in Des Moines, Iowa. 'Sometimes there are folks on college campuses who are liberal and maybe even agree with me on a bunch of issues who sometimes aren't listening to the other side. And that's a problem, too. I've heard of some college campuses where they don't want to have a guest speaker who is too conservative. Or they don't want to read a book if it has language in it that is offensive to African Americans, or somehow sends a demeaning signal towards women. I gotta tell you, I don't agree with that either. I don't agree that you, when you become students at colleges, have to be coddled and protected from different points of view. Anybody who comes to speak to you, and you disagree with, you should have an argument with them. But you shouldn't silence them by saying, "You can't come because, you know, I'm too sensitive to hear what you have to say." That's not the way we learn either.'

Obama's view was shared by Sir Winston Churchill, who said, 'Some people's idea of free speech is that they are free to say what they like, but if anyone says anything back, that is an outrage.' And by a man from the opposite end of the political spectrum to Churchill, libertarian socialist Noam Chomsky, who said, 'If we do not believe in freedom of speech for people we despise, we do not believe in it at all.'

SATURDAY 7 MARCH

More grim news from Italy, where the whole of the Lombardy region of 10 million people has now been locked down – and the country's health system is teetering on the verge of total collapse. Yet here in the UK most people, especially younger people, still seem remarkably relaxed about the virus, insisting it only affects old or sick people, so why do they need to worry about it?

There's a horrible irony that the supposedly socially conscious 'woke' generation, so intent on 'getting older people on board' for things like gay rights, is so determined not to let a silly old pandemic curb their freedoms even if it kills a lot of old people. It's also indicative of my wider belief that they've never had to endure anything really serious to give them perspective, so don't even recognise a proper thing to genuinely worry about when it's staring them in the face.

'I keep hearing people say "stop scare-mongering about coronavirus, it only kills the elderly & those with an underlying illness",' I tweeted, 'as if somehow we shouldn't care about them. Well sorry, I do. And it's time everyone stopped being complacent about this – it's serious.'

I was met with another barrage of abuse for 'scare-mongering' – again – and 'panicking people'. If only the trolls put as much energy into demanding firmer action from the government as they do into being outraged by me.

SUNDAY 8 MARCH

It's International Women's Day, and UN Women, the United Nations Entity for Gender Equality and the Empowerment of Women, posted a tweet to celebrate that read, 'Womxn Trans Genderqueer Femme Mujer 女人 Mulher женщина Donna Mwanamke 女性 Frau Kadın Γυναίκα Կին Femina महिला Mulher नारी Vrouw 여자 Babae Manਰਤ النساء' *Today we celebrate every woman who resists patriarchy, insists on equality and persists for a better future.*

Hilariously, as people soon pointed out, the one category of woman they didn't celebrate, in English at least, was 'women'. Nothing more perfectly illustrates the ridiculousness of the gender debate than the deliberate refusal of organisations like the UN to use the word 'women' in case it offends people.

They aren't the only villains in this regard. In 2018, the Wellcome Collection, a free museum and library in London, promoted an event aimed at 'womxn' to virtue-signal to the transgender lobby. When asked why they didn't spell it 'women', the museum responded, 'We've had some questions about why we're using the word womxn for this event. We're using it because we feel that it is important to create a space/venue that includes diverse perspectives. It was agreed during our conversations with collaborators as the programme developed.'

To which Labour MP Jess Phillips retorted, 'I've never met a trans woman who was offended by the word woman being used, so I'm not sure why this keeps happening. As if internet dissent now replaces public policy. I get what they are trying to do, but why is it only women not men where this applies?'

Twitter user Suzie Leighton was more succinct: 'Bullshixt.'

Today, Sadiq Khan, never a man to miss a virtue-signalling opportunity, tweeted that we should all 'believe women, respect women, promote women, trust women'.

But, as I replied to him, what if the woman is lying? Or are we now supposed to presume every single woman on the planet is a perfect, morally untouchable version of Mother Teresa? Fortunately, many sensible women saw right through this absurd nonsense. Polly Vernon, a good friend and author of a refreshingly non-PC book *Hot Feminist*, tweeted, 'I know some f*cking awful women, but I know some excellent ones too. We're a mixed bunch.'

To round off the International Women's Day farce, dozens of female Extinction Rebellion protestors chained themselves topless to Waterloo Bridge to 'highlight vulnerable women in the face of climate breakdown'. They definitely got people's attention, but judging by Twitter it was largely directed at the quality of their respective cleavages and not climate change, so the whole attention-seeking farce merely served to illustrate the ineffectiveness of this form of activism. 'I bet this was a man's idea,' tweeted well-known 'radical feminist' blogger Jean Hatchet. 'Or a woman who hasn't worked out feminism yet.' Greta Thunberg has achieved a lot more with a zipped-up anorak. One thing it won't have achieved is make anyone think more seriously about how to save the planet.

Extinction Rebellion has demanded that 'the government must act now to reduce greenhouse gas emissions to net-zero by 2025'. This, according to the Energy and Climate Intelligence Unit (ECIU) – which supports XR's demands – could only be fulfilled if all flying was scrapped, 38 million petrol and diesel cars were removed from the roads and 26 million gas boilers were disconnected. The ECIU said this was 'an ambition that technically, economically and politically has absolutely no chance of being fulfilled'.

Notwithstanding this sobering reality check, many stars have clamoured to be seen with Extinction Rebellion, and of course, their own gigantically hypocritical carbon footprints were promptly highlighted by a gleeful media. None of them say they would give up flying. But at least they knew how absurd this sounds, for 100 celebrities, including Jude Law, Benedict Cumberbatch, Mel B and Steve Coogan, signed an open letter supporting Extinction Rebellion and admitting the obvious flaw in their position.

'Dear journalists who have called us hypocrites,' they wrote, 'you're right. We live high carbon lives and the industries that we're part of have huge carbon footprints.'

But naturally, this admission didn't stop them all lecturing us in the same letter about the impending death of the planet and demanding *we* all cut our carbon footprint. 'The stories that you write calling us climate hypocrites will not silence us!' they added. Clearly. This was like 100 morbidly obese people demanding we all stop eating so much food, but admitting they have no intention of doing so themselves – and running straight into the nearest McDonald's to order a barrel load of Big Macs. Common sense, as so often the case, is getting completely drowned out by virtue-signalling and the need to be *seen* to do or say the right thing. And all this means is that real progress becomes impossible.

MONDAY 9 MARCH

I loved the Wombles when I was a kid. Author Elisabeth Beresford's pointy-nosed, burrow-dwelling furry creatures were the first real eco-warriors when they burst onto our TV screens in the 1970s BBC classic – collecting and recycling rubbish, and demonstrating a selfless community spirit and respect for each other and the planet.

Now they're being brought back in a new CGI version and, inevitably, they've been woked – with some of the Wombles now having darker skin tones, not just the original orange and grey tones, to make them 'more relatable' and 'inclusive'. But Wombles aren't real, they're not humans, so why do they need to be made more 'relatable'? This is yet another one of those nonsensical diversity box-ticking decisions that makes no sense, and which I'm sure nobody has ever actually demanded. It also makes a mockery of real diversity issues, and the undeniable need to make many aspects of society more 'relatable' and 'inclusive'.

WEDNESDAY 11 MARCH

This afternoon, I watched on TV as the masses gathered at the Cheltenham Festival horserace meeting, all partying away like there was nothing to worry about. And tonight, I also watched Liverpool play a Champions League match against Atlético Madrid at Anfield, where another 52,000 people massed together – including 3,000 fans who flew in from Madrid, which is in lockdown because of a coronavirus outbreak so bad that no football is being allowed to be played there. Yet we have allowed thousands of people to fly in from a corona hotspot, with no checks on arrival, to potentially bring the virus into the UK, to watch a bloody football match. It seems insane.

As for the constant refrain that we are 'following the science', Richard Horton, editor-in-chief of prestigious medical journal *The Lancet*, tweeted today, 'The UK government – Matt Hancock and Boris Johnson – claim they are following the science. But that is not true. The evidence is clear. We need urgent implementation of social distancing and closure policies. The government is playing roulette with the public. This is a major error.'

It seems to me we're not learning anything from history. One of the reasons the 1918 Spanish flu pandemic killed between 17 million and 100 million people worldwide (the figure is disputed) was because of the shocking complacency by authorities and, as a result, the public.

For my generation, Covid-19 is the biggest threat to civilian life that we will have experienced since World War II, and it represents a particularly dangerous enemy because we still don't know exactly what we're dealing with, or how bad things are going to get. Unlike a traditional foe, this is not something we can 'defy' with conventional weapons. It's a virus, so if you come into contact with it, then it doesn't matter how big or tough you are, you will get infected.

In fact, it's estimated that 80 per cent of the entire planet may end up catching this coronavirus. Most, especially the very young and healthy, should emerge relatively unscathed. But for older people, and those with underlying health issues, Covid-19 is a very serious virus.

What we need now, just as in WWII, are calm heads, common-sense behaviour and stoicism. I can understand why people feel the need to stock up on basic essentials, given many of us will inevitably have to self-isolate. But there have been stunningly stupid, and grotesquely selfish, scenes of people cleaning out toilet roll shelves in supermarkets without a moment's thought for whether some old lady living on her own may need some too, and buying up all the face masks when we know that health workers on the frontline have nowhere near enough.

It's also been repulsive to hear so many moaning about possibly having to forgo their trips to the football, cinema, ski slopes or favourite restaurant for a few weeks or months. Are our elderly loved ones not worth skipping a movie for? No, we're all going to have to make sacrifices for a bit. If that means postponing holidays, missing some sport or drinking at home rather than the pub, then so be it.

The bottom line is this: life's going to get rough for a bit, as rough as most of us have known, and a lot of people are going to get seriously ill or die. But if we come together, act sensibly, put the health of others before our own selfish pursuit of pleasure and show some gritty resolve, then we will come through it.

It won't be easy, but it's the right thing to do. This is not a typical war, not least because we're all fighting a common enemy, but we're still going to need the kind of bulldog spirit as personified by Winston Churchill. 'If you're going through hell, keep going,' he famously urged as the Nazis blitzed Allied forces. But it's another of his quotes that seems more pertinent now: 'Things are not always right because they are hard, but if they are right one must not mind if they are also hard.'

MONDAY 16 MARCH

Having seemingly, finally, woken up to the threat from coronavirus which he now says is the 'worst public health crisis for a generation', Boris Johnson announced new measures this afternoon to combat Covid-19, including a directive that if anyone in a household shows symptoms of it, the whole household immediately goes into 14-day quarantine. Susanna rang this evening.

'I'm self-isolating from you,' she announced.

Notwithstanding our permanently simmering on-screen tension, this seemed a rather dramatic deterioration in our TV marriage.

'Something I said?' I asked.

'No, something that's happened to one of my sons – he's got a persistent cough, and under the new rule, we'll all have to quarantine.'

'Does he have the virus?' I asked.

'I don't know because he's not sick enough to warrant a test, and there's no way of finding out without a test.'

This seems an absurd situation. What if her son, who has no fever, *doesn't* have the virus, they all do the 14-day quarantine, go back out into the world and then one of the Reid household *does* get it? Do they all quarantine again?

A country-wide lockdown, if it comes, will be a massive test for all of us. Nobody wants their freedom taken away. But however tough it gets, it's not going to be anything like as tough as it was for people during the world wars. As someone tweeted tonight, 'Anne Frank and seven other people hid in a 450 sq ft attic for 761 days, quietly trying to remain undiscovered in order to stay alive. You'll probably be fine in your house with your wine, your Grubhub [US version of Deliveroo] and your Netflix until 30 April. Feel grateful yet?'

It's hard to think of a more perfect denunciation of the shocking lack of perspective so many people of this generation seem to have.

WEDNESDAY 18 MARCH

I've often wondered how the 'millennial' (born between 1981 and 1996) and 'centennial' (born after 1996) generations would cope with a real crisis. And I don't mean one of the myriad crises many of them claim to have every second of every day, triggering the biggest explosion of 'anxiety' the planet has ever seen. No, a real one. One that impacts on every one of us, causes genuine hardship and strife, costs huge numbers of deaths and rips the global economy to pieces, and one that is a proper valid reason to feel anxious because it's indisputably frightening and none of us, not even the world's top scientific experts, knows how bad it will get before we come out the other side.

Well, now I don't have to wonder because it's happening. And while some of my younger earthlings are being perfectly stoic and sensible, recognising the gravity of the situation, others are behaving like complete and utter cretins, like the spring break students flocking to beaches in Florida, hugging and kissing each other like it was VE Day. Or the reckless twerps flocking to bars on St Patrick's Day around America yesterday, when even Ireland shut down every pub in the country.

Every crisis draws out 'useful idiots', but this one seems to be drawing out a whole new level of stupidity. They've been dubbed the 'Covidiots' and I fear it's a mutation of the disease that no vaccine can cure.

Two brothers from Tennessee, Noah and Matt Colvin, drove 1,300 miles around the state buying 17,700 bottles of hand sanitiser, hoping to make a massive profit on Amazon by selling them on for $70 a bottle. But the online store moved fast to clamp down on such greedy exploitative pandemic price-gouging and shut down their account after they'd sold just 200 bottles, leaving them with 17,500 bottles of hand sanitiser they can't sell.

'I'm not looking to be in a situation where I make the news for being that guy who hoarded 20,000 bottles of sanitiser that I'm selling for 20 times what they cost me,' said Matt Colvin, who is of course now 'that guy'.

What kind of mentality makes people so brainless?

For the answer, we need look no further than *High School Musical* star Vanessa Hudgens, 31, who reacted to news that the virus may still be wreaking havoc through the summer, by telling her 38.4 million young and impressionable Instagram followers, 'Til July sounds like a bunch of bullshit. I'm sorry, but like, it's a virus, I get it, I respect it. But at the same time, like, even if everybody gets it, like, yeah, people are gonna die. Which is terrible, but like inevitable? I don't know. Maybe I shouldn't be doing this right now.'

No, Vanessa, you shouldn't.

Ms Hudgens perfectly represents a woefully entitled generation that's grown up whining about absolutely everything – yet has so little to legitimately whine about given how much safer, healthier and more prosperous the world is now compared to any other time in recorded history. They mock and scorn the 'boomers' (those born between 1944 and 1964 – I don't quite qualify, having been born in 1965, but this doesn't stop them calling me one for being old, out of touch, boring and narrow-minded). But their response to this emergency is already revealing a shocking selfishness.

The biggest sacrifice we're being asked to make is not go to the pub or beach and sit at home for a while watching TV. Is that really too much to ask? Fortunately, there are some high-profile young people who *do* get it, like pop superstar Ariana Grande, who tweeted the following message to her 72 million followers: 'I keep hearing from a surprising amount of people statements like "this isn't a big deal", "we'll be fine", "we still have to go about our lives", and it's really blowing my mind. I understand that is how u felt weeks ago but please read about what's going on, please don't turn a blind eye. It is incredibly dangerous and selfish to take this situation lightly. The "we will be fine because we're young" mindset is putting people who aren't young and/or healthy in a lot of danger. You sound stupid and privileged and you need to care about others ... like, now.'

She concluded, 'Like, your hip hop yoga class can f*cking wait, I promise. This a national emergency and a pandemic of global proportions.'

THURSDAY 19 MARCH

'Coronavirus Is a Disaster for Feminism,' screamed a headline in *The Atlantic* today.

It was above a lengthy piece by Helen Lewis, author of the book *Difficult Women: A History of Feminism in 11 Fights* in which she argued, convincingly, that feminism's success is down to complicated, bloody-minded women who fought each other with the same passion they fought the cause.

In this new piece, she complains that Covid-19 will 'send many couples back to the 1950s' and 'women's independence will be a silent victim of the pandemic' because the main burden of responsibility for looking after the home and kids if we enter a prolonged lockdown will fall to women. 'Many fathers will undoubtedly step up,' she mused, 'but that won't be universal.'

I was struck by her certainty about what men will do in this pandemic. Imagine if I'd written that 'many mothers will undoubtedly step up but that won't be universal'. I'd have been rightly accused of sweeping sexist, misogynist generalisation.

I know Ms Lewis, and she is not a man-hater by any means, but it grates with me that her instinctive verdict on what the male response will be is automatically negative, without any proof yet that her fears are correct. It plays into the ongoing narrative since the #MeToo movement began that all men are bad unless they prove otherwise. But we're not, just as it would be wrong to presume all women are good until they prove otherwise. I know good and bad men, and good and bad women. And many of both sexes who flirt on the hard deck of both good and bad.

Lewis's piece made me think more seriously about feminism. I've stated that I'm a feminist and I consider myself to be a feminist. Or, rather, I feel very comfortable identifying as a feminist in the manner in which it used to be defined. That is, I believe 100 per cent in a woman's right to full gender equality, and the principle that men and women should be treated exactly the same, politically, economically, legally and socially, and afforded the same opportunities. That, after all, was how the women who originally fought so courageously for equality over one hundred years ago saw it themselves.

As singer Kate Nash pleaded, 'Feminism is not a dirty word. It does not mean you hate men, it does not mean you hate girls that have nice legs and a tan, it does not mean you are a bitch or a dyke; it means you believe in equality.'

Sounds simple enough, right? Yet it isn't, partly because some men remain unreconstructed misogynist dinosaurs who think feminism is a profanity, but also because women themselves have become massively divided over what feminism means. Let's be honest, for some women feminism just means hating men, and indeed hating other women who don't share their angry view of what feminism should be. This squabbling has turned 'feminism' into such a toxic word that many women now decline to even identify as one because of all the controversial connotations that surround modern debate about it. And while women go about shaming and vilifying each other, men like me who believe in gender equality can only stand back and scratch our heads in bemusement.

Feminism has gone on a long and often very difficult journey – the latest wave is typified by the ongoing #MeToo and #TimesUp movements – and in the process its meaning has evolved and been hijacked by many vested interest groups all desperate to redefine it as *they* see it.

Of course, the very last person many women wish to hear define feminism is a man, and especially if that man is me. But that isn't going to stop me, because the battle for true feminist ideals will only be won if men are persuaded to embrace them.

It's time women worked out which feminist role models do their cause a service, and disservice. The absolute nadir of modern feminism, for me, came when Kim Kardashian and Emily Ratajkowski – two of the most followed women on social media in the world – tweeted a topless selfie of themselves in a ladies' restroom as they flipped the bird. It was, according to them, a shining expression of liberating, female sexual freedom. To me, it looked like a couple of fame-hungry chancers deliberately flaunting their naked flesh to make money. I have no problem with that, but please don't pretend it has anything to do with fighting the cause of gender equality.

'RIP feminism,' I tweeted, posting the image next to a picture of Emmeline Pankhurst. This ignited a firestorm of indignation from women across the globe. How dare I say feminism is dead? What right have I got to even question their motives for getting their kit off? Who the hell did I think I was even talking about this subject as a *man*? And those were the responses I can repeat ...

Kim and Emily, revelling as always in all the publicity, were both keen to publicly reaffirm their positions on this matter. Ms Kardashian, accepting an award at the Webbys, said five words: 'Nude selfies 'til I die!' What a magnificently empowering statement to rally the female gender! Right up with there with Pankhurst's demand a hundred years ago to be given the right to vote. Or perhaps not.

The thought of Kim's gazillion young female followers on Twitter and Instagram rushing straight to their cell phones to bombard cyberspace with nude pictures of themselves in honour of their role-model heroine should leave real feminists horrified. How does it promote female equality, to so lamely and publicly titillate men and make them view women purely as objects of sexual desire? Or to encourage women to think that is the only way they can achieve success?

As for Ms Ratajkowski, she, in a sublime moment of chronic self-awareness failure, branded me an 'attention-seeker'. This from a young lady for whom the words 'shall I keep any clothes on today?' never seem to enter her thought process. This week, she posted naked photos of herself, presumably because she didn't know what else to do in a pandemic. 'Every woman,' she declared, 'whether they're comfortable with the term feminist, probably wants to be equal to men and that fundamentally is what feminism is about.'

Well, yes, Emily, it is. So why do you feel the need to hijack the meaning of the word to justify flashing your breasts and middle finger to millions of complete strangers? Men don't do that, and if they do anything similar – as singers Justin Bieber and Usher both did – they get roundly and rightly ridiculed for it.

The kind of feminist battle that Pankhurst would definitely have endorsed, as did I, was *House of Cards* star Robin Wright fighting to be paid by Netflix the same as her co-star Kevin Spacey (before he was brought down by a #MeToo scandal) when she discovered he was getting paid a lot more. 'There are very few films or TV shows where the male, the patriarch, and the matriarch, are equal,' she explained, 'and they are in *House of Cards*. I was looking at the statistics and Claire Underwood's character was more popular than [her husband] Frank's for a period of time. So, I capitalised on it. I was like, "I want to be paid the same as Kevin or I'm going to go public."'

And she did. The result? A contract worth $5 million. Good for her. That, surely, is what feminism is about: unearthing gender inequality and correcting injustice through personal strength, determination and courage.

Women of the world need to ask themselves one simple question: who makes you feel more empowered or liberated? Kim and Emily flashing their flesh? Or Robin fighting for gender parity on pay? The answer, I would hope, is obvious. Feminism, *real* feminism, is surely better than just shameless public stripping. It's about women striving to be treated exactly the same as men and to be paid the same for doing the same job if they do it just as well. I support that ambition 100 per cent.

A good example, to me, of a feminist role model is professional female darts player Fallon Sherrock, who at the end of 2019 became the first woman to ever beat a man in the men's World Championships. In fact, she beat two men, drawing huge media attention, big TV ratings and global acclaim from superstars like tennis legend Billie-Jean King. Darts is not a sport that relies on power, so there is no reason why a woman can't be as good as a man. Sherrock qualified for the men's tournament purely on merit. There was no tokenism, no 'let's go easier on the girls' nonsense. She was there because she was good enough, and she proved it by winning two matches.

In the same vein, I would cite the extraordinary 17-year-old female German racing driver Sophia Floersch, who suffered a horrific crash while she was competing in her first Formula 3 World Cup race at the Macau Grand Prix against male and female drivers. On the fourth lap, Sophia struck another driver's car as she approached a bend at 175 mph. The collision caused Sophia's car to spin out of control and catapult several hundred yards through the air into a wall. It's the most horrifying accident I have ever seen, and everyone who watches it would assume she must have died. But Sophia lived, despite fracturing her spine. And within just a few hours, she tweeted, 'Just wanted to let everybody know that I am fine but will be going into surgery tomorrow morning. Thanks to everybody for the supporting messages. Update soon.' No fuss, no playing the victim. Can you even imagine the scale of self-pitying hell that would be unleashed on the unsuspecting public if any of the Kardashians had a minor 25 mph car prang today in which they broke a diamond-encrusted toenail?

Sophia is now back racing, against men and women, and has both an incredible talent for driving a car and incredible courage too. She is a rising star in a male-dominated sport determined to prove she can mix it with the boys, and I applaud her for it. Both she and Fallon Sherrock have done more for progressing women's rights and the cause of feminism than a million Kim Kardashian topless selfies. And the impact this will have on girls and young women is immeasurably better.

If there's one thing worse than fake female feminists, it's fake male feminists who race to attach themselves to any absurd virtue-signalling feminist bandwagon, all competing with each other as to who can sound the most 'pro-women'.

As the #MeToo and #TimesUp campaigns careered around the world, destroying many undeniably vile men in their wake, they also threw up a lot of men desperate to distance themselves from their own ghastly male gender and firmly establish their woke 'I'm with you!' credentials with women.

Leading this PC-crazed pack has been singer John Legend – a man whose supreme talent as a musician (he is one of my favourite singers) is only matched by his supremely irritating capacity to spout faux virtuous garbage to make himself look good.

For example, my favourite festive holiday song is 'Baby, It's Cold Outside'. Immortalised in the 1949 movie *Neptune's Daughter*, it's a joyous celebration of flirtation, as a handsome charming man tries to persuade a beautiful charming woman to stay the night with him on a wintry night. There's nothing sleazy about it, or nasty, or even remotely 'problematic', to quote the ghastly buzzword of modern-day political correctness. It's fun, sexy, playful, and both the man and woman are completely in control of their own actions during the mutually enjoyable and totally consensual experience. This is a scene that has played out many billions of times in the history of our great planet.

It's called seduction. And that process only becomes something sinister or even criminal when a woman is being forced to do something she doesn't want to do. That is not the case in 'Baby, It's Cold Outside'. It was written by US songwriter Frank Loesser to sing with his wife Lynn Garland at their housewarming party in New York. The original lyrics included these lines:

'My mother will start to worry ...' (Man: 'Beautiful, what's your hurry?')

'The neighbours might think ...' (Man: 'Baby, it's cold out there.')

'Say, what's in this drink?' (Man: 'No cabs to be had out there.')

To 99.9 per cent of all those who've ever heard these lyrics, particularly in the context of the film clip, they are perfectly sweet and innocent. But to the 0.1 per cent of super-woke, permanently offended virtue-signallers out there, this is in fact a sickening depiction of sexual harassment or even sexual assault. To them, the man's obviously a disgusting monster, refusing to understand that no means no, who has slipped some kind of Bill Cosby-style drug into the woman's drink in an effort to render her unconscious so he can attack her.

This ridiculous narrative, started by a few angry radical feminists a few years ago, reached a climax in the wake of the Harvey Weinstein scandal. By late 2018, radio stations began banning the song altogether, led by WDOK Star 102 in Cleveland, Ohio, who attributed its decision to the 'lyric content, based on listener input, amid the #MeToo movement'.

The public, gloriously, reacted by marching out to buy Rat Pack legend Dean Martin's iconic version of the song in such huge numbers it rocketed back into the US Billboard chart, with sales surging 70 per cent thanks to the furore. You might think this would be the end of the matter. But sadly, it wasn't. In fact, it was just the start as John Legend decided the original version of 'Baby, It's Cold Outside' was so despicable the lyrics must be rewritten for the #MeToo era. So that's what he did, writing a new version with *Insecure* comedian Natasha Rothwell, which he then performed with Kelly Clarkson. The new lyrics included:

'I really can't stay ...' (Man: 'Baby, it's cold outside.')

'I've gotta go away ...' (Man: 'I can call you a ride.')

'This evening has been ...' (Man: 'So glad you dropped in.')

'... so very nice.' (Man: 'Time spent with you is paradise.')

'My mother will start to worry ...' (Man: 'I'll call a car and tell 'em to hurry.')

'What will my friends think?' (Man: 'I think they should rejoice.')

'If I have one more drink ...' (Man: 'It's your body, and your choice.')

What a load of nauseating tripe. At this stage, it's worth remembering how Mr Legend himself first got together with his equally annoying, publicity-mad, swimsuit model wife Chrissy Teigen. They met on the set of his music video for the song 'Stereo'. He was the most powerful man on set, the star and therefore, effectively, the boss. She was an impressionable 21-year-old model hired to work alongside him. Ms Teigen told *Cosmopolitan* several years later, 'I walked into John's dressing room to meet him and he was ironing in his underwear. I said, "You do your own ironing?" He said, "Of course I do." I gave him a hug.' After the shoot, she says they went back to his hotel room and 'hooked up'. Hmmm. I'm not an expert on the whiter-than-white standards of super-woke behaviour, but by Legend and Teigen's own yardstick, isn't every part of this story highly 'problematic'? Older, powerful boss hooking up with younger employee after they work together? The CEO of McDonald's was fired in 2019 for doing exactly that.

And when it comes to rewriting inappropriate lyrics, why did Legend pick on 'Baby, It's Cold Outside'? After all, it pales into insignificance compared to the shockingly sexist and misogynist lyrics of so many current rap and pop stars.

Snoop Dogg sang, 'B*itches ain't sh*t but hoes and tricks, lick on these nuts and suck the d*ck.' Kanye West sang, 'I know she like chocolate men, she got more n***as off than

Cochran.' Eminem sang, 'Slut, you think I won't choke no whore, til the vocal cords don't work in her throat no more?' And as for Pharrell Williams's 'Blurred Lines' collaboration with Robin Thicke, he's since admitted the lyrics, including 'I hate these blurred lines, I know you want it,' were 'rapey'.

John Legend hasn't suggested rewriting any of these songs. Why could that be? Oh wait, is it because they're all performed by his good friends? As with most 'woke' campaigns, this one was riddled with sanctimonious hypocrisy.

Legend targeted 'Baby, It's Cold Outside' because it was an easy win for him – something guaranteed to get him lots of publicity and make women go, 'Awwwww, isn't he lovely?' Yet when it comes to the often disturbingly hateful women-shaming lyrics of so many of his contemporaries, the same Legend remains complicitly silent.

Deana Martin, daughter of Dean, perfectly summed up the fake outrage. 'It's mad. It's a sweet, flirty, sexy, fun holiday song that's been around 40 years. This breaks my heart.' As for what her dad's reaction would be, she said, 'He'd be going insane right now. He'd say, "What's the matter with you? Get over it. It's just a fun song."'

Exactly. It is, or rather it was until the woke brigade got their claws into it. There would be zero tolerance for such trivial, meaningless nonsense. And here's the most laughable part of this whole pathetic furore: in *Neptune's Daughter*, the song is actually performed twice. There's the famous version between Ricardo Montalbán and Esther Williams where it's the man doing the persuading. And there's a far less talked about version between Betty Garrett and Red Skelton where it's the *man* who wants to leave, and the *woman* who's trying to persuade *him* to stay.

Needless to say, nobody ever mentions this second one, because it doesn't suit the man-hating theme. Oh, and did I mention that the movie ends with both couples planning their weddings? If John Legend had his way, the movie would now be rewritten to have the men arrested.

FRIDAY 20 MARCH

I had hoped the coronavirus might compel celebrities to quit the virtue-signalling for a bit, given the real stars right now are the health workers risking their lives to save ours. But, sadly, the opposite has happened and it's just given them the perfect excuse to tell us how much they care about us all.

Wonder Woman star Gal Gadot decided that what the world really needs right now is her and a bunch of famous friends, including Natalie Portman, Will Ferrell and Amy Adams, singing a diabolically tuneless version of John Lennon's 'Imagine' line by line from their homes. It was presumably supposed to be the self-isolating version of the iconic aid-for-Africa anthem 'We Are the World' but rapidly became a 'We Are Being Mocked by the World' abomination from the moment Gadot released it yesterday.

Aside from the horrible singing and unctuous self-promoting style of delivery, the message of Lennon's original classic was imagining a world without borders, possessions. So, to see a bunch of multi-millionaire stars singing from within their heavily guarded mansions was particularly hypocritical. As one Twitter user put it, 'A load of millionaire singers and actors singing "imagine no possessions" is not what I need at 8.55 am.'

This pandemic is already exposing an uncomfortable truth for celebrities: nobody gives a shit about them when people are fearful for their lives or losing loved ones. It's also revealed just how fake so many of them are. These shameless, self-absorbed antics aren't really about trying to help other people, they're about helping prop up their brands when they can't do what they normally do to maintain their lucrative star status. But this won't stop their virtue-signalling claptrap.

Perhaps the world's most notable virtue-signaller is Canadian Prime Minister Justin Trudeau, a man so dripping in dubious sincerity it's a miracle he doesn't drown in a pool of his own virtuousness every day. He's the kind of guy who enthusiastically embraces every new woke fad because he is desperate to be seen to look wholesome. In this sense, he's the opposite of someone like his US counterpart Donald Trump, who enthusiastically embraces everything anti-woke because he is desperate to be seen to not give a monkey's about looking wholesome.

The problem with virtue-signalling so hard in order to be a part of a 'movement' like wokery is that you make a complete and utter politically correct plonker of yourself, as Trudeau has done on countless occasions in his race to be their no. 1 public 'ally'. Ironically, he is a handsome young politician constantly drooled over by many of the same women who claim to find male objectification of female flesh so demeaning. Trudeau – who is photographed topless far too often for it to be an accident – knows his fanbase and thinks he knows exactly what they want to hear.

Amid the #MeToo and #TimesUp firestorms he bided his time, waiting for the perfect occasion to throw his virtue-signalling voice behind the feminist cause. It finally came when he addressed students in a Q&A at MacEwan University in Edmonton. In video footage that swiftly went viral, a woman from the World Mission of God, a non-denominational church guided by the ideals of 'God the Mother', stood up to ask him a question.

'We came here today,' she began, 'to ask you to look into the policies that religious charitable organisations have in our legislation so it can also be changed because maternal love is the love that's going to change the future of mankind ...'

On hearing that last word, shirt-sleeved Trudeau recoiled like he'd been shot by a crossbow and instantly raised his left arm in indignant angst. 'We like to say "peoplekind",' he declared, rudely interrupting the woman and flapping the same arm around aggressively, 'not necessarily "mankind". It's more inclusive.'

'There we go!' she cried, excitedly. 'Exactly!'

The crowd erupted with cheers and applause. Or rather, the other women in the crowd did. Most of the men just looked silently bemused.

'We can all learn from each other!' Trudeau added, milking his audience like a greedy dairy farmer.

Trudeau comes over in the clip as the worst kind of hectoring, bully-pulpit smart-arse, dripping with virtuous self-aggrandising sanctimony. He also saw fit to single-handedly rewrite the English language. There is no such word as 'peoplekind'. And he's wrong too about the etymology of the word 'mankind'.

It dates back to a time, many centuries ago, when males were called 'werman' and females 'wyfman', and 'man' was a gender-neutral term meaning all human beings. So 'mankind' was originally intended to signify humanity. Not that Trudeau will care about such trifling details.

After all, he is the single-most PC-friendly, touchy-feely prime minister in the history of world politics. He marched at Canada's version of Gay Pride, he's pro-choice on abortion, pro legalising marijuana and pro just about anything else that he thinks might win him the hearts of global liberals. There's not a diversity box Trudeau hasn't promptly hammered himself inside. He's even called poverty 'sexist'.

'I am a feminist, I'm proud to be feminist,' he declared after acceding to office. And to prove it, Trudeau's first 'gender-parity' cabinet contained the exact same number of men and women, 15 of each. To understand why he's become such a fervent gender trailblazer, look no further than an incident early into his tenure, in which Trudeau stormed across the Canadian House of Commons during a heated debate and accidentally elbowed a female MP, Ruth Ellen Brosseau.

He didn't even know he'd done it, which is hardly surprising when you watch the video of the incident and see an accidental, very mild contact of the kind that happens every second of every day on the subway. But that didn't stop Ms Brosseau reacting like she'd been beaten to within an inch of her life. 'It was very overwhelming,' she wailed, 'and so I left the chamber to go and sit in the lobby.' Her colleague Niki Ashton said she was 'ashamed' to witness the 'deeply traumatic' incident and declared that Trudeau's 'manhandling' was the 'furthest thing from a feminist act'.

'If we apply a gendered lens,' she raged, 'it is very important that young women in this space feel safe to come here and work. [Trudeau] made us feel unsafe and we're deeply troubled by the conduct of the prime minister of this country.'

A horrified Trudeau begged for forgiveness like a serial killer on death row apologising for murdering a hundred people. 'I want to take this opportunity now the member is OK to be able to express directly to her my apologies for my behaviour and actions. Profoundly and unreservedly.' On and on he went, switching between English and French, pouring out his agonised soul until I feared he might collapse in a heap of tearful sackcloth-ridden misery.

Ever since, he's doubled, trebled and quadrupled down on his feminist credentials – cowed into supine submission by the militants in his own parliament and now viewing everything through that 'gendered lens'.

As a result, Canada's senators passed legislation to make the country's national anthem gender-neutral. After a 30-year campaign by protestors, and to the consternation of many Canadians, the second line will now be changed from 'in all thy sons command' to 'in all of us command'. (Nobody seems to have worked out what this all means for the supposedly gender-neutral word 'person', given that it contains 'son'.)

But as with all virtue-signallers, Trudeau just didn't know when to stop. And his denunciation of 'mankind' turned him from caring, sharing feminist heart-throb into a global laughing-stock.

There's been a creeping invasion by the PC language cops for the past few years. University campuses around the world have started banning words like 'sportsmanship', 'right-hand man', 'manpower', 'man-made' and 'gentleman's agreement' – all because they contain the dreaded word 'man' and are thus supposedly offensive. This despite the fact I've never met a single person who actually finds any of those words offensive unless they are urged to do so.

But it's one thing for snowflake students and professors to pull dumb stunts. It's quite another for the culprit to be the prime minister of the world's second largest geographical country. Put it this way: if Justin Trudeau has his way then one of the greatest achievements in the history of mankind (apologies for anyone offended by that word) will have to be banished from our consciousness too.

When Neil Armstrong, the first man – sorry, person … no sorry, human – on the Moon, said it was 'one small step for man, one giant leap for mankind', he could have had no idea just how offensive he was being.

And of course, like so many woke heroes, Trudeau's self-acclaimed virtue turned out to have feet of very non-PC clay. I've not met a high-horse rider yet who doesn't eventually tumble off into a pit of shameless hypocrisy. But I've got to hand it to Trudeau, when he fell, he really FELL.

Last year he was exposed for having repeatedly blacked and browned up his face, which is about the least woke thing that any wokie could do. *TIME* magazine revealed Trudeau had attended an 'Arabian Nights' party in a turban and with his face painted dark brown when he was a teacher at West Point Grey Academy.

'I shouldn't have done that,' a stern, ashen Trudeau said. 'I take responsibility for it. It was a dumb thing to do. I'm disappointed in myself. I'm pissed-off at myself for having done it. I wish I hadn't done it but I did and I apologise for it. I should have known better, but I didn't.'

So far, so predictably self-flagellating; Trudeau knew the only way out of this Grand Canyon-sized hole he was in was to beat himself up. But there were two problems with his statement. First, he wasn't a young student at the time of his Arabian Nights brownface stunt – he was a 29-year-old teacher. And this wasn't 1951, it was 2001, so the explanation that a man of nearly 30 had no idea that painting his face brown at an Arabian Nights party might be racist doesn't fly, especially as *TIME* reports he was the *only* person there in brownface.

Second, it wasn't his only venture into the face-painting arena. Pressed to disclose if there were other incidents like this, Trudeau admitted to wearing 'blackface' at a high-school talent show, where he sang 'Day-O', the song made famous by black singer and civil rights campaigner Harry Belafonte. Sure enough, CBS News soon located a photo of him performing at that show in blackface. And a few hours later, a third incident emerged in which he was seen with blackface in a video, apparently from the 'early 1990s' – laughing, pulling faces and sticking his tongue out.

So, Trudeau's a serial blackface and brownface offender. Of course, he didn't resign. And few liberals called for him to resign. He was one of their own, so didn't need to be cancelled. Contrast this with the way TV host Megyn Kelly was banished from the NBC airwaves after musing that it didn't used to be deemed offensive to wear blackface on Halloween. Kelly never actually blackfaced herself, and what she said is perfectly true, but that didn't matter as she became the sacrificial lamb to a howling mob of outraged liberals who'd never forgiven her for working at Fox News. The way she was destroyed, and Trudeau saved, epitomises the rank hypocrisy and deceit that lies at the heart of cancel culture.

The same high-profile liberals who demanded Kelly's head on a plate didn't do the same with Trudeau, even though he repeatedly did the very thing she only talked about. Instead, they praised his 'honesty' and his 'sincere apology'. This, we were told, was very much a 'teachable moment' that he should survive.

But there's nothing 'honest' about a virtue-signalling prime minister keeping his blackface habit a secret for two decades until the press uncovered it. And as for sincere apologies and teachable moments, Megyn Kelly made an abject, tearful *mea culpa* on air and it made zero difference to the mob. The only lesson she got was that there's one rule for conservatives on such matters and quite another for liberals.

Can you even begin to imagine how the same people defending Trudeau today would react if this was Donald Trump who'd been caught wearing blackface? They would want him instantly hounded out of office. Yet, because it was nice-guy Justin, the one who *really* cares, he got a pass.

In other news, this afternoon Boris Johnson told all pubs, cafés, bars, restaurants and gyms to 'close tonight as soon as they reasonably can' and asked people to 'please' not go out.

Alongside him was Chancellor Rishi Sunak, who announced a staggeringly large rescue plan for businesses – most of which will immediately hit the shutters from today – including a furlough scheme where employees will be paid 80 per cent of their wages for the next three months, up to £2,500 a month per person. The economic fallout from this crisis is going to be monumental.

My increasingly passionate attempts to get people to wake up to the reality of this threat were brought up in Parliament yesterday. 'During times of national emergency,' Conservative MP Lee Anderson addressed Jacob Rees-Mogg, Leader of the House of Commons, 'the media play a vital role in delivering information to concerned viewers, listeners and readers. Scrutiny is good but undermining the national effort by spreading disinformation helps nobody and creates panic among some of the most vulnerable members of our society. Will my right honourable friend raise this issue with broadcasters such as ITV, where Piers Morgan, who has no scientific or medical qualifications, seems to want to make irresponsible comments on a daily basis?' Rumblings of 'Hear! Hear!' filled the House.

Rees-Mogg replied, 'I am grateful to my honourable friend for his question and he is right to point out the role the media plays in informing the public and holding the government to account. One does not have to take every utterance from controversialists as holy writ. Piers Morgan enjoys causing a row and, frankly, I think it would be better to pay less attention to him, rather than more, and listen to the government advisers. Free speech is very precious. If people want to say silly things and look foolish, that is a matter for them.'

Much as I'm amused by the irony that Parliament is now debating whether I should be given any attention, I'm bemused as to what 'disinformation' I'm supposed to have been spreading.

SATURDAY 21 MARCH

'Friend had her birthday yesterday,' texted Susanna. 'Her mum and best friend both gave her loo roll. What a time to be alive.' She then forwarded me a tweet from Irish actor John Connors which read, 'Such a shame we don't have Piers Morgan in Ireland, he's the only journalist with the balls to challenge government day in and out. He's doing more good than all our journalists combined. Fact. When the history books are written, the Brits will thank him greatly.'

Definitely, right after pigs fly over my house.

Susanna and I discussed how this crisis has brought my 'The world's gone nuts' mantra into sharp focus. 'In a way it all plays into your anti-woke theme,' said Susanna. 'How a virus smashed identity politics ... how we woke up to a real problem ... viruses don't respect your self-ID?'

'Yes,' I replied, 'I don't see any way back for the old woke bullshit after this. We can already see zero tolerance for whiny celebs.'

'No one is getting cancelled for not being woke anymore,' she said.

'Weakness is no longer something to celebrate, etc,' I said.

'I don't see it as weakness,' Susanna retorted. 'It's just a privilege, no one has time for it anymore, the virus is the great leveller.'

Is it, though? I'd love to think it is, and we'll emerge from the coronavirus wreckage as better people with a better sense of perspective. But history isn't reassuring on that front. One major hurdle will be people's increasing intransigence to any deviation from their world view. Someone who got this danger better than most was the late *Telegraph* columnist Christopher Booker, who died last year.

In a review of his new book *Groupthink: A Study in Self-Delusion*, published posthumously, another *Telegraph* writer, Allison Pearson, wrote, 'The book begins in early 2019 with the author trying to account for a world "wracked by strains, stresses and divisions which even a decade ago would have been hard to imagine". He singles out Islamist terrorism, the European Union, the secular religion of climate change (very much not a believer!), a rift between the ruled and their rulers and identity politics. Underlying all of them is "the peculiar social pressure to conform with a whole range of views deemed to be 'politically correct' marked out in those caught up in it by their aggressive intolerance of anything or anyone who differs from their own beliefs". For a scientific explanation of this growing zealotry, Booker turned to a thesis put forward more than 40 years ago by Irving Janis, a professor of psychology at Yale University. In *The Victims of Groupthink* Janis observed how "a group of people come to be fixated on some belief or view of the world which is hugely important to them. They are convinced that their opinion is so self-evidently right that no sensible person could disagree with it. Most telling of all, this leads them to treat all who differ from their beliefs with a peculiar kind of contemptuous hostility." Janis used this theory to account for several notorious fiascos of US foreign policy – failure to heed intelligence about Japanese plans to attack Pearl Harbor being one example – in which a group made decisions based on how they would ideally like the world to be, not according to the realities of the situation. What strikes the modern reader is Janis's uncanny premonition of today's "cancel culture" in which an individual expressing a point of view that challenges the liberal orthodoxy can be no-platformed.'

I totally agree with this. It is precisely the problem with modern illiberal liberalism: if free speech is stifled and a rigid set of intransigent opinions is enforced by cancelling any dissenting voices, we end up in a world where debate doesn't exist, so bad decisions inevitably get taken. I wonder if the pandemic will fix this insidious culture, or exacerbate it?

SUNDAY 22 MARCH

Shocking news: the *Sunday Times* is reporting that Dominic Cummings, Boris Johnson's chief adviser and the architect of Brexit, described the government's strategy in a meeting in early February as – and this was apparently a summary of his words – 'herd immunity, protect the economy, and if that means some pensioners die, too bad'.

This is horrific and astounding on many levels. Why the hell is Dominic Cummings leading government policy anyway? I never voted for this unelected, grim-faced, casually dressed bully-boy.

Boris's sister Rachel tweeted, 'As it's Mother's Day here's one of my own mother's unbeatable instructions which is what she always says to me in a crisis: "It is urgent ... to do nothing."' This seems to be an instruction Boris has taken firmly to heart. He's *still* just 'advising' people not to gather in public and *still* trusts the public to take his advice, even when it's obvious that many aren't, and when countries like Italy and France are in total lockdown. I'm sorry, but this isn't leadership.

This weekend, we're seeing the result of his refusal to order people to stay in. The sun shone over Britain and many have treated it like a bank holiday weekend – flocking to beaches, parks and tourist sites where they mingled with each other in direct contravention of their prime minister's friendly advice. The scenes made me sick. These people are morons, imperilling their own lives and those of others. But ultimately, I blame the spineless sheep leading the country more than the brainless lemmings jumping off the coronavirus cliff. If the guy at the top is saying, 'Please stay home but go out if you need some fun,' then it's hardly surprising if many think this can't be too bad.

The people who will really suffer are the health workers desperately struggling to save people's lives all over the country. So many doctors and nurses have gone public to say they're being exposed to terrible personal risk due to the chronic lack of suitable protective clothing, masks, gloves and sanitiser. These are the people we need to prioritise – selfless heroes who epitomise the essence of unity and communality as they battle together all day every day to save the lives of complete strangers. They're the perfect antidote to selfish, woke individualism, and to the spoiled egotistical celebrity culture that society has so ill-advisedly put on some kind of higher pedestal.

Aside from failing to give health workers adequate protection, the most egregious failing in this crisis has been with coronavirus testing. 'Test, test, test,' has been the WHO's mantra since January. Yet ten days ago, the British government announced it was stopping general testing and would only now test the seriously ill in hospital. Now we've done a U-turn on that insane decision, but the damage has been done. Britain needs massively higher levels of testing as a matter of extreme urgency, not least to ensure our health workers can do their jobs. We also need to lock down immediately in a proper enforced national quarantine because the sad but entirely predictable truth is that many stupendously selfish people in Britain don't give a damn about Boris Johnson's cheery 'advice'. But we've let the genie out of the bottle and freed it to do its worst for much longer than we should have done.

Tonight, *Mail on Sunday* journalist Caroline Graham, a long-time friend, emailed to say her mother is seriously ill in hospital with Covid-19. 'Mum's not great,' she wrote, 'the virus is consuming her, I've never seen anything like it. People have no idea what's about to hit.' She said the hospital staff were enraged by people ignoring social distancing rules. 'The nurses are furious people aren't staying at home and feel utterly betrayed by Boris. I've been here since Tuesday and the mood has gone from stoic to one of f*cking outrage. One of the nurses has been up since 5 am, and has asthma and two kids but has been coming in every day to try to save patients like Mum. They have no proper gear and there's a staff shortage because care assistants and even the phlebotomists refuse to enter the Covid-19 ward. This is a national disgrace. If anyone spent five minutes on a coronavirus ward, they would self-isolate in a heartbeat.'

We've got Matt Hancock on again tomorrow. It's time to take the gloves off.

MONDAY 23 MARCH

In the car to work, I was still simmering with anger over what Caroline had told me. It's disgraceful that we're sending our frontline health workers into this war without the right protective equipment. Why haven't they got it? It's been two months since the WHO called this a global health emergency, and we've surely prepared for a pandemic like this.

Not bothering with the usual niceties, I got stuck in to the health secretary straightaway. 'Mr Hancock, the NHS frontline is reeling from what is already happening, and at the thought of what may be coming quite soon. They are ill-equipped, they don't have enough equipment, enough PPE, enough masks, enough anything, and they're terrified and many of them are now falling sick themselves. What reassurance can you give to NHS staff that you and your government are going to get them the protection they urgently need?'

'Well, you're right, Piers, this is incredibly important,' he replied, 'and our NHS staff and staff in social care have got to have the equipment they need. What's happened is that there's been a sudden sharp increase in the amount of protective equipment that is needed.'

No shit, Sherlock, I could have predicted that for him six weeks ago. Irritated by his response, I interrupted him. 'Why are we so late though? Given the World Health Organization alerted the world to a possible global pandemic at the end of January, given that we saw the scenes in China, so we knew what was happening, why is this country, this government, and I say this respectfully, so woefully ill-prepared in terms of the equipment we need to fight this virus?'

Hancock's eyes, with the tell-tale dark bags of acute tiredness lurking beneath them (I don't underestimate how hard he must be working, but if you want to be health secretary then this is what you signed up for), narrowed slightly.

'Well, that's *not* the case,' he snapped, 'and I think you know it.'

This is a Trump-esque interview technique, telling the journalist he agrees with you even when you know he doesn't. It's quite effective if the journalist doesn't instantly rebut.

'That *is* the case,' I retorted. 'Literally, yesterday, all day long, doctors, nurses, consultants were hitting the airwaves, and hitting social media, telling appalling stories. I've got a friend of mine whose mother is in a critical condition with coronavirus in a south London hospital and she says the nurses are absolutely desperate, they have very little protection, they're worried sick about themselves and about the avalanche coming their way. They don't feel protected and I don't think it's good enough for you to sit here and just say, actually they are.'

'No, I wasn't saying that,' he replied, tersely, 'getting the equipment to the frontline is mission critical. There's been a sudden increase in the need for it, which is totally understandable and right, and I have to get it to them. And of course, we knew there was going to be this increase, but getting the distribution of this huge quantity of equipment right across the NHS is a very significant challenge. The point is this: if you ask people to go out and look after and care for others, then we've got to make sure they have the equipment they need.'

Yes, it is. And they haven't.

'If you really care for the people who are doing all the hard stuff and risking their lives for us, Health Secretary, why is the government doing nothing to lock down this country that bears any relation to what most other countries are doing? Why is it that Spain, France, Italy, Belgium, almost all the other countries around us in Europe are in almost total lockdown and we are seeing these catastrophically stupid scenes all over the country – people piling into pubs, the Cheltenham Festival not cancelled, all weekend people going out partying like it's a bank holiday, and still the prime minister stands at the podium and says, "My advice is that you don't do this." People are not listening to his advice. They want clear direction, these people, because they're too stupid to make that decision themselves. We are risking lives, in my humble opinion, and by all means tell me I'm wrong, but I believe that every day we are not locking down properly as a country, we are putting the very health workers that you are talking about at greater risk.'

'Well, I share your frustration, Piers,' Hancock replied. 'The number of people not following the advice is incredibly damaging to the effort to stop the spread of the virus.'

'But given we all agree, including the prime minister, that it will cost lives, why is he not mandating it and locking down the country? If that is the new strategy, then lock the country down.'

Hancock looked irritated again, but this time I wasn't sure if this was from irritation at my own frustrated angry tone, or his own angry frustration that perhaps Boris is not doing what I'm suggesting. The *Sunday Times* report yesterday suggested Hancock's been pushing for a proper lockdown for several weeks. If so, there can be few more difficult things for a politician to have to do than defend something you yourself don't agree with, especially if you believe lives depend on it.

'The strategy has been the same all along,' he insisted, 'which is to protect life, and to make sure we stop the spread of this virus ...'

I interrupted him again, prompting him to shake his head with irritation. 'With respect, Health Secretary, your strategy has not been the same all along. There was a massive report by Tim Shipman in yesterday's *Sunday Times* highlighting how dramatically it changed. *You* actually came out of that quite well because *you* were one of the few people that appeared to get it and were pushing for a lockdown. But there was a sentence in that piece that you'll be very well aware of involving a guy called Dominic Cummings, one of the prime minister's senior aides, who at the end of February outlined the government's strategy. Tim Shipman, one of the best political reporters in the country, reported those present say it was "herd immunity, protect the economy, and if that means some pensioners die, too bad". Not a direct quote but a summation of Dominic Cummings's view of the government strategy, and we know herd immunity was the strategy for the next two weeks, and then dramatically it changed to the complete opposite. So please don't insult my intelligence by telling me we've followed the same strategy. We haven't.'

'Herd immunity has never been the strategy ...' Hancock insisted.

'Your own chief scientific adviser said on the radio literally ten days ago, herd immunity was the strategy,' I exclaimed. 'Was he lying?'

'No, he didn't say that. And I don't want to get into who said what in the *Sunday Times* in what wasn't a direct quote.'

'Let me play it to you ...' I suggested.

'No, Piers, NO. If you will listen ... then I will tell you the answer.' I ignored him.

'Let's listen to what the chief scientific adviser said. You say he didn't say it, let our viewers make their own minds up.'

I then played him the tape of Sir Patrick Vallance saying the strategy was herd immunity.

'That was your chief scientific adviser literally spelling out herd immunity, the strategy you say we weren't following.'

'No, we weren't, and we aren't. The message I would give to your viewers, and I know you've got your frustrations ...'

'I've got more than frustrations, to be frank with you!' I hit back. 'I'm seeing an NHS getting run over, morons out all over the streets ignoring the friendly advice of our prime minister, and I am seeing the leader of this country refusing to take draconian measures to lock down the country when almost everywhere else has done so. He's a libertarian, we keep being told. He believes it's wrong to remove people's liberty. I couldn't give a stuff [about their liberty], honestly, Health Secretary. I don't think you agree with it either. I think from what I've been reading you should think we should be locked down.'

'What I'm going to do is tell the people watching this programme what needs to happen,' he replied, speaking slowly to buy time. 'The tittle-tattle that you're talking about, I'm not going to get into.'

'TITTLE-TATTLE?' I erupted. 'Really? How dare you! You think what I'm saying to you is tittle-tattle?'

'I think that picking up on bits and pieces in the Sunday newspapers is less important in terms of broadcasting to the nation what needs to happen at this incredibly difficult time,' he replied.

Hancock said more draconian action would follow if the advice was not taken and went through a robotic checklist of all the current government advice. When I interrupted him again to talk about testing, he visibly tensed up, pursed his lips and stared back slightly murderously at me.

'Only ten days ago,' I continued, 'the prime minister announced we were not going to be continuing any testing with anyone but the seriously ill in hospital. Literally as the World Health Organization ...' Hancock began furiously shaking his head.

'Well, you can shake your head,' I said, 'but this is what was said from the [news briefing] podium by the prime minister, and the World Health Organization was saying at that very moment "testing, testing, testing, testing, testing". Why did we abandon testing for all but the seriously ill? Why are we still only testing 8,000 a day when we were promised it would be 25,000? The lack of testing is a massive problem, isn't it?'

'We are absolutely ramping up the testing,' Hancock replied.

I've noticed ministers now repeatedly using the phrase 'ramping up' when they have to defend the lack of PPE or tests. It's obviously a line pumped out from the Number 10 press office to deflect criticism.

'Again, what you said in the question isn't right ...' he stammered.

'Well, which bit is wrong?' I asked. 'You can't just say that, which bit is wrong?'

Hancock sighed again audibly. 'We are ramping up the testing ...'

'What did I say that was wrong?' I persisted. 'You said what I said wasn't right, what was wrong?'

He shook his head again.

'Don't shake your head, just tell me what I was wrong about?'

'You said the prime minister had said we were stopping testing ... not true.'

'He did, apart from the seriously ill in hospital, we would be doing no more testing, that's what the expert team at the podium said. Do you dispute that?'

'Erm, yes, as you characterised it ... but, Piers, there's a more important thing going on here ...' This was an old Tony Blair tactic when cornered – decline to answer the question and tell the interviewer what's 'more important' to discuss.

'I know that people are worried and angry, I want to increase the amount of testing too ... and I want to communicate to people the things that we are doing and we should have a responsible conversation based on the strategy that we have as a country to get through this. And as health secretary, my top priority of protecting lives is the basis of everything I do, including increasing the testing, which of course is critical.'

We moved on to argue about people in supermarkets not maintaining social distancing – which most aren't – and again I asked him why we don't make it mandatory and enforce it.

'If we were the only country involved in this,' I said, 'then I would say, OK, fair enough, you must know best. But every other country around us has locked down more than us, which prompts the question: what do we know that they don't?'

Hancock said the other countries were ahead of us in 'the curve' – but that would surely make it even more urgent for us to take quicker action, wouldn't it?

'Health Secretary,' I said, 'stop trusting people when they're ignoring you.'

This whole lengthy exchange with Hancock was riveting viewing but also potentially very significant from an evidential viewpoint. What the UK's health secretary says publicly at this stage of a global crisis like this might well come back to haunt him in any subsequent public inquiry into how we responded.

Twitter blew up after the interview, with the most unlikely people rushing out to applaud me for going after Hancock so aggressively. Ash Sarkar, the self-proclaimed communist writer and political activist who has roundly abused me for years, tweeted, 'I never thought I'd say this either, but Piers Morgan is doing what every broadcaster ought to at this time – holding the government's feet to the fire over their botched pandemic strategy.'

She was joined by another hardcore left-wing activist Owen Jones, whom I've also regularly locked horns with, who tweeted, 'Yes, I'm going to say it: huge kudos to Piers Morgan for holding the government to account, and it's an example other journalists should follow.' If someone had told me in January that these two would be publicly praising me, I'd have thought them stark raving mad. But I already sense this pandemic is changing everything.

The reaction wasn't all positive. One old newspaper colleague struck a note of caution. 'Piers,' emailed Steve

Sampson, a former *Sun* executive whose opinion I always value, 'I'm a big supporter, you don't need to hear that repeated. You need to slightly change the tone. We are now at war – the Falklands, Iraq. Whatever. Holding the government to account means something different now. The country needs you to question them closely, ask all the questions they can't. You're the bridge. No one else around you has the heft. Whether we like it or not, Hancock and the others are running it. This is going to get way worse. You need Hancock leaving the studio to go and get on with it, not in ribbons. Still push him and the rest, just with a change of emphasis. Steve.'

Others were far less polite with their critiques. As fast as I was gathering new unlikely admirers, I was losing old ones – for much the same reasons Steve was politely getting at. I received a stream of abuse all day from ardent Brexiters on social media for being 'disloyal' and 'unpatriotic' in the way I questioned Hancock. These were the same people who've loved me since the EU referendum for being a Remainer who loudly campaigned for the result to be honoured but seem to think I must now be slavishly loyal to Boris Johnson's government. But I don't care what party is in power during this crisis, only how they handle it. Partisan politics, and Brexit, seem utterly irrelevant.

Tonight, Boris addressed the nation and announced we were now finally going into proper lockdown. All non-essential shops will close with immediate effect, as will playgrounds and libraries. We will only be allowed out for one hour of exercise alone, essential shopping for food or medicine, or for work if we can't work from home. Even though I've been shouting for this to happen, it's still a stunning moment – the biggest loss of freedom for the British people in 70 years. It won't be too bad for those with nice houses and big gardens, but imagine being cooped up in a high-rise council flat with three kids for weeks or even months on end?

With her usual dreadful tone-deafness, Madonna posted a video of herself at her lavish mansion, naked in a candlelit bath full of rose petals while prattling on about the virus being the 'great equaliser'.

Yeah, right. It's self-evident that wealthy stars in vast secure homes will be far safer from the virus and more comfortable in lockdown than poor people living in cramped conditions on vast council estates. Madonna was savaged for her self-indulgent tripe, an early sign that the public will have no truck with spoilt celebrities showing off during lockdown.

TUESDAY 24 MARCH

America is on the same trajectory as Italy was several weeks ago, and if the carnage that's unfurled there now unfurls in the USA, as many experts predict, then it may decimate human life like no other single entity in the nation's history.

Right now, the only thing that can possibly stop this happening is a complete and total shutdown of the kind Trump himself ironically once demanded on all Muslims entering the USA after the ISIS terror attacks. Coronavirus will kill many more Americans than Islamist terrorists ever have.

Governments have been scrambling to find a way – any way – to contain it, and almost all of them have now arrived at the conclusion that the best way to stem the tide of infection is a lockdown similar to the one we now have, finally, in the UK. This means a complete cessation of any 'normal' activity. This means people whose jobs don't directly contribute to fighting the virus stop working and stay at home. This means everyone exercising draconian social distancing. This is how China, where the virus emanated, finally got on top of it – along with massively intensive testing of the kind America has abjectly failed to deliver. If Americans think their current lack of 'freedom' is bad, they should see how an authoritarian state like China handled its lockdown. But it worked.

As with his fellow populist Boris Johnson, President Trump's natural political skills that made him so electorally popular sit uncomfortably with this crisis. The American people are incredibly fearful, for very good reason. They want firm, calm, decisive action, unambiguous, accurate advice and constant reassurance that their government is doing everything it can to fight the virus. What they don't want is a blustering, bravado-laced leader shooting from the hip every day, lying about being 'in total control' of the virus, espousing unproven 'cures', picking idiotic fights with the media or political opponents, and giving false hope about when this will all end.

Trump, like Johnson, has been flailing through this crisis because all his natural instincts are to maintain everyone's 'rights' and 'freedoms', and because he appears to be motivated more by a desire to save the economy than to save lives. I don't think he's a callous, uncaring human being, contrary to what some believe. I'm sure that beneath Trump's typical self-aggrandising 'I'm handling this beautifully' self-confidence lies a guy secretly panicking at the rapidly escalating US coronavirus infection rate and death toll.

And I'm also sure he believes with every fibre of his being that getting the economy going again will be crucial to America's recovery from this crisis. After all, Trump's a money man to his bootstraps who has spent his entire life driven by a craven love of business, success and cash. So, for him to now see his presidency consumed by the greatest disintegration of the economy in US history will be hitting him harder than he is letting on. One minute, Trump was cruising to re-election, the next he is staring down the barrel of a disaster of epic proportions that threatens to derail everything, including his chances of winning again in November.

But Trump needs to understand very clearly that lives matter more than money. The economy will eventually recover because it always does. Lives lost to the virus will never be recovered.

WEDNESDAY 25 MARCH

During my clash with Matt Hancock on Monday, I asked him about the issue of nurses and doctors racking up parking tickets at hospitals due to their long shifts in the crisis.

I've complained many times on air before about how absurd it is that health workers have to pay to park their cars where they work to save people's lives. When I asked Hancock if he would scrap all charges, at least for the duration of the pandemic, he replied, 'I will look at it, yes.'

Nothing's yet been done, though, and I woke up today to a number of health workers tweeting me copies of their parking tickets. This incensed me so much that I ripped into Housing Secretary Robert Jenrick on *GMB* for the government still not ordering free parking for all NHS staff as they fight the virus.

'We're already indebted to them,' he blustered, 'anything further we could be doing, Piers, we should be considering.' As he blathered away without making any firm commitment, I decided to do something myself, and vowed on air to personally pay for any and all parking fines sustained by NHS staff. Talking to them straight down the camera, I said, 'I will pay them and then go to the government and have the battle with them – you don't get involved.' Sometimes, you just have to publicly shame people into doing the right thing.

'That could turn out to be a very expensive gesture,' chuckled Susanna after the show. I hadn't really given much thought to that. Bit late now!

At 9 pm tonight, the government announced free parking for all NHS staff and care workers for the duration of the crisis, and I was bombarded with messages on social media from health workers thanking me for standing up for them, which made a nice change from all the abuse for my 'scaremongering'. It feels good to be able to wield my platform in such a positive way.

THURSDAY 26 MARCH

A campaign was launched a few days ago for everyone to step outside our homes tonight at 8 pm and 'Clap for the NHS'.

It's a lovely idea, but I was doubtful about the public's willingness to actually do it. I shouldn't have been so cynical.

At 8 pm, I walked out with Celia and Elise and began clapping, and to my astonishment so did almost everyone else in our part of Kensington. There were cheers and roars too, and people hitting pots and pans. It was an extraordinary, rousing and intensely moving moment. I found myself giving a thumbs-up to neighbours I've barely ever spoken to, smiling in solidarity.

And when we went back inside after five minutes and turned on the news, we discovered that the same scene had been replicated everywhere around the country in the most spine-tingling act of national unity I've ever seen and one which will have surely given our health-care heroes such a boost when they most need it, on a day when it emerged that 39 doctors have already died from coronavirus in Italy.

The great national clap might also go a long way to healing Britain too after all the horrible toxic feuding over Brexit. And if it does, how ironic that we've finally found a way to come together – by being forced to stay apart.

FRIDAY 27 MARCH

An astonishing, tumultuous, unnerving day. First it was announced that Boris Johnson has tested positive for coronavirus, then a few hours later that Matt Hancock has too, and that Professor Chris Whitty has self-isolated, fearing he also may have it. As we digested these stunning developments, Dominic Cummings was seen running out of Downing Street.

The instant sense of national panic and worry at this unprecedented and unpredictable turn of events reminded me of the first few hours after 9/11 when all hell was breaking loose and nobody was quite sure how things would end.

It also raises immediate, urgent questions about who's now in charge of our fight against the virus.

'If Boris has a #Coronavirus fever, as he says,' I tweeted, 'then he surely shouldn't still be trying to run the country? Too many huge, crucial decisions to be made for someone who may be feeling very rough to be at the helm. Who is the designated survivor PM – Raab? Sunak? Gove?'

'Piers,' replied the *Financial Times* chief feature writer Henry Mance, 'don't know how to break this … but after the last couple of weeks, it's actually *you*.'

News of Boris's diagnosis lit up Twitter, and the troll cesspit began gleefully celebrating the fact he had the virus and hoping it kills him. There are perfectly legitimate reasons to feel Boris was stupid and reckless to boast of shaking hands in a hospital containing coronavirus patients just three weeks ago. But for people to actively want him dead, and I saw many tweets to this effect, is just disgusting.

It also shows that for all the #BeKind bullshit since Caroline Flack's suicide, many people have learned absolutely nothing. Not least super-rich celebrities who continue to be extraordinarily tone-deaf in this crisis.

Billionaire movie mogul David Geffen posted a photo to Instagram of his gigantic $590 million gin-palace yacht with the caption, 'Sunset last night ... Isolated in the Grenadines avoiding the virus. I'm hoping everybody is staying safe.' Like Madonna, he was promptly ripped to shreds. The public has zero tolerance for wealthy, privileged stars rubbing their noses in it right now.

MONDAY 30 MARCH

My 55th birthday. Had a fun chat with the family on Zoom, the video-conferencing platform that's exploded in popularity since the pandemic started and is now, staggeringly, worth more than every US airline combined.

It's not the same as seeing people in the flesh, but it's a lot better than not seeing them at all. Technology is at least allowing us to maintain visual contact – what the hell would this kind of lockdown have been like a hundred years ago?

TUESDAY 31 MARCH

Neil Thompson, *GMB*'s editor, phoned me this afternoon to tell me that our presenter Kate Garraway's husband Derek is critically ill in hospital with coronavirus. They're both good friends of mine, and when I spoke to Kate on the phone tonight, she was calm but understandably frightened. Derek's just 52 and had no underlying health condition, but is now fighting for his life. This virus is terrifying.

APRIL

PM in ICU. No PPE for NHS

WEDNESDAY 1 APRIL

I'm having to do my own make-up at work, and today I accidentally picked up the wrong pot and managed to paint myself bright orange. I only realised when viewers bombarded me on Twitter with gleefully mocking messages.

'How bad is it?' I whispered to Susanna, now back at work after her enforced quarantine.

'It's not great,' she giggled, 'there are some … blending issues.'

Lorraine Kelly was less polite when she saw me later. 'It's like a satsuma had a fling with a tangerine and then they both went to a tanning booth.'

I've had a lot of uncomfortable moments on live TV, but trying to present the most serious news story of my lifetime while knowing I was resembling a human pumpkin is possibly the most excruciating. It didn't stop me getting into a heated debate with Housing Minister Robert Jenrick, again, over the government's failure over testing. He confirmed that we're currently carrying out just one-tenth (8,000) of the daily tests Germany (80,000) is doing – but couldn't explain the disparity.

'Why is Germany testing ten times as many of its citizens a day as we are?' I demanded. 'That is a complete disgrace. We're supposed to be the sixth biggest economy in the world. How can we have got to this position given we've known for a while that intensive testing is the absolutely crucial thing to be doing?'

'Different countries have different strategies,' Jenrick stammered. 'That's the advice we've had from the scientists.'

This constant deferring to the scientists is driving me nuts. These politicians were elected to make decisions, not pass the buck to anyone but themselves. And why do we have a different strategy to testing anyway? The WHO has said for months that testing is the key to getting on top of this virus. Our chronic lack of testing means we have no idea how many people have the virus, or have had it, and without that information it's impossible to let people go back to work and restart the economy, which will be crucial to our ability to recover when this is all over.

It also means most health workers can't be tested and many are therefore forced to self-isolate for two weeks if they or a household member shows any symptoms, without even knowing for sure they have it. One paramedic this week revealed he and his three fellow paramedic flatmates have all been forced to do this – taking them off the frontline for 14 days at the most intense, vital time.

'Why can't any of you give a straight answer?' I asked Jenrick, about Germany's superior testing. 'No government minister can give a straight answer to that very simple but very important question.'

'Well, I don't have the latest figures for Germany,' he replied. 'We believe we have the capacity to test 12,700 people.'

The wording of this sentence was extraordinary. Having the 'capacity' to do something doesn't mean you're actually doing it. I have the capacity to sleep with 1,000 supermodels, but I'm not sleeping with any.

I quoted Jenrick the words of *The Lancet*'s Richard Horton, who tweeted while we were on air, 'The handling of the Covid-19 crisis in the UK is the most serious science policy failure in a generation. Last week the Deputy CMO said, "There comes a point in a pandemic where that [testing] is not an appropriate intervention." Now a priority. Public message: utter confusion.'

'No one can understand how we got this so wrong,' I said. 'Can you explain?'

'We have a particular strategy,' he said. 'We don't test in the same way.'

That much is painfully obvious. I then asked him about the government's inexplicable decision to keep all the airports open for business.

'Just to clarify,' I said, 'if you land from Italy right now, or New York, which are both being ravaged by coronavirus, what happens to you when you land?'

'For most of those individuals they wouldn't be tested,' he admitted. 'They enter the country if they are able to do so.'

'So, they just come in, there's no mandatory quarantining?'

'Those individuals who have symptoms are taken down one route, those who are not symptomatic are allowed to enter the country. That is on the basis of medical opinion. We have been guided in our approach at airports, as elsewhere, by scientific and medical opinion, and I appreciate that other countries have different approaches there.'

So, the UK is behaving in a completely different way to other countries – but nobody in government can explain why, other than 'we're following the science'.

I cannot help but feel that we simply didn't prepare for this kind of pandemic and have now caught the mother of all colds.

On social media, aside from the general fury – mainly stemming from people with pro-Brexit and Boris slogans in their Twitter bios – that greets any criticism of the government, there's also still an ugly growing sentiment of, 'If it only attacks the old and sick, why do the rest of us have to stay in?'

Infuriated by this attitude, I tweeted, 'I don't give a damn how old someone is, or if they have an underlying condition, every single life is equally important. Those casually suggesting they should be sacrificed in this coronavirus crisis for the greater economic good are disgusting. Where's our humanity?'

It was one of my most-liked tweets ever, suggesting it struck a chord and many others feel the way I do. We need the compassionate voices to be as loud, or louder, as the selfish ones.

FRIDAY 3 APRIL

One of the most haunting tragedies of the crisis has been the case of a 13-year-old boy named Ismail Mohamed Abdulwahab, the youngest person in Britain so far to die from coronavirus. Ismail, from Brixton in south London, died alone in hospital this week because two of his siblings are displaying symptoms of the disease, forcing the whole family to self-isolate, including his mother. For a young boy to die like that, and for a mother to be unable to see him as he did so, is utterly heart-breaking. Today, photos emerged of him being buried by men in hazmat suits lowering his coffin into the ground. It was one of the saddest things I've ever seen and stung me to tears. I imagined that being one of my own sons, left to die alone. Just horrendous.

SATURDAY 4 APRIL

Another 708 UK coronavirus deaths were reported today, the worst day of the crisis so far. Each one is a person, a loved one, someone's grandparent, parent, sibling, child, friend. It's devastating.

Today's *Daily Mail* splashed on the growing horror in our care homes, where staff have little PPE and there is barely any testing for them or the residents. There are 11,000 care homes in Britain, housing over 400,000 elderly people.

'This is incredibly serious,' I tweeted, 'so many old & vulnerable people at grave risk, and who is properly protecting the care workers at all these homes? Hospitals are not only the [sic] war zones in this battle.'

By horrible coincidence, an old schoolfriend, Annali-Joy Middleton, emailed me to say her mother has tested positive for Covid-19 in her care home and won't recover. Even more heart-breakingly, none of the family is allowed to go and see her, so their last conversation will have to be done on FaceTime using a carer's mobile phone. I can't imagine having to say goodbye to a parent like that. The way coronavirus separates loving families from each other at their darkest moment is so cruel.

SUNDAY 5 APRIL

Tonight, the Queen addressed the nation. These are extraordinarily unsettling times and much more loss and grief will sadly ensue, interspersed with flashes of hope and the ecstatic joy of people surviving against all odds. With our current prime minister incapacitated, and a series of bumbling government ministers having the combined comforting effect of lying on a bed of rusty nails, all eyes turned tonight to a 93-year-old woman sitting in a castle where she has been self-isolating with her 98-year-old husband.

Queen Elizabeth II has reigned in the United Kingdom for a staggering 68 years. During that entire time – the longest period served by a current world ruler of any kind – she has barely put a regal foot wrong and on only four occasions has she felt compelled to address the nation outside of her annual Christmas speech: at the time of the first Gulf War in 1991, after the deaths of Princess Diana and then her mother in 1997 and 2002, and on the occasion of her Diamond Jubilee celebrations in 2012. But this was her most important address, one that came when every single person in Britain has been profoundly affected by a deadly virus that is destroying lives as fast as it is destroying jobs and economies.

And in just five short minutes, Her Majesty gave the greatest speech of her life. It was eloquent, powerful, evocative and perfectly pitched – thanking health workers for risking their lives to save ours, and the public for (largely) obeying government lockdown rules, but also urging all of us to dig deep into our individual reservoirs of stoic strength to get us collectively through this endurance test. This is Queen speak for 'Stop being so damn selfish!'

'Together we are tackling this disease,' she said, 'and I want to reassure you that if we remain united and resolute, then we will overcome it. I hope in the years to come everyone will be able to take pride in how they responded to this challenge. And those who come after us will say Britons of this generation were as strong as any. That the attributes of self-discipline, of quiet good-humoured resolve and of fellow feeling still characterise this country. The pride in who we are is not a part of our past, it defines our present and the future.'

Then she got personal. The Queen could have done this by saying that her own 71-year-old son and heir Prince Charles was infected by the virus last week, a worrying time for any mother given his age. But she didn't. Instead, she reminded us of the time during WWII when thousands of young children were evacuated from British cities into the countryside, separated from their parents for their own safety. She and her late sister Princess Margaret, themselves both very young at the time, recorded a radio message to those kids to offer them comfort and hope.

It was the Queen's first-ever broadcast and was also taped at Windsor Castle, where she taped the latest one. 'Today, once again,' she said last night, 'many will feel a painful sense of separation from their loved ones. But now, as then, we know, deep down, that it is the right thing to do.'

The Queen ended with this rallying cry: 'We should take comfort that while we have more still to endure, better days will return; we will be with our friends again; we will be with our families again; we will meet again.'

I felt a tear in my eye well up when I heard those words, and I'm sure I wasn't alone as social media instantly exploded with emotional praise. In her own uniquely influential way, the Queen made the British people feel better, lifted our spirits and gave us hope for the future.

'A magnificent speech from a magnificent lady,' I tweeted as soon as the address finished. 'Thank you, Your Majesty – this was your finest moment as our Monarch.'

And I meant it.

MONDAY 6 APRIL

A day of endless irritations began with Meghan and Harry announcing (is there any day they're not announcing something?) plans to launch a new charitable organisation, Archewell – named after their son Archie, whom they insist they want to keep private – that we're told aims 'to do something that matters'.

Aside from the grotesquely tone-deaf inappropriateness of doing this immediately after the Queen addressed the nation about coronavirus, I imagine the total number of f*cks the British public currently gives about these two self-regarding brats, announcing their 'plans' as they do nothing that matters in a Hollywood mansion, could be written on the back of a postage stamp.

I was also incensed by news that Liverpool Football Club, owned by US billionaires, is furloughing its staff after making £45 million profit last year. As I said on *GMB* this morning, why would such a great club, riding so high under their brilliant manager Jürgen Klopp, trash its reputation like this? Getting the British taxpayer to pay 80 per cent of employee salaries, when they're paying their players £5–10 million a year and making tens of millions of pounds in gate receipts and fees for winning the Champions League, is an astonishingly stupid decision. I was attacked by Liverpool legend John Barnes for saying this but supported by many of the club's fans on Twitter – and this evening, Liverpool's owners announced they would no longer be furloughing staff. It's the right thing to do, just a pity they had to be shamed into it.

The most shocking news, however, came around 8 pm with the announcement that Boris Johnson has been taken into intensive care after his condition worsened. It's obviously very serious, as it is for anyone admitted with the virus to ICU, where the survival rate is said to be no more than 50 per cent. Sadly, even this didn't spare Boris the vicious wrath of the vile #BeKind Twitter troll mob, who began joyfully celebrating the news and, disgustingly, wishing him dead.

As we watched the shocking news, Cory, our long-time Filipino housekeeper and nanny, told me that one of her friends works in the very intensive care unit at St Thomas' Hospital where Boris is now fighting for his life.

'Do you have many friends working in the NHS?'

'Oh yes,' said Cory.

'Give me their names and jobs,' I replied.

They were: Aeron Aquino, a nurse manager at Guy's Hospital and Nightingale Hospital; Cherifer Mamuyac and Venus Daquiz, nurses in the infectious diseases team at Northwick Park Hospital; Princess Shorter, a nurse at St Mary's Hospital; Louie Nuesa, a nurse at Queen Alexandra Hospital in Portsmouth; and Ayesha Nuesa, a senior staff nurse at the intensive care unit at Guy's and St Thomas'. To my astonishment, I then discovered there are nearly 20,000 Filipinos in the NHS, out of a total of over 55,000 immigrant health workers. I had no idea it was that many. How shameful that they've had to spend the last few years having their very existence in this country so belittled and abused during the vicious and sometimes openly racist Brexit debate. 'Why do we let all these damn foreigners come over 'ere?' was the repeated question.

To save our damn lives, it would seem.

TUESDAY 7 APRIL

Boris was still alive, but in critical condition, when I got to work at 5.15 am. Once we got on air, amid all the drama, I suddenly remembered Cory's friends and read out their names.

'We forget about this extraordinary workforce who comes from all round the world to help the NHS,' I said.

'I think we particularly value them right now,' agreed Susanna, whose mum is a nurse.

'An amazing number of Filipinos work in our NHS,' I said. 'Unsung heroes. It's worth bearing in mind when we talk about immigrants in this country, that these are the immigrants currently saving people's lives, coming here and enriching our country and doing an amazing job. So, thank you to all the Filipinos who are here and doing all this amazing work, and to every other immigrant working in the NHS currently. At the end of this, I hope we have a different sentiment, a different feeling about what immigration has done for this country.'

A clip of what I said went viral on social media and got over five million views. Former Home Secretary Sajid Javid, himself the son of a Pakistani bus driver, retweeted it with the words, 'We should all take a moment and reflect on the invaluable contribution of immigrants (and their adult children) to our NHS. Without them – however challenging things are now – so many more lives would be lost.'

We should do more than just reflect. When this is all over, we need to radically change the way we show our appreciation for these people. Clapping is fine but it doesn't pay the bills.

WEDNESDAY 8 APRIL

I got into a blazing argument on *GMB* with Mayor Sadiq Khan when he tried to defend not providing London's bus drivers with proper PPE despite nine of them so far dying from coronavirus. He protested that he was 'following the advice of experts' who said the drivers don't need full PPE. To which I retorted it was high time he followed common bloody sense, because self-evidently they do need it urgently – and more will die if they don't get it. I suspect Khan knows this and agrees with me.

But the shameful truth he doesn't want to admit publicly is that we simply don't have enough PPE for frontline NHS health workers, let alone others in the coronavirus war support system like bus drivers, shop assistants, pharmacists, teachers, police officers, binworkers and mail workers. We're sending all these brave warriors out to fight this war for us with their hands tied behind their back. And they're dying as a result.

Meanwhile, there are many selfish fools who think it's fine to break the lockdown rules, like footballer Jack Grealish, the Aston Villa captain, who has been charged with driving without due care and attention after he reportedly crashed into two parked cars after attending an all-night party at a mate's house. What made his behaviour so particularly outrageous was that less than 24 hours before the alleged incident, Grealish had issued a public appeal to his social media followers to 'Stay home. Protect the NHS. Save Lives'. Having lectured us all, he then apparently went out, failed to protect the NHS and might have cost lives.

Thankfully, it's not all misery and selfishness. Extraordinary tales of inspiration are shining through the darkness, via the mouths of those who survive the virus against all the odds and emerge blinking into the sunlight again, clapped and cheered as they leave hospital by the NHS heroes who saved them. One of them was Hylton Murray-Philipson, 61, a remarkably eloquent farmer from Market Harborough who survived a week in intensive care with Covid-19 and told us on *GMB* today how the experience has given him a new appreciation for life and the little things he will no longer take for granted. 'Honestly, I'm seeing the world with fresh eyes, as if I am a child again,' he said. 'Every little thing is magic.'

Of the medical staff who saved him, he became emotional as he said, 'It doesn't really matter what age you are, you go back to a state of childhood and complete and utter dependence on the kindness of others for every little thing in your 24 hours. How can you not bond with somebody who is washing your back, who has just been stroking your brow and whispering in your ear, "You're going to be OK. You're going to make it"? The individuals have come from all over the world but the quality of human compassion is just absolutely phenomenal.'

And what did he fantasise most about as he lay fighting for his life?

'A piece of toast and marmalade. That's enough for me.'

Susanna and I both felt very emotional after the interview. It's been utterly draining covering this story, with its seemingly unrelenting horror. These little stories of hope lift the heart and are incredibly important to balance all the grimness.

Boris is out of intensive care. I'm very relieved and pleased he is on the mend. I've known him for 30 years and we've always got on well personally. But the health of one man, however important he is, shouldn't turn attention away from the horrifying new coronavirus death figures for the UK. Nearly 1,000 deaths were recorded in the past 24 hours, a massive spike in fatalities that now puts us on a trajectory to potentially having the worst death rate in Europe.

SUNDAY 12 APRIL

Boris has released a video of himself recuperating at Chequers. He looked OK, if a little pale and slimmer, and spoke in a serious, heartfelt way about how grateful he is to the NHS heroes who he said had 'saved my life, no question'.

As I was watching him at home, someone asked me on Twitter what's the first thing I'll do when this is all over. I thought for a bit then replied that I'd jump in my car, head down to Newick, rendezvous with my cricket club mates at the Royal Oak, drink 12 pints of Harvey's best bitter, then stumble joyfully to the next-door Tandoori restaurant for a chicken tikka masala. That's what freedom would taste like to me.

'Can you walk 100 laps of your garden, Piers?' replied someone named Captain Tom Moore. I wasn't sure what he was getting at until I discovered he's a 99-year-old World War II veteran who is currently walking 100 laps of *his* garden before his 100th birthday on 30 April – to raise cash for the NHS.

Apparently, he originally hoped to make £1,000 but after a regional ITV station picked up his story, his endeavour has gone viral and money is now pouring in.

'Haha, no Tom!' I responded. 'Love what you're doing – keep pounding.'

Then I told the *GMB* team to book him for tomorrow's show.

Tonight, Cory told me that one of her Filipino NHS friends, whom I mentioned on air, has contracted Covid-19 from treating patients and is very sick in the same St Thomas' Hospital where Boris had been.

MONDAY 13 APRIL

By the time Susanna and I spoke to Captain Tom Moore, his JustGiving donation page had soared to £350,000, and he'd set himself a new target of £500,000.

He explained his motivation: 'When our nurses go into work at the moment,' he said, 'they must feel like Daniel going into the lion's den because they don't know what's going to happen, but they know they're in for a pretty tough day and by gum they're brave.'

Captain Tom, appearing with his daughter Hannah, whom he has lived with since his wife Pamela died in 2006, added, 'In the war, we had to carry on whatever was going on and we knew eventually we were going to win and it's the same with this virus. There's no doubt we're on the winning side. We shall survive and we shall all get through it well in the end.'

This rousing rallying cry to the nation moved me so much I told Captain Tom I would donate £10,000 myself and urged viewers to chip in too. Within four hours of our interview, he'd reached the £500,000.

'I can't thank you enough, sir,' a delighted Tom tweeted me (I suspect with a bit of help!), 'hats off!'

'Hey, Captain Tom,' I replied, 'why stop at £500k? Let's go for £1 million ...'

I then urged my 7.5 million followers to donate, and watched the total surge all day.

TUESDAY 14 APRIL

America is now the epicentre of the coronavirus crisis, and what is abundantly clear is that President Trump and his administration, like the UK government, was shamefully late to recognise the severity of the Covid-19 threat and as a result has played catastrophically bad catch-up ever since. This complacency has left the USA, and Britain, woefully under-prepared when it comes to having enough of the right tools to fight the virus – from PPE for health workers to tests, ventilators, masks and other vital pieces of kit.

From the start of this crisis, President Trump has tried to rely on his usual political methodology – attacking opponents, trashing the 'fake news' media, blaming anyone and everyone but himself, pretending things are better than they are, and congratulating himself repeatedly for making all the right decisions. But his tactics aren't working this time because Americans are dying in their droves from coronavirus at a rate faster than almost anywhere else in the world, and they're seeing the stark, horrific reality in the shape of mass open-air graves being prepared and field hospitals being set up in parks. They're also seeing the US economy tank like never before, jobs being destroyed in historically bad numbers, and vast swathes of the American public being plunged into poverty, homelessness and misery.

This is as bad as it gets; a grim Ground Zero for most Americans who've never had to even contemplate such terrible hardship, let alone actually endure it. Yet every day their president pops up for several hours on TV to pontificate about how it's not really that bad, how things will all bounce back quickly and how he couldn't possibly be doing a better job. Blah blah bloody blah. It's become an increasingly nauseating spectacle and last night President Trump reached a new low with a press briefing performance that was frankly an utter disgrace.

Time and again reporters asked him perfectly legitimate questions about his administration's handling of this crisis, and time and again Trump furiously abused, denounced and dismissed them with sneering contempt. He ranted, raved, mocked and derided in such an appalling manner that by the time he finished, the hashtag #TrumpMeltdown was the no. 1 trending topic on Twitter in America.

This was worse than just a meltdown. This was the most undignified and pathetic display I have ever seen from any world leader in a global crisis, let alone the president of the United States. And where once I could occasionally defend his combative, abrasive style against what I have often felt has been an unfairly hostile media, I cannot defend this and have become increasingly vociferous in my criticism of him on air, and in my columns and tweets.

WEDNESDAY 15 APRIL

'I'd like to see the magnificently inspiring Captain Tom be knighted for his services to his country in WWII & now to the NHS,' I tweeted. 'Who's with me?'

Almost 90,000 people liked the tweet, showing just how much this doggedly determined, charming old man has inspired us all. His rapid ascent into the national and indeed global consciousness, and conscience, has been an astonishing thing to watch. Captain Tom's most admirable quality is his humility. He doesn't see himself or what he's doing as anything special. Yet we all do because there's something so incredibly moving about watching him shuffle slowly up and down his garden to do his bit for the NHS. We interviewed him again today after his total reached £900,000.

'It's marvellous that so many kind people are helping those on the frontline,' he said with typical modesty, 'our army in this war are wearing nurse and doctor uniforms.'

Captain Tom surged past £1 million a few minutes after we came off air, and carried on surging all day to £4 million by midnight, with people from all around the world joining in.

I've been really enjoying throwing the full power of my TV and social media platform behind him. It feels so much more meaningful than throwing it behind taking another whack at Meghan Markle or venting my rage at papoose-wearing radical vegans. Helping Tom help the NHS in its toughest moment is something that unites everyone rather than inflaming division.

The same cannot be said for the procession of hapless government ministers being sent out to defend the indefensible with shockingly poor knowledge and interview skills. Today, the Care Minister Helen Whately appeared on *GMB* and was unable to tell me how many NHS and care home workers have died from the virus.

'Your focus on figures slightly belies the fact we are talking about individual people's lives here,' she replied.

'I just asked you how many health workers and care workers have died from coronavirus on the frontline,' I persisted. 'Do you know the answer?'

'The latest information we have for NHS workers is that 19 NHS workers have very sadly died.'

'That's complete and utter nonsense,' I retorted. 'The *Mirror* had 38 yesterday.'

'I don't get my data from newspapers,' she said. 'The official figure I have been given for health workers is 19, but we do also know that some workers have died in social care and I'll be straight with you, we don't have a figure for that.'

I then asked her if it was true, as the *Daily Mail* screamed on its front page this morning, that as many as 4,000 people may have died in care homes, but she hadn't got a clue. In fact, she laughed – I assume, let's be generous here, from nerves – as I asked the question, just as she laughed again later in the interview during a startlingly inappropriate and jarring performance that exposed both her shocking ineptitude and the government's worrying reliance on incredibly inexperienced people to handle this enormous crisis.

There were over 600 complaints to OFCOM that I was too hard on her, but she's the care minister at a time when there is an epidemic of coronavirus in care homes due to government incompetence and it is my fundamental duty as a journalist to hold her accountable. 'Apparently some people found my interview with care minister Helen Whately today "uncomfortable",' I tweeted. 'For perspective, it probably wasn't as "uncomfortable" as what our under-protected NHS & carer frontline heroes are going through.'

Many viewers approved of my bombastic style though. 'BOOM @piermorgan,' tweeted Rose McGowan, 'this is like watching a fly get stuck on sticky paper.' Former Tory MP Anna Soubry agreed. 'What irresponsible idiot put up a badly briefed, inexperienced minister for interview by @piersmorgan?' she raged. 'He takes no prisoners & yes he interrupts when he shouldn't (nothing new) but he's trying to get the answers & action that millions are demanding.'

Matt Hancock released a video message to the nation later. 'Throughout this crisis,' he said, 'we've been working incredibly hard to protect people in social care and today we can announce that everybody going from hospital into social care will be tested and will be isolated while the result of that test comes through, because that helps to protect people who are in social care, who are after all some of the most vulnerable people in the country.'

I had to watch this several times before I could fully comprehend what I'd just heard.

So, let me get this absolutely straight: we've spent the past few weeks sending hordes of elderly people out of hospitals, where coronavirus is rife, back into care homes without testing them for the virus? This is the very epitome of the phrase 'lambs to the slaughter', isn't it? Yet this strategy supposedly constitutes 'working incredibly hard to protect people in social care'?

The result of this appalling negligence – and there's no other word for it – is that Britain's care homes are now exploding with coronavirus, both among the residents and the heroic care workers trying to look after them, often without adequate PPE. The situation is so catastrophically bad that the government has no idea how bad it is.

I'm on a WhatsApp group chat with a few top TV news journalist mates and we all agree that we can't recall a time when both the government and opposition ranks seemed to be so lacking in calibre, with the honourable exception of Chancellor Rishi Sunak, who has been commendably authoritative during his press briefing stints.

Nobody pretends it's an easy time to be running this country, or indeed any country. But it feels, increasingly, disconcertingly evident that many of the people charged with doing so in Britain don't have a clue what they're doing.

There's also been stinking self-serving hypocrisy by our leadership. Michael Gove, one of the most senior government ministers, was forced to self-isolate when his daughter showed symptoms of coronavirus. If that situation happens to anyone working on the NHS frontline, it's almost impossible for them to get a test for their child, so they are compelled to stay at home for 14 days without even knowing if there is a good reason to. But Gove spoke to the Chief Medical Officer Chris Whitty and asked him if he could have a test for his child. He was told he could, his daughter was tested, thankfully found to not have the virus, and Gove was free to go back to work. Yet most politicians are doing their work from home, and I see no good reason why Gove can't either. Instead, he got an incredibly valuable test to free himself from restrictive isolation when most NHS staff and care workers can't. That too is shameful.

The first duty of any government is to keep its people safe and to protect public health. This government has spectacularly failed in that duty during this crisis so far. The only questions now are how many lives will it cost, how much damage will it cause to our economy and what impact will it have on our already divided society?

THURSDAY 16 APRIL

Captain Tom has now raised £12 million, making him the biggest single fundraiser in JustGiving history.

'This is absurd!' I told him when he came back on *GMB*.

'It certainly is!' he agreed.

Hannah told him about my knighthood campaign, which made several newspaper front pages today.

'I've never anticipated anything like that,' he chuckled. 'Our Queen is perfect, and we should all be so proud of her.'

'If she did knight you,' I asked, 'what would you say to her?'

'I would say, "Your Majesty, this is the greatest honour anyone could get, because you are such a marvellous person," and then I would remind her that she and I both served in her father's army in the war.'

As for this war, Captain Tom remained resolute: 'The future is in front of us all, and things will get better and we will get through this very difficult time. We've fought so many battles as a country and we've always won, and this time we will win again. Remember, tomorrow will be a good day.'

There's something so extraordinarily powerful about his simple but inspiring rhetoric. If only the woke brigade, with their ludicrously misaligned focus on what matters, would take note. Captain Tom passed his 100 laps later in the morning but vowed to keep going. 'I'll continue walking as long as people are generous enough to donate to the NHS.'

Matt Hancock was back on *GMB* and, during a series of further testy exchanges, I pushed him on how many people are still flying into the UK.

'Fifteen thousand a day,' was his answer.

That's 105,000 people a week flying in from all over the world, including from corona-ravaged countries, with no checks or quarantine.

Yet the rest of us are under enforced lockdown to 'save lives'.

It's madness.

Hancock recently targeted footballers, saying they should 'do their bit' financially to help.

Given that New Zealand Prime Minister Jacinda Ardern – one of several detail-oriented female world leaders, including Germany's Angela Merkel, who seem to be handling this crisis a lot better than their blustering male counterparts – has just announced she and her cabinet are taking 20 per cent pay cuts for six months, I asked Hancock if he would be 'doing his bit' and following the New Zealand government's lead.

'No,' came the answer.

FRIDAY 17 APRIL

For the past few years, feminist writer queen Caitlin Moran has repeatedly, and with great linguistic relish, whacked and ridiculed me in her weekly Celebrity 'Top 10' Watch column in *The Times*. This week, to my astonishment, I appeared in her no. 1 slot under the headline: 'Piers Morgan uses his powers for good instead of evil.'

Ms Moran explained, 'As I noted a few weeks ago, "the Awfulness" is bringing out unexpected changes in people – and one of the most notable is the Epic Coronavirus Journey of Piers Morgan. Morgan is a fascinating character for those who have a Blakean tendency to see the world in just one grain of sand – or, in this case, in one breakfast TV presenter and prominent contrarian ... picking fights with feminists, trans activists, mental health campaigners, sundry "snowflakes" and, most quixotically, vegan sausage rolls.

'Since coronavirus hit, though, everything has changed, for Morgan seems to have furloughed his beef with vegans, and

Madonna's bum, and has become one of the few presenters on TV trying to hold others to account for their tactics during the pandemic. Morgan has been mauling the Work and Pensions Secretary Thérèse Coffey for saying she had "no idea" how many care workers have died from Covid-19; savaged Care Minister Helen Whately; shouted "How dare you!" at Health Secretary Matt Hancock's claim that the British strategy hadn't changed; and called out Boris Johnson's "failure of leadership", even when Johnson was in hospital. He has also defended immigrant workers.

'Most notably of all, he has used his *Daily Mail* column to round on Donald Trump – Morgan's friend, and one of the few people he follows on Twitter – calling him "undignified, pathetic, ludicrous, shameless ... an emperor with no clothes", and ridiculing the President's rambling boasts about his "ratings figures" with "I don't want to hear that you're a ratings hit – the reason you're a ratings hit is because people are terrified because of the death count, and infection rates are going through the roof in your country." If I were friends with the President of the United States, I probably wouldn't slag him off. But it seems that now Morgan has something he can genuinely get his teeth into, he has no fear at all. Perhaps, all this time, Morgan has just been bored and spoiling for a fight – with only a sausage roll or a princess for an outlet. He is, at the moment, Right-On Piers. Definitely not the hero Gotham wanted – but the hero, it turned out, Gotham needed.'

Ms Moran may be onto something. I probably have been waiting for something meatier than a vegan sausage roll to sink my fangs into.

MONDAY 20 APRIL

'Daddy, what did YOU do in the Great War?' screamed the famous recruitment posters across Britain during World War I. That was the first time British civilians had been asked to enlist in large numbers to fight alongside regular professional armed forces. And the recruitment campaign, featuring young children sitting on their father's knee after the war was over asking a very simple question, was a deliberately brutal, emotion-charged, guilt-inducing assault on an individual's conscience. No man wanted to be the guy who had to reply: 'Nothing, kids, I stayed at home and did nothing.' Millions of men signed up as a result, answering the call to duty, and Britain and our allies eventually prevailed.

Ironically, in this new world battle with coronavirus, most of us are being asked to do what people then were shamed into NOT doing – stay at home and do nothing. That's literally all the vast majority of us have to put ourselves through to help defeat the deadly enemy, Covid-19, as our heroic health workers do all the heavy fighting in hospitals and care homes at huge personal risk to themselves and their families.

Some, like Captain Tom, are doing a little bit more than just sitting at home. He won't be around for future generations of his family to ask him what he did in the war on coronavirus, but he won't have to – because everyone else will tell them. By stark contrast to this wonderful man's attitude and commitment, which has now raised £27 million and rising fast, the coronavirus war has also brought out the very worst in far richer and more privileged people.

Take, for example, Victoria Beckham. She and her husband David popped up on Lady Gaga's excellent *One World* version of 'Live Aid' last night – Gaga, to her great credit, personally raised over $30 million from corporate sponsors to help fight coronavirus – to speak of their deep gratitude to all health workers. They've also posted a series of videos of themselves applauding the same workers. Yet when it comes to doing *their* bit for their country, what have the Beckhams done? It turns out they've decided to fleece the British taxpayer of money that should be going to support the NHS, that's what.

Yes, arguably the most famous couple in Britain, worth a combined £335 million, have planned to furlough staff at Victoria's failing VB Fashion company so the government has to fork out £2,500 each a month for 30 people. (I include David in this decision because he has repeatedly intervened to financially bankroll his wife's business due to heavy losses it continues to incur, so is clearly a partner in all Victoria's big decisions regarding it.) That works out at £75,000 a month, which is way less than the Beckhams will earn in interest alone on their vast wealth during the period of this furloughing.

But that is £75,000 a month that could and should be going to the NHS, who so desperately need more PPE.

This decision comes several weeks after it was revealed the Beckhams have recently splashed out £17 million on a new penthouse apartment in Miami, and after they posed with a £2,000 bottle of wine they were drinking for dinner. So, this is a hugely rich couple who can easily afford to continue paying a few dozen employees through this tough time. Instead, they've decided to take taxpayer money that is desperately needed elsewhere.

It's a perfectly legal move, but it's also a perfectly immoral one for those who don't need to do it. In fact, just as it was when big football clubs like Liverpool and Spurs announced they were doing the same (decisions they were shamed into reversing by justified social media outrage – one of the times when it can be a useful tool), it's hard to think of a more selfish, shameless, greedy or exploitative decision or a more disgustingly hypocritical one, given how keen the Beckhams have been to show us all how much they care about the NHS.

Elsewhere, Meghan and Harry have resurfaced. We were told they wanted a 'quieter, more private life', especially for their young son Archie. So naturally, they've now washed up in Beverly Hills, the paparazzi epicentre of the world, where they're living in a palatial home owned by TV star Tyler Perry. (I wonder who's paying for it this time.)

I really don't want to have to think about these two anymore as the crisis rages, but they keep hurling themselves into the news cycle as if they're desperate to wrestle our attention back from a mere pandemic.

The timing of their move couldn't be worse. Meghan and Harry have gone to Hollywood to relaunch their careers as full-time celebrities, only to find the whole world shutting down due to coronavirus, and celebrities being displaced by health workers as stars in most people's eyes. To compound their irritation, the other senior royals back home in Britain, led by the Queen, Prince Charles and Camilla, and the Cambridges, have been doing their duty in a quietly, stoically magnificent way.

Last night, the Sussexes inexplicably decided this was a good time to launch yet another front in their pathetic ongoing war with the media. In a statement of breathtakingly haughty arrogance, they announced they were banning four British newspapers from their lives, including the *Daily Mail*. They made one of their usual rambling, poorly written, whiny assaults on how awful the tabloids are, and got their new Hollywood PR firm Sunshine Sachs to send it – don't laugh at the back – to the world's media.

'That'll show 'em!' they clearly thought to themselves, as they sat back in their luxurious mansion to wait for the inevitable applause and attention they've been missing for so long. Only, all it showed us was what a repellent pair of preening tone-deaf little twerps they really are.

Even more disgracefully, Prince Harry accused the British media of exaggerating the scale of this coronavirus crisis. How the hell does he know how bad it is from his Hollywood hideaway – did he call his father Prince Charles, who has been suffering from the virus many thousands of miles away?

It's almost impossible to exaggerate how bad this crisis is: it's causing unimaginable, relentless horror and grief and affecting all of us in a way we couldn't have comprehended a few months ago. Lives are being destroyed, jobs are being destroyed, whole economies are being destroyed and almost everything we took for granted has been taken away.

Yet we're supposed to think this is all some whipped-up hysteria by the media?

I won't take such ill-informed lectures from a massively privileged man who quit his family and his country to pursue a vacuous new life of pampered self-indulgence in the world's most shallow and media-frenzied city.

Nor will I take any orders about how I can or should behave as a journalist from a pair of spoilt little brats who contrary to their statement are still spending millions of pounds of taxpayers' money on British royal protection squad officers. Imagine thinking the middle of a global pandemic is the right moment to declare another war on the media? Or being so deluded that you think anyone gives a shit about your bruised egos when so many health workers are being slaughtered on the frontline of this war? Or being so dumb that you think the public right now have even one ounce of interest or concern in how you're portrayed by newspapers?

But then like the Beckhams, it's sadly, pathetically clear that all the Sussexes care about, like so many self-obsessed privileged wokies, is themselves. They live in a me-me-me bubble that doesn't allow for anything more important, like the worst global pandemic in a century, to interfere with their self-promotion.

When their grandkids sit on their knees and ask, 'Granny, Grandpa, what did YOU do in the Great Coronavirus War?' the Beckhams will be forced to reply, 'We spent taxpayers' money that should have gone to nurses,' and the Sussexes will be forced to reply, 'We moaned about our own beastly media coverage.' Meanwhile, Captain Moore quietly got on with pounding his garden and raising tens of millions of pounds for those on the frontline. *He* is what we should all aspire to be. *They* are what we should all aspire not to be.

WEDNESDAY 22 APRIL

The United States has now had more coronavirus deaths than anywhere else in the world, and the rate of American infections (827,093) and deaths (over 45,000) continues to soar to horrific heights.

Yet despite this, thousands of protestors have begun marching all over the country in fury at the lockdown measures, from North Carolina and Missouri to Alabama and Oregon. They're blocking streets, honking horns and angrily demanding their right to 'freedom'. Many are armed with guns, the preferred instrument of protecting liberty for many Americans. And they are largely, though not exclusively, conservative and pro-Trump as can be seen from their banners, T-shirts and rhetoric.

In one particularly unedifying incident outside the state capitol building in Austin, Texas, the far-right American radio show host and notorious conspiracy theory whack-job Alex Jones fuelled chants of 'You can't close America!', 'Let us work!' and even 'Fire Fauci!' in reference to Dr Anthony Fauci, America's most brilliant and impressive medical expert.

The protestors have been actively encouraged by President Trump, who in a tweet storm several days ago blasted, 'LIBERATE MINNESOTA!', 'LIBERATE MICHIGAN!' and 'LIBERATE VIRGINIA!' – all states, and this was not a coincidence, run by Democrat governors.

By doing this, Trump encouraged the idea that coronavirus lockdowns are the enemy of liberty, even as his own experts were advising people to stay at home and obey them. And even as his own government advice remains that no state should reopen until they see 14 days of declining infections.

It would be easy to dismiss all the protestors as a bunch of Neanderthal idiots, but I will resist that temptation because it wouldn't be accurate or fair. Some definitely are, judging by their inflammatory nonsensical ramblings when they've been interviewed. But others I've seen speaking out have seemed genuinely fearful and concerned for what the lockdowns mean for the crashing US economy, for jobs, and for public health from the inevitable poverty and homelessness that will escalate the longer this crisis goes on.

And there is a perfectly legitimate, indeed essential debate to be had about the merits of how strict a lockdown should be and how long it should last. One of the best things about America and its open democratic society is that this debate is being had publicly and loudly, in a way that shames countries like my own, Britain, where the government is behaving during this crisis like a Soviet-style regime intent on suppressing the truth.

However, when I see protestors squaring up angrily to health workers, as has begun happening more frequently in recent days, my heart sinks at the abysmal lack of respect for people on the frontline of this coronavirus war, who know they will soon be treating many of those protesting, and for the lack of basic common sense being applied by those demanding their 'liberty'.

My question for the protestors is this: what kind of 'freedom' do you think ignoring lockdowns will bring? I imagine it is the kind that would allow them to go to a nice restaurant with their families and have a meal. I'd love to do that too, but I understand that to do so would be to put my life at risk, and the lives of others. Why don't the protestors understand this?

I suspect the main reason is that they don't believe or trust the 'experts' telling them not to. So, they see lockdowns as some kind of tyrannical threat being driven by politically motivated opponents who want to control their lives, a belief that has been disgracefully fuelled by their president.

I once had a very friendly conversation with a Texan oil tycoon about guns, at a time when I was engaged in a series of very unfriendly gun-related conversations on air at CNN following the Sandy Hook massacre. He explained to me that the reason so many Americans believe so passionately in the right to bear arms is that they genuinely fear the government may turn tyrannical on them and they need to be armed to defend their liberty for when that time comes.

I didn't agree with that argument – not least because the US government has 5,800 nuclear warheads at its disposal so the fight wouldn't last very long – but I understood it. I think this mindset explains why so many Americans are taking to the streets to protest against being locked down. They see it as an assault on their liberty, which is the very cornerstone of every American's constitutional rights.

But it's not. In fact, it's the opposite: the lockdowns are designed to protect life and preserve liberty. Until there is a successful vaccine for Covid-19, or enough mass testing to work out who has had it and whether they have developed an immunity, the lockdowns are going to be an absolutely vital tool in fighting the virus.

And those who flout the rules may pay the ultimate price. Consider the story of a man named John McDaniel, 60, from Marion County in Ohio. On 15 March, he was so enraged by Governor Mike DeWine's lockdown measures that he posted the following on Facebook: 'If what I'm hearing is true, that DeWine has ordered the bars and restaurants to be closed, I say bullshit! He doesn't have the authority. If you are paranoid about getting sick just don't go out. It shouldn't keep those of us from living our lives. This madness has to stop.'

Two days earlier, McDaniel, married with two children and boss of an industrial equipment supply company, suggested the dangers posed by the coronavirus had been massively exaggerated. 'Does anybody have the guts to say this Covid-19 is a political ploy? Asking for a friend. Prove me wrong.'

John McDaniel died from Covid-19 last week.

FRIDAY 24 APRIL

I woke up to news that President Trump has suggested people suffering from Covid-19 should be injected with bleach. Trump made his absurd claim after William Bryan, the Department of Homeland Security under-secretary for science and technology, gave a presentation about new research which supposedly shows 'emerging results' that coronavirus degrades faster in warm conditions and dies quickest when exposed to direct sunlight. He didn't explain why, if this is the case, the virus has wreaked havoc in warm-weather parts of the USA like Florida and Louisiana. Bryan added that his research also indicated bleach can kill the virus in five minutes, and a concentrated isopropyl alcohol solution can kill it in 30 seconds.

The president loved what he was hearing and decided to proffer his own ideas after Bryan had finished. His first was that irradiating patients' bodies with UV light might work too.

'Supposing we hit the body with a tremendous – whether it's ultraviolet or just very powerful – light,' he said, turning to Dr Deborah Birx, the White House coronavirus response coordinator, whose blinking face remained wearily impassive as he added, 'and I think you said that hasn't been checked but you're going to test it? And then I said, supposing you brought the light inside of the body, which you can do through either the skin or in some other way. And I think you said you're going to test that too. Sounds interesting.'

He then asked Dr Birx if she had ever heard of the 'heat and light' approach to treat the virus. 'Not as a treatment,' she replied. 'I think it's a great thing to look at,' he countered. But this, it transpired, was just the warm-up – literally – for his BIG idea. 'And then I see the disinfectant where it knocks it out in a minute,' Trump mused. 'One minute. And is there a way we can do something like that, by injection inside or almost a cleaning? So, it will be interesting to check that.'

At this point, Trump stated the only fact he uttered during this medical diatribe of nonsense: 'I'm not a doctor. I'm like a person that has a good you-know-what.'

No, I don't know what, actually. I just see a president pretending to be a medical expert and spewing theories that might have disastrous consequences.

Throughout this coronavirus crisis, Trump has turned the daily White House task force briefing into a rambling two-hour self-promoting rally – trashing the media, attacking political opponents, telling us how great he is and rewriting history as he tries to defend all the mistakes he's made since the virus first erupted. And he's done all this while 50,000 Americans have died from Covid-19, the worst death toll in the world, and nearly a million cases have now been reported across the country. But by far the most reckless and dangerous thing Trump has done is use the most powerful podium on earth to air his batshit crazy theories about how to beat the virus. And this is a horrible new low.

It's hard to imagine a more stupid thing for a president to say than publicly float a completely unsubstantiated 'idea' like that, which will inevitably make some Americans believe having bleach inside them will cure the virus. For him to use his platform to fly absurdly delusional and dangerous medical 'cures' during this crisis is an outrageous abuse of his position.

Several weeks ago, he repeatedly pumped up a malaria drug hydroxychloroquine, and was joined by a number of enthusiastic conservative TV hosts and pundits. Then he, and they, suddenly stopped. Why? A study of coronavirus patients in a US military veterans' hospital found *more* deaths among those treated with hydroxychloroquine than those treated without it.

So, it was doing more harm than good.

When Trump first began saying in mid-March what a good idea the drug was for coronavirus, a Phoenix man died after he and his wife attempted to self-medicate against the virus by drinking chloroquine phosphate, a fish-tank cleaning additive that they wrongly thought was the hydroxychloroquine Trump had been talking about on TV. His wife, who was left critically ill but survived, said, 'We were scared of getting sick.' How many Americans, also scared of getting sick now the crisis has escalated dramatically, will now be tempted to try taking bleach to combat Covid-19?

Some found Trump's latest ridiculous medical theories amusing, and myriad Trump and bleach memes have gone viral on social media. But I don't find any of this funny. In fact, I found his remarks breathtakingly stupid, reckless and dangerous. I posted a *Daily Mail* column saying all this, with the uncompromising headline: 'SHUT THE F*CK UP, MR PRESIDENT: Trump's batshit crazy coronavirus "cure" theories are not just shockingly senseless and stupid – they're going to kill people.'

It was full-on, but he needs to understand how insanely dangerous his behaviour is becoming. I'm reminded of what Trump himself once told me about success. 'You gotta win,' he said. 'That's what it's all about. Muhammad Ali used to talk and talk, but he won. If you talk and talk but lose, the act doesn't play.'

Exactly. The president is currently talking and talking – but losing. And the act isn't playing.

SATURDAY 25 APRIL

President Trump unfollowed me on Twitter overnight. I guess he didn't like being told to shut the f*ck up.

MONDAY 27 APRIL

OFCOM has emphatically ruled in my favour about all the complaints over my fiery interview style with ministers, and done so with a significant statement of support for freedom of speech. 'We assessed a number of complaints about Piers Morgan's conduct while interviewing politicians about the UK's response to the coronavirus public health crisis,' the statement read. 'Piers Morgan is well known for his combative interviewing style, and viewers would expect him to challenge senior politicians and hold them to account. His guests were given adequate opportunity to put their points across and counter the presenter's criticisms. In OFCOM's view, in line with freedom of expression, it is clearly in the public interest that broadcasters are able to hold those making political decisions to account, particularly during a major national crisis, such as the coronavirus pandemic.'

It's great to see a regulatory body understand the vital importance of free speech and put it above the hysterical partisan attempts to suppress it.

There's been an interesting debate raging in the *Yorkshire Post* about my conduct, fuelled by the paper's columnist Anthony Clavane, who declared, 'Hardly a morning goes by, these days, without Morgan tearing into a hapless minister on the show. It has become something of a national sport. [...] Piers divides people. To some, he is a smug, name-dropping, arrogant buffoon who bullies hapless ministers. To others, he is, on this issue at least, the voice of reason, a champion of transparency and a presenter who robustly holds the powerful to account. I tend towards the latter view. True, in the past I've found his goading of liberals, his sycophancy towards Donald Trump and his all-round oafishness to be the breakfast TV equivalent of pickled eggs in pubs. But he has emerged as Britain's answer to Howard Beale. You might remember that, in the 1975 film *Network*, Beale – played by Peter Finch – memorably raged, "I'm mad as hell and I'm not going to take it anymore."'

It's not a bad analogy, though a slightly disconcerting one given that Beale ends up being shot dead on TV after going completely bonkers and tanking his ratings. But the response from his readers in the *Post*'s letters page reflects the bitter divide between so many Britons right now. One, David Warnes, raged, 'During recent mornings, I have witnessed two female Cabinet ministers being subjected to rage and abuse by a TV presenter on *Good Morning Britain*. This trial by television was an obscenity. The bumptious and holier-than-thou Piers Morgan, and others of his ilk, need to be reminded that this country and indeed the world is at war. Could one imagine that sort of behaviour going on in the last war? No, in those days we had a supportive media which boosted morale against a common enemy and, in no small way, helped us win that war. Perhaps Mr Morgan and others like him could do with a spell of reflection in the Tower of London. Isn't that what we do with subversives?'

To which another reader, Paul Harrison, replied, 'I was intrigued by the somewhat draconian assertion of your correspondent that TV presenter Piers Morgan should be consigned to the Tower of London on the grounds that the journalist was subversive. Mr Morgan apparently had audaciously cross-examined two evidently inept Conservative ministers on the government's failings during the current pandemic crisis. Mr Warnes goes on to remind us of the high moral standing of a "supportive media" during World War Two. I would, in turn, respectfully remind him that the conflict was fought in the defence of democracy, including the right of free speech, and an independent press.' Quite right.

TUESDAY 28 APRIL

Home Office minister Victoria Atkins appeared on *GMB* after a shocking episode of *Panorama* last night exposed Britain's abject failure to properly prepare for the onslaught of Covid-19.

It focused on the massive pandemic drill in 2016 named Exercise Cygnus, attended by all major government departments and health chiefs, that was an almost exact parallel to what is now happening and concluded that Britain was woefully short of many things, including, specifically, personal protective equipment for frontline health workers.

Yet as *Panorama* revealed, nothing was done to fix this shortage. And 134 NHS and care-home staff have now died from coronavirus. This is an absolute disgrace. Astonishingly, Ms Atkins, who hadn't bothered to watch *Panorama*, had never heard of Exercise Cygnus despite being a Home Affairs Select Committee member at the time.

When I expressed my horror at her admission, she brazenly lied and suddenly announced she *had* heard of it, but when I asked her to reveal one single finding, she couldn't, other than to repeat back what I had just told her. It was the single worst performance by any government minister on *GMB* since the crisis began, and the bar was sadly already very low.

'Who in government takes the decision to send such under-prepared ministers on to *GMB*?' tweeted BBC broadcaster Andrew Neil after watching it. 'It's not a car crash, it's a massive pile-up. Is the government that bereft of talent? If so, better not to send anyone. It's excruciating.'

Incredibly, it seems to be a deliberate policy. The *Sun* reported that my 'ferocious coronavirus maulings' apparently 'boost ministers' standings' because Downing Street focus groups suggest the public feels sorry for them. The paper quoted a Number 10 insider saying, 'He doesn't know it, but Piers is doing us a big favour. That's why we keep sending ministers in front of him.'

Wow. A government actively celebrating its ministers getting exposed as woefully ill-informed imbeciles during the biggest crisis of our lifetime is beyond parody.

Tory MP Simon Hoare ripped into me on Twitter. 'I'm afraid @piersmorgan is not acting as a journalist. As a barrack room lawyer? Yes. As a saloon bar bore? Yes. As a bully? Yes.

As a show-off? Undoubtedly. He is not a seeker after truth: he's a male chicken.'

To which Anna Soubry responded, 'I'm more afraid of sycophantic MPs. Piers Morgan is doing his job. Tough questions must be asked of Govt & the scientists we are all placing our trust in. This MP would do better to demand proper answers from his Govt Ministers not spin & lies.'

WEDNESDAY 29 APRIL

Number 10 has thrown in the towel and decided not to put up any ministers on tomorrow's show. I'm only surprised it took them this long.

I had an idea.

'How long would it take to read out the names of every health and care worker who has died?' I emailed the team. 'Just their name and occupation – with their photo where one is available? It might be a powerful thing to do in the 8.30 am slot where we would normally interview the minister.'

THURSDAY 30 APRIL

Susanna and I spent six minutes slowly reading out all the names. It had a hugely emotional impact on viewers, and us.

Philip Collins in *The Times* wrote about the shocking quality of ministerial performances in TV interviews. 'The standard of ministers being fielded is so lamentable,' he wrote, 'that Tory MPs are starting to worry. Victoria Atkins, the safeguarding minister, was the latest to collapse into incoherence on *Good Morning Britain*. Piers Morgan will be getting very fat with all the junior ministers he is having for breakfast.'

As #BeKind Twitter swiftly pointed out when I posted this quote, I'm definitely getting fat but that's more down to the delights of Deliveroo during lockdown. More worryingly, the pandemic is starting to have the opposite effect on people than I had hoped. Rather than come together in a united spirit to fight the common enemy of coronavirus, we're using it as an excuse to become even more divided. Yes, there are wonderful heroes like Captain Tom to lift our spirits. But there is also an increasing resentment building between those who have the means to survive the lockdown in comfort and those who don't.

Far from being 'the great equaliser' as Madonna claimed in her rose-petalled bath, Covid-19 has turned out to be 'the great divider'. The data emerging shows it predominantly attacks the poorest, oldest, sickest and therefore most vulnerable members of society. And it has shone a grim light on the selfishness of many younger, fitter and less vulnerable people that it spares from its deadly wrath, the ones who don't want to accept that they need to make sacrifices for others.

We need to wake up. But will we?

MAY

'What about you, Fatso?'

FRIDAY 1 MAY

Matt Hancock proudly boasted of reaching his target of 100,000 tests a day by the end of April. What he didn't mention during his victory lap at the daily briefing was that 40,369 of them were posted out the day before, with no confirmation of any of the tests even being done. Nor did he mention that only 73,000 actual people were tested. The original pledge still sits, entirely unambiguously, on the prime minister's official Number 10 Twitter account from 5 April: 'We'll test 100,000 people a day by the end of this month.'

So, Hancock failed to reach the actual target but behaved like he'd just won an Oscar. His desperation to claim any kind of 'success' in this debacle grows ever more absurd.

SATURDAY 2 MAY

I've been experiencing a weird breathlessness sensation for a couple of days that I put down to bad hay fever. But today, it got significantly worse, to the extent that I was having trouble breathing properly, was left panting after walking up or down the stairs, and then I started sporadically coughing too. I also feel oddly tired and was disconcerted enough to call a respiratory consultant, who treated me for a rough bout of bronchitis a year ago, for his opinion.

'Breathlessness, cough and lethargy are all possible symptoms of Covid-19,' he said. 'You should get a test as soon as possible.'

I'm not easily fazed but felt a sudden wave of panic. I watched an ICU doctor on TV last week saying they were seeing more and more men in their fifties carrying a bit of excess timber who were seriously ill with coronavirus. Boris Johnson is my age, 55, and nearly died. Kate Garraway's husband Derek, who is a similar height and build to me, is just 52 and still fighting for his life, poor man. So, this was an unnerving moment.

'What would you say my chances are of having the virus?' I asked, nervously.

'Five to ten per cent,' he replied.

I've always been a glass half-full person, so would normally view those odds very confidently as 90 to 95 per cent in my favour. Yet right now, all I can think is that I might have a disease that is killing a lot of people in a particularly horrible and vicious way.

MONDAY 4 MAY

After two poor nights' sleep, partly from the symptoms and partly from worry, I paced around all day waiting for the result of my test like a condemned man on death row desperately hoping for last-minute clemency. Eventually, early this evening, my doctor rang and uttered one word: 'Negative.' I like a man who gets straight to the point. How ironic that this was such positive news – well, for me anyway.

I tweeted the development: 'UPDATE: My Covid-19 test was negative. I was advised to take the test by my doctor after developing possible coronavirus symptoms and was entitled to do so as a Govt-designated essential worker. I'll be back on *GMB* as soon as my doctor advises I'm OK to return to work.' To which a young woman named Chloe replied, 'Personally, I was hoping for death, so this is a shame to read.'

I shook my head slowly at the brazen awfulness of this tweet. I saw so much of this vile stuff when Boris was seriously ill, and it's staggering to me that people are happy to commit such despicable thoughts to public gaze. They're usually the same people who scream 'BE KIND!' at others, oblivious to their own viciousness. Social media has many qualities, but it's increasingly becoming a hypocritical cesspit where those who scream loudest about 'tolerance' and 'kindness' are the least tolerant and most unkind people imaginable. It's why I have such a huge distrust of wokeness: I see so few who profess to be woke actually practising what they preach.

TUESDAY 5 MAY

The Department of Health and Social Care tweeted today: 'There is emerging evidence to suggest that #coronavirus may be having a disproportionate impact on some ethnic groups, as well as certain genders. We're launching a review into the factors impacting health outcomes to address health inequalities.'

By 'certain genders', they obviously mean men, as it is men who are dying at a far faster rate than women. But they can't say that in case they offend someone. This is how ridiculous the gender debate has become: even governmental guidelines in the midst of a global pandemic are pandering to hypersensitive, woke nonsense.

An incredible story broke late tonight: one of the government's top science advisers Professor Neil Ferguson – the man in charge of the data modelling on which all the big decisions have been taken – has resigned after the *Daily Telegraph* caught him breaching his own social distancing lockdown rules to be with his married lover. I don't give a damn about his sex life, but the hypocrisy stinks and suggests the government is 'following the science' of scientists who don't even follow their own science. Ferguson even tried to claim he thought he was immune from Covid-19 after having had it – despite there being no scientific evidence to prove this yet. And this guy is the no. 1 'expert' on whom the government's been basing its entire coronavirus strategy? No wonder it's been so shambolic.

WEDNESDAY 6 MAY

Meghan Markle released a home video of her and her son Archie reading *Duck! Rabbit!* to celebrate his first birthday. On every level, this seems completely at odds with her and Harry's professed desire to protect their son from public attention, and just more pathetic hypocrisy. I started to compile a tweet along those lines, but then stopped halfway through.

What *am* I doing? There's a pandemic raging, so am I seriously going to waste even more time bitching about Meghan being a hypocrite again? Who cares? I've been asking myself these same questions for the past few months since the crisis started, then lazily succumbed to old click-baiting habits. It's time to stop being distracted by this trivial crap and focus on what matters. I pressed delete and went back to watching the real news on TV.

THURSDAY 7 MAY

Adele has unveiled a new photo of herself on Instagram looking slim, fit, tanned, healthy and happy to celebrate her 32nd birthday. The singer, who has reportedly lost seven stone in an intensive training regime after splitting from her husband, was pictured standing in front of a large floral arch at her LA home, wearing a black mini-dress and puffball sleeves.

On every level, this should have been one of the least fury-inducing posts in social media history, and indeed it quickly received more than a million 'likes', with thousands of people wishing her happy birthday, thanking her for praising health workers and complimenting her on her stunning new appearance. But her new look generated utter rage too. Apparently, she's now TOO slim, TOO fit, TOO tanned, TOO healthy and TOO happy. It seems utterly absurd that so much energy can be expended on something so innocuous during these times of crisis. But the extremity of the rage this photograph has sparked is far more concerning. Why were so many of Adele's fans so angry?

The answer, apparently, is that by losing so much weight, she has betrayed all fat women! This is not the Adele people had come to know and love – the hard-partying, overweight one who joked to *Vogue* about having 'three bums'. As she told the magazine at the time, 'Fans are encouraged that I'm not a size zero – that you don't have to look a certain way to do well.'

Unfortunately, those same fans aren't so encouraged by her losing two of those bums, which is why she's been deluged with hate by 'fat activists' appalled that she has got herself into better shape and accusing her of only doing it to appease fat-shaming societal standards.

'The Fatphobia is STRONG this morning,' tweeted 'Hayley' under the account name @curvesncurlsuk. 'Everyone acting like weight loss is an important milestone in Adele's illustrious career – this is what DIET CULTURE looks like.'

What kind of world do we live in where someone like Adele is not allowed to stop being fat and unhealthy? Like so many woke firestorms, there is such a ridiculous illogicality to this fury. Sadly, this kind of nonsense is a direct result of the absurd glorification of fatness in recent years. In an effort to broaden 'inclusivity', the favoured cause of all wokies, it seems that everything must be celebrated, even when it's detrimental to someone's health.

The weird trend culminated in *Cosmopolitan* magazine putting super-sized model Tess Holliday on its August 2018 cover, wearing a green swimsuit and blowing a kiss under the headline: 'A SUPERMODEL ROARS! TESS HOLLIDAY WANTS THE HATERS TO KISS HER ASS.' Ms Holliday is 5 ft 3 in and weighs over 300 lb. As such, she is suffering from morbid obesity. That's not me being a 'fat-shaming douche-bag' as some spat when I questioned the wisdom of this decision by *Cosmo*. It's just an inarguable fact.

The medical establishment gives that definition to anyone who is more than 100 lb overweight or has a BMI (body mass index – the ratio of an individual's height to his or her weight) of 40 or more. Morbid obesity, as its name suggests, is a very serious, potentially lethal health condition. Those who are diagnosed with it are at far greater risk of illnesses like diabetes, high blood pressure, gallstones, osteoarthritis, heart disease and cancer. In other words, it can literally kill you.

Yet *Cosmo* sat Tess Holliday on a throne and declared she was 'a role model for others who've been excluded this way', 'downright honest' and 'everything the fashion industry needs right now' because she 'doesn't conform to the narrow standard of beauty that's been set by society'. What a load of disingenuous piffle.

As with size-zero models, Holliday's body image is one that people should be actively deterred from celebrating because it's unhealthy. In *Cosmo*'s accompanying interview, she explained why she started an online campaign with the hashtag '#effyourbeautystandards'. 'I created it out of frustration,' she said. 'I was angry and sad that people kept commenting on my pictures saying, "You're too fat to wear that!" or "Cover up!" And then one night, I was lying in bed and thought, "F*ck that!" So, I posted an image with four photographs of myself wearing things that fat women are often told we "can't wear" and encouraged others to do the same.'

I can understand the desire to do that. But then she said, 'I'm at the heaviest I've ever been in my life now and it took me being the heaviest to finally love myself.' Sorry, but I just don't believe her. Nobody, male or female, could see their weight surge to over 300 lb, if they're just 5 ft 3 in tall, and be genuinely happy. And I would argue it is socially irresponsible to suggest otherwise. But on a human level, I can see how easy it is to become trapped in such a hellish spiral of self-delusion when soaring fame and fortune are entirely dependent on you remaining morbidly obese.

Tess Holliday only got the cover of *Cosmo*, and a barrage of other media off the back of it, because she's a dangerously overweight model feigning joy at her massive size. The publishers and editors paying her large sums of money to glamorise her morbid obesity cynically exploited her; they were her enablers.

And before everyone reading this screams, 'What about you, Fatso?' I fully admit I'm no body-perfect myself. I am 6 ft 1 in and weigh around 215 lb. My doctor says I'm reasonably fit for a man of 55, but he'd like to see me get under 200 lb. I completely agree, which is why I try to work out as often as I can, and watch what I eat and drink. Unlike Tess Holliday, when I see a fat-looking photo of myself, I don't cheer, I cringe.

When the predictable furore erupted over her *Cosmo* cover, she proudly posted a photo of herself in just her underwear to her 1.7 million Instagram followers with the caption, 'Damn ... that look good.' When I saw the photo, which quickly went viral on Twitter, my heart sank.

'This is very sad,' I tweeted. 'She badly needs better friends, who are going to be more honest with her & explain she is dangerously overweight & should do something about it.'

Holliday snapped back at me. 'Makes me feel like you're almost into thicker girls & too afraid to admit it.'

OK. Well, first, I love women of all shapes and sizes. But second, I wasn't criticising her for a bit of social media fun or to score a few cheap points at her expense. I did it because I genuinely feel she is promoting a very dangerous message that others will follow, and because I am concerned her life will be in danger if she continues down this path. The most inspirational thing Tess Holliday could do right now is *lose* weight like Adele, not put even more on.

Imagine what a powerful message it would send to the millions of other Americans with morbid obesity. The bottom line is that there's nothing remotely powerful or inspiring about a 5 ft 3 in person breaking the scales at over 300 lb. It's just a guaranteed pathway to sickness, misery and possible death.

So, let's stop pretending this radiates some great 'positive image' to the world. It doesn't.

I feel exactly the same about the glorification of size-zero models too. Victoria Beckham – who last week announced she will not now be furloughing staff at her fashion company after a public outcry – regularly uses painfully thin models to sell her fashion lines. To flog her 'VB Eyewear' collection two years ago, Beckham hired an emaciated Lithuanian. As Dr Amanda Foreman, a *Wall Street Journal* columnist, tweeted, 'A model who looks like a teenager with severe anorexia is the face for the #VBEyeware 2018 summer collection. This is the reason why every study on social media and advertising calls the threat to young girls' mental health "dire".'

I don't think I've ever seen such an instantaneous and furious backlash to a modelling campaign. Or one so warranted. Beckham loves to talk about 'empowering women' but there's nothing empowering about making them think this is the type of body they should covet. In fact, it is far more likely to have the complete reverse effect of crushing young women's confidence and driving them to emergency diets. There's also a stinking hypocrisy at play here, as Victoria's been very vocal in her career about supposedly avoiding the use of these kind of models.

I don't blame the models themselves. For all I know, this one is perfectly healthy. But the way she was dressed and photographed for that campaign was deliberately intended to propagate a message that very thin is good. And I'm sorry, but it's not. Yes, it's true that some girls – and boys – are born naturally very thin and have a metabolism that means they struggle to put on weight however much they eat. But they are in a tiny minority, and in our modern technological age the vast majority of young girls suffer from very real body image and self-esteem issues that are made immeasurably worse by the likes of Kim Kardashian and Emily Ratajkowski, who cynically promote unattainably 'perfect' body images. These girls also look to people like Victoria Beckham for guidance, and she is giving them entirely the wrong guidance. She is someone who makes millions of dollars selling merchandise to predominantly young women, so she should be mindful of a very serious duty of care with regard to the imagery she deploys.

As the father of an eight-year-old girl the same age as Victoria's own daughter Harper, I don't want her growing up thinking this is the body image she should aspire to, or comparing her own body to this size-zero human stick insect and hating herself for not being that thin. Nor do I want her looking at magazine covers and craving to look like the heavily airbrushed female stars beaming out of them. Many of these stars seem in total denial about their own complicity in this unhealthy process. In a blog, actress Jennifer Aniston wrote, 'The objectification and scrutiny we put women through is absurd and disturbing. The way I am portrayed by the media is simply a reflection of how we see and portray women in general, measured against some warped standard of beauty. [...] Little girls everywhere are absorbing our agreement, passive or otherwise. And it begins early. The message that girls are not pretty unless they're incredibly thin, that they're not worthy of our attention unless they look like a supermodel or an actress on the cover of a magazine is something we're all willingly buying into. This conditioning is something girls then carry into womanhood. We use celebrity "news" to perpetuate this dehumanizing view of females, focused solely on one's physical appearance, which tabloids turn into a sporting event of speculation.'

Of course, there's another reason why the media objectify and scrutinise famous women, and why little girls get confused about beauty and body image, and it's because stars like Jennifer Aniston deliberately perpetuate the myth of 'perfection' by posing for endless magazine covers which have been airbrushed so much that in some cases the celebrity is virtually unrecognisable.

If you Google 'Jennifer Aniston magazine covers', a veritable avalanche of results appear: there she is on the cover of *Elle*, *GQ*, *Rolling Stone*, *InStyle*, *Grazia*, *Vogue*, *Red*, *Marie*

Claire, *Allure*, *Harper's Bazaar*, *Vanity Fair*, *Hollywood Reporter*, *Cosmopolitan*, *People* and ... just about everything else. I don't know the inner workings of each magazine or photoshoot, but I do know with my old newspaper editor hat on that almost all these cover shots were 'cleaned up' to make Jennifer look more perfect than she is. Cellulite had been removed, crease-lines decreased, pimples expunged. In many of them, this detailed work continued to the rest of her semi-naked or even fully naked body: thighs trimmed, butts toned, the vaguest suggestion of bingo wings eliminated. It's the same type of forensic cover photo cover-up which goes on all day every day on magazine picture desks the world over. The aim? To sell a false image of perfect beauty. Why? To sell magazines and to sell the cover star's personal brand. These covers, and I estimate Jennifer Aniston has done over a hundred in her career, have made both her and the magazines a ton of money.

I don't blame them for the cover-up – after all, who wants to see imperfection if you don't have to? I myself proudly demand full-on protective airbrushing and chin-removal in every photoshoot I do. 'Nobody wants or needs to see the real me,' I explain to photographers, who invariably concur. Neither do I blame them for raking in cash on the back of such false imagery. If people want to buy it, so be it. And nor, frankly, do I blame the paparazzi for wanting to get in on this scam themselves by taking and selling revealing photos of these cover-girl stars without all the airbrushing. They are, after all, merely 'setting the record straight' in time-honoured journalistic fashion. Once you put your body up for lucrative personal gain, I'm afraid you have to accept a level of scrutiny and debate that comes with it.

However ... I do think the least stars like Jennifer Aniston can do in return for the massive financial and career boost these fake covers bring them is to stop pretending it's all everyone else's fault that impressionable young girls struggle with their own beauty and body images as a result of seeing perfect photos of Jennifer Aniston. That would be a giant leap for feminism and this is where our focus should be, not hysterically and irrationally glorifying and defending fat or thin women on social media.

FRIDAY 8 MAY

There's been a spate of footballers behaving like idiots during the lockdown. But Kyle Walker, the Manchester City and England footballer, is a repeat offender and his behaviour has pointed to a real problem in society with the woke misappropriation of mental health for cynical self-defence reasons.

Last month, Walker hosted what was described as a 'sex party' at his Cheshire apartment, after inviting over a friend and two prostitutes for the night. He apologised profusely when he was caught: 'I understand that my position as a professional footballer brings the responsibility of being a role model. As such, I want to apologise to my family, friends, football club, supporters and the public for letting them down. There are heroes out there making a vital difference to society at the moment, and I have been keen to help support and highlight their amazing sacrifices and life-saving work over the past week. My actions in this matter are in direct contrast to what I should have been doing regarding the lockdown. And I want to re-iterate the message: Stay home, stay safe.'

Unfortunately, it seems he didn't receive his own reiterated message, and has now been caught breaking lockdown rules twice more to visit his parents and sister at different addresses. But rather than apologise again, this time Walker went on the attack – lambasting the media and claiming he was being 'harassed'. Then he played the mental health card, so beloved of many famous people these days when they get caught doing something stupid or hypocritical. He even managed to play the Covid card too for good measure, a new favourite of the 'unfairly' vilified wokie.

'My family has been torn apart,' Walker said, 'this has been dragged through the press, and I ask: when is enough, enough? At a time when the focus is understandably on Covid-19, at what point does mental health get taken into consideration, an illness which affects every sufferer differently? I am a human being, with feelings of pain and upset just like everybody else. Being in the public eye as a professional athlete does not make you immune to this.'

Walker's lengthy statement ticked every key box of modern-day damage control: a) blame the press, b) play the victim, c) use mental health as an excuse. Even Bill Clinton has started pulling this trick, claiming recently that cheating on Hillary with 22-year-old intern Monica Lewinsky in the Oval Office helped manage his anxieties. What a load of poppycock.

What made Kyle Walker's ridiculous outburst so particularly tone-deaf is that today is VE Day, the 75th anniversary of the end of World War II. For a millionaire footballer to be moaning about his life like this on the day we remember those who sacrificed theirs for our freedom is not just infuriating, it also gives a shocking insight into just how molly-coddled, needy and self-obsessed so many in this generation have become.

It has got to the stage where all you have to do when caught misbehaving is blame it on your 'mental health' and everyone has to immediately cease any criticism and applaud your bravery. I don't think Walker's a victim, or remotely brave. I think he's a selfish, spoilt brat who decided the rules don't apply to him, so he was happy to go out and risk spreading the virus whenever he felt like it. For that recklessness, he deserves our reproach and opprobrium – not praise for his courage and sympathy for his 'issues'. Taking any personal accountability for your actions has become unnecessary. In fact, it's now seen as a weakness. Far better to blame someone or something else – like your 'anxieties'.

Before the pandemic struck, I often said that what these people lacked was proper perspective on what's really important in life, hence the high incidence of anxiety over stuff that really doesn't matter in the general scheme of things. Until now, it's been a pretty damn good time to be a human being – as I said in my introduction to this book, we are safer, healthier, more prosperous, better fed and more peaceful than ever. A World Values Survey last year revealed that in 85 per cent of countries studied, happiness has increased. And this despite the global population soaring to over seven and a half billion people.

Yet for some inexplicable reason, many young people appear convinced this is the worst, scariest time to ever exist. Rates of anxiety and depression, and even suicide, have soared in recent years, despite an almost 24/7 media obsession with talking about mental health. I put some, perhaps a lot, of this down to people taking a lot more drugs – legal and illegal – than ever before. I don't know anyone who's taken any form of narcotic, including many prescription pills, for a sustained period of time who hasn't suffered from increased 'anxiety'. So, it seems entirely logical that as the consumption of drugs has rocketed, so has the increase in anxiety issues. But that doesn't explain why, before coronavirus erupted, so many other people who don't abuse drugs were wandering around in a state of extreme anxiety without much reason to be.

Some blame ignorance. 'The fact that something is bad today doesn't mean it was better in the past,' argues Steven

Pinker. 'The world has made spectacular progress in every single measure of human well-being. Here is a second shocker: almost no one knows about it.'

New York Times columnist Nick Kristof raised an interesting suggestion as to why we've grown so inexplicably anxious. 'I fear the news media and the humanitarian world focus so relentlessly on the bad news that we leave the public believing that every trend is going in the wrong direction. [...] I worry that deep pessimism about the state of the world is paralysing rather than empowering; excessive pessimism can leave people feeling not just hopeless but helpless.'

I think he's right. Everything is recorded, everything is shared, and bad, scary stuff will always draw more attention than fluffy, nice stuff. That's just human nature, and the instinctive 'if it bleeds, it leads' mentality of the media.

I spoke to Dr Phil McGraw, the legendary daytime TV host in America, about why youngsters feel so much more anxious, and he suggested it was because they're so much more aware of the world's horrors than previous generations.

'When I was young, if a man got eaten by an alligator on a golf course in Florida, I almost certainly wouldn't hear about it. Today, a video of the deadly attack will be posted online in minutes and the whole world will hear about it very quickly. Kids are being bombarded 24/7 with terrible imagery via social media of bad stuff happening, often in real time, and it understandably makes them anxious. My generation was far more protected from that kind of thing. We just didn't hear about most of it. I suspect there is actually less horrifying stuff happening now, but it feels like there's a lot more of it.'

A constant sensory overload of negativity has to take its toll. But I think there's another more pressing reason why young people seem so overwhelmed by life when they should be feeling ecstatic that they're living in such comparatively good times: bad parenting.

Many mums and dads are breeding a generation of pampered, cotton wool covered snowflakes who have no clue what the real world entails, pandering to their kids like never before, showering them with love and affection from dawn 'til dusk, giving them more money, holidays and general comfort blankets than any previous generations could have dreamed of, and sending them off to schools where losing, at anything, is virtually forbidden.

The combined effect of all this is that we're producing kids who can't handle the real world and don't understand the concept of things going wrong. 'Success is stumbling from failure to failure with no loss of enthusiasm,' said Sir Winston Churchill, who was voted the Greatest Briton of All Time in a major nationwide BBC poll. Churchill was the living embodiment of his own words, enjoying triumphs and disasters throughout his life, yet never losing the enthusiasm to 'Keep Buggering On', another of his memorable quotes.

I too have regularly enjoyed the twin arrows of outrageous fortune and misfortune throughout a chequered and varied career and life – and I can honestly say that I've learned more from failing than succeeding. When I was fired in 2004 as editor of the *Daily Mirror*, for publishing photos of British troops abusing Iraqi civilians that were denounced as fake (members of the regiment the *Mirror* accused of abuse have since been court-martialled for abusing Iraqi civilians), I was frog-marched into the street by a security guard and not even allowed to return to my office to retrieve my jacket or personal possessions.

Even though I was ready to move on after ten years of editing the paper, the brutal nature of my dismissal still sucked. I got home to find myself leading all the news bulletins and being ridiculed, shamed and abused by all and sundry. Nobody gave me a participation prize, literally or metaphorically. I was left to pick up the pieces from the wreckage of my career, and it wasn't easy. I didn't even know that stamps were now self-adhesive as I hadn't posted a letter for years.

Yet the whole experience of being turfed out on my backside was one of the best things that ever happened to me. It forced me to leave a job I loved but that I had become bored doing, and it taught me a lot about people's character by the way they responded to me at such a calamitous moment in my life. When you win, it feels so good you rarely stop to really think about why or how you won. Yet when you lose, you agonise over why you lost, and if you're smart, you learn the bitter yet vital lessons from defeat that stop you losing next time.

Yet the youth of today aren't allowed to lose.

At school, the concept of 'participation prizes' was laughable anathema to my generation. If you came last in a race on Sports Day, you won nothing but well-deserved ignominy and ridicule. (I was no athlete, but I made damn sure I won the non-finalists' race.) Today, in many schools, if you come last you get hugs, cuddles, coos of 'Well done!' and you are handed a prize for participating. In other words, there is no failure, or loss. You win too, by coming last.

So, the incentive to win is automatically reduced. Why bother putting in the extra yards of practice if you're going to win anyway? We're told this is done to protect children from the emotional and psychological trauma of losing. But how does it do that? The real world doesn't do 'participation prizes'. In the real world, you win or lose on a daily basis, and you suffer or enjoy the consequences of both eventualities.

I don't really blame the 'snowflake generation' – by which I mean millennials and younger – for their hypersensitivity to everything and their crippling self-doubt and anxiety. I blame the environment they've grown up in. Rather than prepare kids properly for the real world, warts and all, we've been smothering them in cotton wool at home and at school, ensuring they are protected from any of the tough stuff they're going to face when they're released into reality.

We're teaching them that there is no such thing as losing, when, in fact, they will lose quite regularly. They'll lose jobs, homes, friends and family. Life is a never-ending fight, and you've got to keep taking the punches and getting back on your feet.

But how to do that when we now live in a victimhood culture where weakness is celebrated and strength frowned upon? Barely a day goes by now without some big celebrity 'confessing' to some problem or ailment, usually in a tearful interview to some magazine or TV show.

It's not enough anymore to be great at your job. That won't get the headlines like it used to. Today's stars have to be 'vulnerable' and 'real' and 'damaged' and emote 24/7 to their broken body or heart's content. Suddenly, they're all suffering from PTSD, or vague 'mental illness', or 'surviving' cancer scares, or enduring crippling anxiety and depression. And they can't wait to tell us all about it, every spit and 'possible bubonic plague' cough.

In return, they are cheered and revered by the PC language cops who now dictate that phrases like 'stiff upper lip' and 'manning up' are deeply offensive. It's no longer acceptable for any public figure to celebrate toughness because it supposedly denigrates those who aren't tough. You can't boast about being 'mentally strong' because it might upset the mentally weak. If you don't cry regularly in public, whether you're a sportsman or entertainer, you're deemed a cold-hearted freak who is best avoided. When did we go so damn soft? And why? What, exactly, does it achieve?

We know that young people are highly impressionable and will follow the lead of their heroes. So why do we encourage all their heroes to wallow in self-obsessed woe-is-me bullshit? All it does is make millions of young people think that's the way to be. They're not just absurdly overprotected from the real world, they're also actively encouraged to celebrate stuff that's wrong with them and wear it as a badge of honour.

Frankly, I feel nauseated every time I see people I know, famous or otherwise, posting self-aggrandising nonsense on Twitter or Facebook celebrating their ever-longer lists of weaknesses and ailments – accompanied by clichéd 'empowering' quotes that only make me feel empowered to laugh out loud.

'I failed my driving test for the fifth time!' they proclaim. 'But I'm so proud of myself for the way I dealt with my anxiety while driving the car.'

I think we attack the mental health issue in entirely the wrong way. The debate has focused on a basic premise that we're all mentally unwell, rather than the vast majority of us actually being mentally well. It's perfectly normal to feel occasional anxiety or get down about stuff. Life's tough and throws a lot of curve balls. Nobody's happy all the time. We need to drum into kids that being anxious, which is a perfectly understandable reaction to many small problems in life, is not the same as suffering from anxiety, which is a debilitating mental illness. And pretending that they're the same thing is very damaging to getting the right kind of help to those with genuinely serious medical illness who really need it.

John Marsden, the acclaimed Australian author and school principal, believes we're wrecking our kids by overly protecting them. In his book *The Art of Growing Up*, he accused parents of being in love with their children, rather than loving them, and warned of 'toxic parenting' that is leading to kids exceeding past generations in terms of academic achievement but being left emotionally fragile and ill-equipped to deal with the real world.

'The scale of the problem is massive. The issue of emotional damage is pandemic,' Marsden told the *Guardian*. 'The level of anxiety is something I've never seen before, and I don't know how it can be improved.'

He said that by limiting children's exposure to danger and to fear, we are limiting their ability to mature, develop resilience and independence. Marsden despairs at parents who don't even allow four-year-olds to peel their own mandarins. 'They're capable of helping themselves and we have to be forceful in making sure we step back.'

As the father of four kids, I couldn't agree more.

SUNDAY 10 MAY

The government has issued a new slogan: 'STAY ALERT, CONTROL THE VIRUS, SAVE LIVES.'

What the hell does that even mean? Alert to what? Coronavirus is an enemy we can't see, hear, smell or feel. And as for controlling it – how? The only way to 'control' Covid-19 is to either find a vaccine that works, drugs that can stop people from dying with it, or an antibody test that is 100 per cent reliable and can prove we get immunity if we've had the virus. None of these things exist yet.

Nobody else has a clue what this slogan means either. 'Is Coronavirus sneaking around in a fake moustache and glasses?' tweeted J.K. Rowling. 'If we drop our guard, will it slip us a Micky [sic] Finn?'

Ministers just added to the confusion. 'Stay alert by staying home as much as possible,' declared Housing Secretary Robert Jenrick, 'but stay alert when you do go out.'

As mockery grew, Number 10 was forced to issue a lengthy clarification of their slogan, which of course is always the death knell of any slogan. Then Boris appeared on TV this evening to babble away about it with his usual bluster, blather and fist-banging – and managed to make things sound even more baffling.

Even chat show star Jonathan Ross, who hardly ever dips his toe into controversial political opinion waters, felt compelled to tweet, 'I rarely comment on politics, and avoid publicly siding with one party (all pretty useless at the moment) because no one should give a shit about celebs' opinions. But it's hard to imagine a greater display of inept leadership and muddled thinking then [sic] Boris just displayed.'

Aside from the incomprehensible messaging, there's also a splendid irony in the prime minister now preaching about alertness, given how stunningly *unalert* he was to the threat of coronavirus in the first place.

James Corden emailed me from LA. 'Seeing how you're doing? Hope you and the family are doing OK.'

'All sort of OK here,' I replied. 'Working flat out obviously, but surrounded by a lot of Covid misery – several good friends losing parents, Kate Garraway's husband in a coma, etc. Been very grim. Had a bit of a scare myself last week but tested negative. You OK over there? All so weird isn't it?'

'It's so weird,' he replied. 'All of it. I'm very grateful to work in the entertainment industry and have a job.' James revealed that one of the team on his US talk show recently lost her husband to the virus, but another friend had thankfully survived after two weeks on a ventilator. 'It's just so strange to be in the midst of things, the uncertainty of it all,' he wrote. 'We're all trained to deal with definite and finite moments. Terror attacks or natural disasters. It's the timeline of this which I think makes it so strange and difficult. Keep fighting the fight.'

His personal stories resonated strongly with me. One of my cousins-in-law lost his father last month, after he contracted coronavirus in hospital. He'd never spent a single night apart from his wife in 58 years, but she couldn't be with him as he lay dying. So heart-breaking.

I wonder if those like James and me, who've been directly affected by the virus through people we know dying or losing loved ones, have a different perspective to those who haven't?

WEDNESDAY 13 MAY

Ruth Binsley, a TV producer I've worked with many times, including on a documentary we filmed together in South Africa, emailed me: 'Hey, I wanted to say thanks for all you're doing to challenge the government response to this crisis and to share with you that my mum passed away on 2 May from Covid-19. She was a patient in a care home as she had Huntington's disease. Obviously, it's heart-breaking, but I'm also so angry that she and thousands of others were just left, discarded as the old and the ill, when in fact my mum was severely disabled by her illness but could have lived another 10 or more years. Why was her life worth any less than yours or mine? Anyway, thanks for beating the drum – it's so important that journalists hold our leaders to account for some appalling decisions. I'm so angry – it's one thing when someone you love dies and there's nothing anyone could have done to prevent it, but quite another when you know that's not the case.'

What's happened in care homes is a growing scandal. A Covid cardiologist at a top London hospital, and a personal friend of Boris Johnson, was quoted in an article by Ambrose

Evans-Pritchard in the *Telegraph* as comparing it to the Siege of Caffa in 1346 during the Black Death, 'when a Mongol army catapulted plague-ridden bodies over the walls'.

'Our policy was to let the virus rip and then "cocoon the elderly",' the doctor said. 'You don't know whether to laugh or cry when you contrast that with what we actually did. We discharged known, suspected, and unknown cases into care homes which were unprepared, with no formal warning that the patients were infected, no testing available, and no PPE to prevent transmission. We actively seeded this into the very population that was most vulnerable. We let these people die without palliation. The official policy was not to visit care homes – and they didn't (and still don't). So, after infecting them with a disease that causes an unpleasant ending, we denied our elders access to a doctor and denied admission to hospital. Simple things like fluids, withheld. Effective palliation like syringe drivers, withheld.'

The doctor, who slammed many other aspects of the way we've handled the crisis, concluded, 'The striking thing is how consistently the government failed, in every single element of the response, everywhere you turn (the Army excepted). This is probably the most expensive series of errors in the country's history. Basically, every mistake that could have been made, was made.'

Yet at today's Prime Minister's Questions, Boris Johnson claimed 'we brought in the lockdown in care homes ahead of the general lockdown'. This, as Reuters swiftly proved, was a brazen lie. No such early care home lockdown was ever ordered, which is why we now have the second-worst reported coronavirus-related death toll in the world.

Of course, the government doesn't want us to know this, which is why it has suddenly stopped showing the daily 'global death comparison' chart at the daily briefings. Asked why,

Robert Jenrick said today, 'We want to be as transparent as we can.'

It's beyond parody. The government and the woke brigade now seem to be matching each other in their level of self-contradiction.

THURSDAY 14 MAY

I seem be gaining new fans as fast as I'm losing them. Even former *Guardian* editor Alan Rusbridger, with whom I've had a love–hate relationship for several decades, has been saying nice things about me, telling the millennial website Joe, '[Piers] has had a good virus, if I can put it like that, because he's done what journalists should which is to challenge these hapless ministers who are going on under-briefed and have not been very impressive in the messages they have tried to advance. So, it doesn't take much to dismember them. In general, I think Piers is quite erratic. He's had some wonderful moments in his career. He was rather brave over the Iraq War, he was rather magnificent over gun control in America, and then, to my mind, his chumminess with Donald Trump where he abandoned any kind of pretence of being an independent journalist and wanted to be Trump's friend, and now of course, he's turned on Trump. So, there's a slightly sort of zig-zagging pattern. But I have to take my hat off to him at the moment, he's been doing what any journalist should be doing.'

It's hard to disagree with any of that assessment. This crisis is certainly changing many things, though sadly some of the pre-corona 'woke' nonsense continues to rear its ugly head.

It was so depressing to read today that plans for an online Virtual Gay Pride charity parade next Saturday, featuring stars like Andrew Lloyd Webber and Dannii Minogue and campaigner Peter Tatchell, have been abandoned because one of its organisers, Charlie Shakespeare, is a Tory supporter who backed Brexit.

His further crimes were that he 'liked' a Nigel Farage tweet saying, 'I witnessed first-hand our Border Force acting as a taxi service for illegal migrants in Dover this morning. This scandal continues and people have got every right to be angry about it' – and he 'liked' a tweet posted in support of actor Laurence Fox.

'My brand will not be associated with anybody who RTs [retweets] Toby Young and Nigel Farage,' denounced Linda Riley, publisher of *DIVA* magazine, one of the sponsors of the event.

When Shakespeare, 26, replied, 'That seems a little politically bigoted', Ms Riley told her 76,000 Twitter followers, 'Apparently I'm a "political bigot" because *DIVA* magazine has withdrawn any support of Virtual Pride, as one of the organisers supports Nigel Farage & Toby Young. For clarity, any LGBTQ event which supports the likes of these, will not have my support. #proudtobeapoliticalbigot.'

Following her message, a wave of scheduled acts and speakers cancelled, leaving organisers no choice but to abandon the show. Shakespeare told the *Mail on Sunday*, 'There has been a massive smear campaign to get us cancelled. They were determined to find something, anything, to put pressure on performers to back out. As soon as Linda Riley sent that tweet, performers started dropping out like flies. Artists were contacting us apologising but said that they worried about getting gigs in the future. They were coming under pressure to pull out. It seems to be that there is no place for you in the LGBT+ community if you are right-wing. Just because I liked a tweet by Nigel Farage, I'm now blacklisted.'

Arguing that Virtual Pride 2020 has become the latest victim of a 'cancel culture', he said, 'Who benefits? The charities do not, the performers do not. They just didn't like me, so they had it cancelled.'

This is absurd, and the fact it's happened during a global pandemic shows how deep the 'woke' rage runs. People like Linda Riley love telling us how tolerant they are. Yet what could be more intolerant than forcing a charity event to be scrapped just because one of the organisers doesn't share your views? The human rights of the LGBTQ+ community should surely transcend political divide? The fact this kind of nonsense is still happening in the middle of an appalling global health crisis just proves how inherently divided society has become. We're eating ourselves alive at the altar of political correctness.

FRIDAY 15 MAY

Boris Johnson is apparently planning a 'war on obesity' following his brush with death. As an Irish friend of mine, Karl Brophy, tweeted, 'If it's anything like his war on the virus then he'll be encouraging Brits to have kebabs and chips for breakfast.'

But perhaps Boris has reached some genuine epiphany over his weight amid mounting evidence that fatter people have been more susceptible to the virus. There's no doubt that Britain has got one of the worst obesity problems in Europe, with an estimated one in three British adults now clinically obese, with a BMI above 30. New research has found that being obese doubles the risk of needing hospital treatment for coronavirus, and Boris is apparently convinced the reason he ended up in intensive care was because of his weight, which was 17½ stone, making his BMI score (given his height of 5 ft 9 in) around 36. He is reported to have said, 'It's all right for you thinnies' when discussing the disease in Downing

Street, and now believes the pandemic should trigger a more interventionist government approach to tackle obesity.

He's right, it should. But to effect real change, we need to also tackle the cripplingly self-defeating PC nonsense that's stopped dangerously fat people from facing up to their condition by its active celebration of models with morbid obesity like Tess Holliday, and which thinks it's OK to shame stars like Adele when they get fit and lose weight.

Jonathan Ashworth, shadow health secretary, was recently harangued by a woman named Angela Chesworth for attending a meeting of an all-party Parliamentary Group on Obesity and using the wrong language. 'Could I ask you use #peoplefirst language?' she tweeted him. 'I am a person living with obesity. I am not an obese person. You wouldn't say a "cancerous person" it's a person living with cancer.'

To my horror, Ashworth replied: 'That's a very fair point and I will certainly do that in future.'

Ms Chesworth then sent back an extract from guidance notes handed out at the meeting about how to express 'positive communication about obesity'. This included instructions to avoid using terms such as 'obesity' or 'overweight' as 'adjectives' and 'combative language' like 'the war on obesity' and 'fight against obesity'.

We'll never win the war on obesity if we can't even call it a war on obesity.

Once again, the PC language cops are preventing proper debate over what needs to be done by turning people off with their absurd antics.

Dame Joan Collins has vented her spleen in the *Spectator* about being locked up on government orders due to her age, and even I wasn't spared my friend's wrath. 'I've always thought Western society was terribly ageist,' she raged. 'Then our government insisted the "over-seventies" (horrible expression) were part of the "vulnerables" (an even more horrible expression) and should remain in lockdown (the most horrible expression of all) until a vaccine is found. That was utter discrimination against the hardy individuals who have no health issues. But more harmful was bolstering the existing belief among the general public (and prospective employers) that the old should keep out of everyone's way. Just before lockdown we were planning to have dinner with Piers Morgan and when I texted him to check if it was still on, I received a manifesto explaining that he "didn't want to be responsible" for my untimely death!'

This is entirely true, and for my concerned pains I received a withering tongue-lashing back that made it quite clear where I could stick my manifesto. But I understood Joan's irritation then, as I do now. She may be 87 but she's extremely healthy and packs more into her hectic social life than most people half her age. As she wrote, coronavirus has created another form of discriminatory ageism: 'Sadly, ageism is the last tolerated prejudice,' she wrote. 'We are not allowed to refer to people as fat and yet it has now been proven that to be obese (almost one-third of the UK population) is one of the major contributing factors in Covid deaths. However, if the government had dared to propose that they too should remain confined, it would cause outrage.'

She's right.

MONDAY 18 MAY

For the first time, a majority of the British public disapprove of the government's handling of the coronavirus crisis, according to a poll in yesterday's *Observer.*

It continues to amaze me that more people are not as enraged as I am about it. In Belgium, which has also had a terrible Covid war, fury spilled over into an extraordinary scene on Saturday when health-care workers turned their backs on Belgian Prime Minister Sophie Wilmès as she arrived for a hospital visit, in protest at her disastrous handling of the pandemic. I wonder if we'll soon see protests like that here if the death toll keeps surging.

Almost as bad as its crisis management is our government's defiant refusal to admit to making any mistakes – from PPE to testing, and especially with care homes. Preposterously, and offensively, Matt Hancock has now claimed that 'right from the start, we've tried to throw a protective ring around our care homes … we've made sure care homes have the resources they need.' This is just another abject, demonstrable lie.

Ruth Binsley appeared on *GMB* with her sister today, after their mum Susan's funeral on Friday, which was attended by just six people. 'We're so angry,' said Sarah. 'We feel completely let down by the system. There was never any shielding there for care homes. They were the bottom of the pile for this crisis. Nobody ever put any plans in place for the care homes and we feel not only desperately sad for the loss of our mother, but we feel so angry that this wasn't her time. She should not have died. If the right shielding was put in place, our mother would not have died from this virus.'

Ruth wept as she said, 'I'm just at a loss as to why they didn't have a plan. I know that the home and many of the staff in the home felt like they themselves were at the bottom of the pile, they weren't getting instructions, they were often having to ring Public Health England to get information about what they should be doing. That's the hardest thing, this feeling angry.'

The government's lies are compounding their terrible mistakes.

TUESDAY 19 MAY

We've started sub-interviewing government ministers as they speak to rival morning media outlets. Thérèse Coffey, one of the more useless ministers, told *BBC Breakfast* today that there had been a 'handful of days' when over 100,000 people had been tested in the UK for coronavirus. This, as I pointed out to *GMB* viewers when we quickly cut and replayed the clip, is a lie. There have been *zero days* when 100,000 people have been tested.

It was quite fun letting her have it in her absence, and our viewers loved it. I'm beginning to think this government boycott is very good for us; it makes them look weak and cowardly, and we can still hold them to account in the same aggressive way, albeit once removed.

WEDNESDAY 20 MAY

Captain, now Colonel, Tom Moore (he was given an honorary promotion) is to be knighted.

'We should have put some money on it,' he chuckled on *GMB* today when I played him back the clip of him telling me not to hold my breath when I first told him about my campaign. He's so chuffed though. I think it means more to him than almost anything else. And again, using my platform to help win him a gong feels so satisfying.

This afternoon, a massive row broke out after Boris Johnson stood up in the House of Commons and revealed a staggering 181 NHS staff and 131 care workers have now died from coronavirus. To put this in perspective, that's far more than the 179 British military personnel who died in the Iraq conflict from 2003 to 2011. The majority of those health and care workers who have died are foreign migrants.

Yet far from rewarding the migrants still working to save our lives, the government recently announced it is going to *increase* an NHS surcharge slapped on all migrant workers, including those employed in the NHS, who come from outside the European Economic Area, and on all members of their families. It was £400 a year, a lot of money for many of those asked to pay it. Particularly as they already pay taxes and national insurance that contribute to the NHS.

But in March, Chancellor Rishi Sunak announced the government was increasing the Immigration Health Surcharge to £624 from October. And from next January, it will be extended to all EU citizens when Brexit is completed – apart from those with settled status in the UK.

So, all migrant workers who come from outside the UK to work in the NHS will have to pay thousands of pounds extra for them and their families to the NHS that they serve, on top of the taxes and national insurance they will also be paying from their salaries. This is being done, Sunak said, 'to ensure that new arrivals to the UK contribute to the funding of the NHS' and that 'what people get out, they also put in'.

At the time, this seemed an astonishingly tone-deaf thing to be doing to the very people risking their lives to save others from coronavirus on the NHS frontline. Today, given the shocking NHS staff death toll, which includes many of the 153,000 migrant workers, it seems utterly disgusting. Even former UKIP leader Henry Bolton told us on *GMB* this morning that he thought it was wrong and the surcharge was a 'flawed approach'.

It was quite a moment to hear someone like that support scrapping a policy that unfairly punishes migrants to this country. Yet an important one, too. If someone like Bolton can be that open-minded about an issue like this on which you might expect him to take an alternative view, then why can't the woke brigade do the same, about anything? Intransigence is the enemy of democracy, and it's the opposite of liberalism. You would think that Boris Johnson, of all people, would want to scrap such a grotesquely unfair financial burden on the very people who helped save him.

But he doesn't. He wants to increase it. In the Commons today, he said he'd 'thought about it a great deal' but decided to go ahead with the massively hiked surcharge.

'I do accept and understand the difficulties faced by our amazing NHS staff,' he said. 'I've been a personal beneficiary of carers who have come from abroad and, frankly, saved my life. On the other hand, we must look at the realities. This is a great national service, it's a national institution, it needs funding and those contributions actually help us to raise about £900 million and it's very difficult in the current circumstances to find alternative sources.'

He's going to further punish foreign NHS workers like some of those who saved his life because he WANTS THEIR MONEY? I've seen some disgusting acts of ingratitude in my time, but this is the worst. And it gets even more diabolical. *The Times* reported today that despite the government announcing that families and dependants of migrant NHS workers who die from the virus could stay in the UK indefinitely, Priti Patel's Home Office has now revealed the scheme will only apply to certain occupations like nursing, not to care workers, hospital cleaners or porters. So, the families of many heroes who have died now face being kicked out of Britain because their loved ones gave their lives to save others.

Syrian filmmaker Hassan Akkad, who made a big impression on *GMB* a few weeks ago when he revealed he is now working as a hospital porter on a coronavirus ward, posted an incredibly powerful 90-second video imploring Boris to change this rule.

'I've been really enjoying the clapping that you and your fellow ministers in the government do every week,' Akkad said directly to the prime minister, welling up with tears. 'Today, however, I felt betrayed, stabbed in the back. I felt shocked to find out that you've decided, your government decided, to exclude myself and my colleagues who work as cleaners and porters and social care workers, who are all on minimum wage, you've decided to exclude us from the bereavement scheme.'

The video quickly went viral, horrifying everyone, and late this afternoon the government caved in to public pressure and announced it would now include all NHS and care workers in the bereavement scheme. I suspect a second U-turn will soon follow on the surcharge.

To encourage it, I tweeted, 'Come on Britain. We've shamed Boris Johnson into a U-turn on all bereaved relatives of health/care workers staying here indefinitely. Now let's shame him into scrapping the NHS surcharge on migrant health/care workers.' The tweet got a massive response.

Spencer came over for a socially distanced chat in our local square, following a relaxing of the rules on being able to see anyone from another household. It's been three months since I last saw him, and it felt very strange not even being able to hug him or even shake his hand. He's my eldest son, yet I'm not allowed to touch him. This is all so weird.

THURSDAY 21 MAY

Hassan Akkad appeared on *GMB* and I congratulated him for his video that changed government policy. After revealing that he gets paid just £8.50 an hour for cleaning a Covid ward, I angrily demanded the government scrap the outrageous surcharge, prompting some viewers to then tweet *their* anger, claiming people like him would get nothing like such good treatment back in Syria and he should stop complaining. I read one of them out, then told Hassan, 'I value you, and I think everybody watching, every decent person, values what you are doing, and we appreciate you.'

'I value you too, Piers,' Hassan responded. 'And I have to say that you have changed recently, and I am really proud of you.' I wasn't expecting this and paused before answering.

'Well, you know what?' I replied. 'We can all be better people after this, Hassan. I do not exclude myself. I think it's brought so much perspective, I really do. It has changed me a bit, actually, I have to say. Made me look at things in a different way, and it's made me look at what we as a society value in a different way, and how materialistic we've become. How petty, how kind of obsessed with culture wars and division and toxicity, all that kind of thing. A virus, a common enemy like this, if it doesn't change everything, I don't know what does.'

After the show, I tweeted Boris, 'Your NHS surcharge for the migrant NHS workers who stopped you dying is a disgrace. Do the right thing – scrap it.' I was very encouraged to see that many others from both sides of the political divide have also spoken out, recognising the terrible injustice of this surcharge.

This afternoon, the surcharge was scrapped. When we come together to right a wrong, a lot can be achieved. We just need to stop screaming loud enough to understand that.

FRIDAY 22 MAY

Unbelievable breaking news tonight: the *Daily Mirror* and *Guardian*, in a rare joint operation, have exposed Dominic Cummings, Boris Johnson's right-hand man, for breaking lockdown rules that he helped create. Turns out that after he was seen running away from Number 10 when Boris was announced to have tested positive, he later that day drove his wife and young child 260 miles to his parents' home in Durham, where they self-isolated for two weeks. He did this at the end of March, at the very peak of the virus and a few days after full lockdown had been implemented.

The hypocrisy is staggering.

SATURDAY 23 MAY

The Cummings story has exploded. He's trying to cling on to his job, and cabinet ministers have clearly been ordered to post pathetic tweets of support, including Matt Hancock who said, 'I know how ill coronavirus makes you. It was entirely right for Dom Cummings to find childcare for his toddler, when both he and his wife were getting ill.' So, we now have the health secretary formally endorsing lockdown rule-breaking?

This, I fear, will signify the end of the lockdown because Cummings has driven a sledgehammer through the government's messaging. As Stan said tonight, 'Dad, why should we obey the rules if the people making them ignore them?' I don't have a sensible answer.

SUNDAY 24 MAY

Boris Johnson has publicly supported Cummings at the daily briefing, and by doing so managed to achieve the impossible: unite Twitter. Journalists, pundits, politicians, celebrities and the public are all enraged by him sticking by his aide, regardless of their political persuasion. We all know people who have lost loved ones and couldn't be there for them because they obeyed the rules.

I tweeted Boris a picture of 13-year-old Ismail Abdulwahab who died and was buried alone, saying, 'This poor boy's family stayed away from his deathbed & funeral because they obeyed the Govt rules. Imagine how that family is feeling now, knowing that all they had to do was follow their "instinct", not the rules? You're a disgrace.'

Someone named Kev Shimmin replied, 'Father in Law died 15 April. We obeyed rules & didn't travel 45 mls despite being desperate to see him & say goodbye. Mother in Law had to care for him alone & watch him die alone. If only we followed our instincts. My wife is inconsolable after that shameful press conference.'

A cardiology registrar, Dr Dominic Pimenta, tweeted me to say, 'Heading back into the Covid ICU where I've worked for the last two months. This stuff is hot and hard work. Haven't seen my parents since January. Frankly, Cummings spits in the face of all our efforts, the whole #NHS. If he doesn't resign, I will.'

I wonder if any ministers will have the principle and guts to resign over this, given how damaging it is to the entire government coronavirus public health messaging? Robin Cook's resignation over Iraq gave him a legacy of courage, integrity and principle that few politicians ever achieve. Do any of this cowardly cabinet have it in them to say to Boris, 'No, I'm not having this. Either Cummings goes, or I do.'

What's extraordinary is how desperate the prime minister is to save an adviser. Imagine if Boris had protected care homes with the same ferocity with which he's defending Dominic Cummings?

MONDAY 25 MAY

Cummings held a lengthy press conference today in the Rose Garden at Number 10, a place normally reserved for statements by the prime minister or world leaders.

In a rambling, self-pitying account of what he did, Cummings revealed he broke at least three lockdown rules: he returned to work when his wife was sick with possible Covid symptoms, he then drove his family to his parents' home in Durham; and he took his wife and son on a 60-mile round trip to a tourist attraction, Barnard Castle, on her birthday. To explain the last breach, he claimed he did it to test his eyesight, which had been giving him problems during his Covid isolation. He must think we're utter mugs. Who would put a young child in the back of a car, as he did, if their eyesight was poor and they wanted to test it?

Cummings's excuses were contemptible. Millions of people obeyed the rules *he* helped create – and he brazenly ignored them multiple times. Now he's lying away, playing the victim and taking the whole country for morons.

How many people will now use their 'instinct' to avoid obeying the government's crucial public health guidance regarding Covid-19? How many of those who do will get infected by the virus and then infect others? How many people will die? This is the direct consequence of what Cummings did.

THURSDAY 28 MAY

Tonight was the last official 'Clap for Carers'. It was such a fantastic idea when it started and really seemed to galvanise the country and pull us all together. But I could feel the energy for the communal clapping dissipate after a few weeks, and a surge in general disunity replace it.

The sad reality is that this pandemic has begun to deepen the sores in our society, not heal them, and I fear things will only get worse as the full economic fallout really kicks in later this year. When millions of people come off furlough to discover their jobs no longer exist, there is going to be so much anger. It could get very nasty.

I went outside at 8 pm with Celia, Elise and Cory to give one final rousing ovation to all the heroes who have worked so hard over the past few months.

Kate Garraway posted an Instagram video of her and her kids doing the same outside their house, with the caption, 'Hear this might be the last clap for carers ... it's been such a source of weekly comfort and I must admit I felt the tears come tonight to think it's coming to an end while our fear for Derek goes on. But even if we don't clap next Thursday it won't diminish my eternal thanks to all in the NHS. They are keeping Derek alive & every one of them is fighting as hard as Derek is to give us the chance to be reunited. Hope has to keep us all going, doesn't it? I am having to find new ways of staying strong every day for Darcey & Billy, as I know Derek would want me to. It's not easy but when I think of how hard Derek is fighting & the bravery of all in the NHS, it helps. Thanks so much for all your messages. Standing together & learning from each other has to get us all through.' Paparazzi pictures soon appeared online of her in tears, looking utterly exhausted.

'This made me so sad,' I texted her. 'You look at the end of your bloody tether and I don't blame you. Just know we're all here for you.'

'I really am,' she replied. 'So tearful tonight. It's a living hell to be honest. I keep saying I can't bear it but then somehow do. It's managing feeling and holding in the same moment your greatest hope, greatest fear and total uncertainty about what way it's going to go – all the time. I don't think I've ever loved him more or felt more at risk of losing him. But at least I still have hope which lots of people have had taken away from them. Am going to watch *Darkest Hour* tonight, cry properly and fight back tomorrow.'

I tried to think of a suitably Churchillian reply to rally her spirits, but another great leader's words rang louder in my head. 'Remember the words of Mandela,' I replied. "It always seems impossible until it's done."'

FRIDAY 29 MAY

Horrendous footage has emerged in the United States of an African-American man named George Floyd slowly dying on a street in Minneapolis as a white US police officer kneels on his head for eight minutes and 46 seconds. I watched it in full, aghast at what I saw, and now I can't get the horrifying imagery out of my head.

Floyd, 46, repeatedly begs for his life as the burly, sneering, uninterested police officer, Derek Chauvin, presses his large knee on his neck.

'I can't breathe, man! Please!' pleads Floyd, handcuffed and pinned face-down on the road. Chauvin, a man with 17 complaints against him during his 19-year career, continues pressing.

'I can't breathe,' Floyd cries out again, 'please, the knee in my neck!'

Chauvin ignores him and carries on kneeling heavily on his neck. Floyd groans loudly and in a moment of desperate poignancy shouts for his dead mother: 'MAMA! MAMA!' Chauvin keeps pressing.

'Please, please, please,' Floyd begs again. 'I can't breathe!' In total, he shouts 'I can't breathe' 16 times in under five minutes. But all his pleas fell on deaf ears even as shocked bystanders scream at Chauvin, 'Let him breathe!' and 'Get off of him now!'

One even exclaims, 'Bro, he's not f*cking moving!'

Chauvin never wavers, and never stops pressing his knee on Floyd's neck. For the last two minutes and 53 seconds, Floyd fell silent and unresponsive, his head slumped unconscious on the cement.

'You think this is OK?' shrieked one member of the public as he saw Floyd's motionless body. 'Check his pulse! The man ain't moved!'

Others, equally stunned, shouted, 'Get off his neck!' and 'Get off him!'

Yet Chauvin still pressed his knee on Floyd's neck. Even when an ambulance arrived, and a medic checked Floyd's pulse, Chauvin kept his knee pressed down. Chauvin finally released his knee but only when he was told to by the medics. Floyd was rolled onto a stretcher and taken to a local medical centre where he died an hour later.

What had led to him being apprehended by police? He'd allegedly used a counterfeit $20 note to buy some cigarettes in a grocery store. There have been some despicable racist acts in America in recent weeks, also exposed in graphic detail by camera phones.

A young black man Ahmaud Arbery, 25, was killed while he was out jogging in Georgia by three white men, Gregory and Travis McMichael, and William Bryan, in a pick-up truck. They have since been charged with murder but have pleaded not guilty. Then a white woman, Amy Cooper, reacted to a black man, Christian Cooper, who was politely asking her to leash her dog in New York's Central Park, by phoning 911 to claim hysterically and falsely that an 'African-American man' was threatening her life.

But nothing quite prepared me for the undiluted horror of seeing George Floyd being slowly killed in such an astonishingly callous manner. What I saw made me feel physically sick. The devil of it was in the diabolical detail, played out in real time like some kind of hideous snuff movie.

George Floyd's death would have been just another sad statistic, doubtless framed as a tragic accident involving a man using fake money who resisted arrest so hard that he caused his own life to end. But there was just one problem for the police officers – three others helped to hold Floyd down – who might have concocted such a defence: the whole thing was captured on film and streamed to Facebook Live for the world to witness.

So, we've all now seen with our own eyes what Derek Chauvin did: the sickening heartless brutality in his cold, hard face, the despicably ugly self-satisfied power trip he goes on as he exercises the full power of his knee on a defenceless man's neck. We've seen, at first hand, the terrifying reality of what it really means to be black in America right now.

And we've seen, with terrible irony, how right NFL star Colin Kaepernick was to take the knee to protest about police brutality against black people – an act that cost him his career.

George Floyd was killed because he was a black man whose life just didn't matter to Derek Chauvin. That much is crystal clear from the nonchalant, staggeringly callous way Chauvin allows Floyd to slowly expire from life under his knee. Even by the dreadful standards of police violence against black people in America, and I covered much of it when I was at CNN, this is a new low. It's the moment everything Kaepernick said about the discrimination against black people by the criminal justice system is shown to be shockingly, inarguably true.

Tonight, protests sprang up all over America. This could get very ugly, very quickly. The country is already on its knees from the pandemic. Now a police officer's knee has poured fuel onto the raging fire.

SATURDAY 30 MAY

Bob Weighton, the world's oldest man, who appeared on *GMB* last month a day after his 112th birthday, has sadly died. His family issued a statement saying, 'Bob was an extraordinary man. A role model to us all, he lived his life interested in and engaged with all kinds of people from across the world. He viewed everyone as his brother or sister and believed in loving and accepting and caring for one another. He had many, many friendships and read and talked politics, theology, ecology and more right up until his death. He also cared greatly for the environment. The second bedroom in his flat was a workshop, filled with furniture, windmills and puzzles he made and sold in aid of charity, often from bits of wood pulled from skips. We are so grateful that until the very end Bob remained our witty, kind, knowledgeable, conversationalist father, grandfather and great grandfather, and we will miss him greatly.'

Epitaphs don't get much better than that. We could all do a lot worse than take Bob Weighton's philosophy away from this pandemic. Our lives, most of them, would be immeasurably improved if we did. As they would, too, if we bottled up the spirit of 103-year-old Jennie Stejna, who recently spent two weeks fighting for her life from Covid-19 in a Massachusetts nursing home. When she recovered, she asked her carers for one thing: 'A Bud Light.'

By contrast, some of the younger generation continue with their self-absorbed neuroses, seemingly oblivious to the world around them. Actress Daisy Edgar-Jones, a very talented star of the new hit TV drama *Normal People*, has spoken about her 'battle with hypochondria'. The 22-year-old revealed she would often 'spiral into doubts' over 'missing out' on university after taking a gap year to prioritise her acting career. And this further manifested itself as 'health anxiety' when she lost out on parts at an audition.

'I auditioned and I got close and I found that very anxiety-making and I really struggled for a while ... when I feel anxious it comes out in different ways for me. One of the ways is that I struggle with hypochondria. I had a lot more free time because my friends were away at university and I did think, "Gosh, am I missing out on life experience?" and so I would get quite anxious.'

This, right here, is the problem with wrapping our kids in cotton wool. They end up having a 'struggle with hypochondria'. What's extraordinary is that there's no in-built alarm bell inside Ms Edgar-Jones that tells her this may not be the best time to be talking about such a 'struggle'. Especially as it's just been revealed that the UK now has officially the worst reported coronavirus death rate in the entire world. Until the younger generation gets a proper grip on life, then struggles with hypochondria will keep happening. If a pandemic can't give them proper perspective, then what the hell can?

SUNDAY 31 MAY

Took my filthy lockdown-battered Aston Martin to a local car wash in Hammersmith. They only recently reopened, and the boss asked me if I'd post something on my Instagram to help give them a push on getting their business back on track. Of course, I was happy to do so, captioning a picture of my gleamingly revitalised car with the words, 'I never knew how much I'd miss a car wash. Thanks to the guys @ atlanticcarwash for restoring my Aston to its former glory after Lockdown rendered it an unsightly stained blot on vehicular humanity.'

I thought nothing more of it, until I checked back a few hours later and saw a barrage of abuse among the comments. Instagram is normally a relatively safe haven from trolls, but as I scrolled down, I saw loads of offensive messages. One read, 'People are dying and Piers is washing his Aston Martin. People in care homes are losing their lives and Piers is driving out for a non-essential car wash. Why on earth, when so many lives have been lost, would you do this? It shows the utter contempt you have. You should be sacked and door-stepped without hesitation.'

Another raged, 'So you're putting other people's lives at risk to get your car washed? Why don't you do it yourself?'

A third sneered, 'So many people lost their jobs and can't afford to pay their mortgage bills etc this is disgusting.'

I was taken aback by the vitriol, though it calmed down when I explained why I had posted the picture. What's clear though is that the public's tolerance for what they perceive to be celebrity show-offs rubbing their noses in it has reached a new low, and that social media is more vitriolic than ever.

Two months ago, when lockdown started, I felt quite optimistic about how we would emerge from it. I genuinely believed that losing our basic freedoms would be such a massive wake-up call that all the woke, self-pitying, virtue-signalling bullshit that was sending the world nuts before coronavirus came along would come to an abrupt halt as people, even diehard wokies, realised what actually matters in life and where the focus of our energies should be. But now I feel increasingly despondent.

We're screaming even louder, the partisan divisions are even wider, and people are dying, grieving, fearful and losing their jobs in vast numbers. I can sense a build-up of stress and tension everywhere. Far from bringing us all together, the pandemic seems to have hardened our tribal allegiances. I've even come off various mates' WhatsApp chat groups because they're getting consumed by arguments about Trump, Brexit, Covid and George Floyd. I need some peace and quiet from the maelstrom. But will there be any?

JUNE

'When the looting starts, the shooting starts.'

MONDAY 1 JUNE

Huge George Floyd protests have exploded across America, with millions taking to the streets to show their fury at his sickening death. There's been nothing like this, on such a massive scale, since the assassination of Martin Luther King in 1968.

Sadly, there has been a lot of rioting, looting and arson too as some of the protestors express their rage in a criminal manner. I was stunned to see a terrifying video clip of what resembled a war zone in Los Angeles, and suddenly realised it was adjacent to The Grove, a very genteel retail and entertainment complex that I've gone to dozens of times with the kids.

I don't condone any of the looting and violence. It's shameful, wrong and self-defeating. As MLK himself said, 'Hate begets hate; violence begets violence. Toughness begets a greater toughness.' But my God, I understand the rage of the protestors. And it's just not good enough for white people like me to watch George Floyd die in the way that he died, shake our heads and say how awful it is, rant about the looters, then turn away and get on with our comparatively privileged lives. This is a wake-up moment for all of us. Things have to change.

Yet the one person who could most powerfully effect that change is doing the complete opposite.

President Trump had one job to do after this terrible killing – and that was to heal the raging wounds of fellow Americans. To speak to them from the Oval Office, with love and respect and empathy. To say he understood their anger and would do everything in his power to stop more black people like George Floyd being killed by the very people charged with protecting their lives. Instead, as America burns, Trump is pouring fuel onto the fire.

'When the looting starts, the shooting starts,' he tweeted on Friday. This was a direct quote from racist Miami police chief Walter Headley in 1967, who referred to civil rights protests by saying, 'There is only one way to handle looters and arsonists during a riot and that is to shoot them on sight. I've let the word filter down: when the looting starts, the shooting starts.' Earlier that month, Headley had 'declared war' on crime and said his primary target was 'aimed at young Negro males, from 15 to 21'.

So, here was the president of the United States effectively telling people protesting at the murder of a black man by a police officer that more black people were now going to be killed by police officers. It's hard to imagine a more reckless, incendiary thing to say at such a tense time. When his comments sparked fury, Trump tried to pretend he didn't know the history behind the phrase.

But he knew what he was saying.

We all knew what he was saying.

And as with his spectacular ineptitude during the coronavirus pandemic that's led to over 100,000 deaths in the USA, Trump's loose-tongued rhetoric has made things ten times worse.

Where he should heal, he's divided.

Where he should calm, he's inflamed.

Where he should lead, he's failed.

As he always does, Trump has reacted to justified criticism by repeatedly lashing out at the 'fake news media', and unsurprisingly a large number of journalists have been targeted by police in the past few days – arrested, pepper sprayed and shot at with rubber bullets. The president, not content with encouraging police to shoot black protestors, wants them to see the media as the enemy too. It's a total disgrace, aimed to show his base supporters what a big tough guy he is.

But where did the big tough guy go when his comments led to large numbers of protestors converging outside the White House over the weekend? The president was taken by Secret Service agents to a secure underground bunker for his own safety. That's where. He even boasted he couldn't have felt 'more safe', and warned there were dogs and heavy weaponry waiting for anyone who tried to get near him. What a shame there were no dogs, heavy weaponry or Secret Service agents around to stop George Floyd being murdered.

The world is in crisis from a deadly virus and crying out for strong leadership. Normally, this would be provided by the United States of America. But America is today in utter chaos, with the worst Covid-19 death toll, 40 million job losses, a devastated economy and now the worst racial equality riots since the 1960s. And the president's response, which must be delighting rival superpowers like China, is to self-implode – hurling off his own verbal firebombs and then hiding in his bunker as they explode.

On Saturday, Trump went down to Florida to watch Elon Musk's rocket Falcon 9 fire up into space. It was a reminder to the world of America at its pioneering, buccaneering, inspiring best and a moment for millions of Americans to feel pride in their country. But it was just a fleeting moment amid the mayhem that's brought the country to its knees and left the rest of the world looking on aghast.

In AD 64 Rome burnt for six days in an enormous fire that destroyed nearly three-quarters of its buildings and left half its citizens homeless. Emperor Nero, so legend has it, was safely tucked away in his villa 35 miles away, playing the fiddle. His people never forgave him. America, already reeling from coronavirus, is now engulfed in anarchy. And the president is shamefully fiddling as it burns.

TUESDAY 2 JUNE

The UK has introduced quarantine for people flying into the country. Home Secretary Priti Patel explained the decision by saying, 'We must keep the country safe from potentially infected passengers unknowingly spreading the virus [...] and ensure that public health comes first.'

Yes, I couldn't agree more. So why are we only doing this now, five months after this virus erupted and after allowing 20 million people to fly in without any checks whatsoever? Like so much this government has done during this pandemic, it makes no sense.

A social media campaign gathered momentum to declare today 'Black Out Tuesday' to honour George Floyd, in which everyone was encouraged to post only a black square with the hashtag #blackouttuesday. I don't really like these kind of enforced shows of social media solidarity, as they're usually just an excuse for people to virtue-signal.

I'd also been so busy with *GMB* and writing two columns that I hadn't really picked up on how many were doing it, until I Instagrammed a photo of a bottle of rosé I was drinking this evening when I finally got time to relax – and promptly got monstered for it.

'No respect shown from Piers Morgan today,' said one follower. 'Despite what he says on TV, today was a day for us all to unite and to black out social media for #blackouttuesday. Obviously way too much to ask from some of those who are not directly affected.'

I replied, 'We did over an hour on racism on *GMB* today, I think that had more impact than me posting a black square.'

'Brave,' messaged Spencer on the boys' WhatsApp chat.

'Why?' I replied.

'The idea was no one to post as a sign of solidarity, you're the only person on my feed all day who did one that wasn't a black square.'

'I prefer to do things my way.'

'I think it's actively provocative not to post today,' said Stanley. 'It was a day of not posting. Surprisingly out of touch.' This got my back up.

'This morning, we interviewed the mother of Ahmaud Arbery, the young guy who got lynched last month, and George Floyd's lawyer, then a half-hour panel with four black activists, before an interview with Ashley Banjo about it all. Don't tell me I'm out of touch.'

'That's great,' said Stanley, 'but why is there a limit to what you can do?'

'Why do I have to do what everyone else feels they have to do? I've done a lot more today than most of them.'

'Solidarity is literally about everyone doing what everyone else is doing,' Stanley retorted. 'Don't post about wine.'

'I'm not a lemming,' I replied.

It's fascinating to see how strongly they feel about it. I suspect there's a lot of peer pressure going on, too, with all their friends looking to see who *isn't* doing the black square, ready to berate them for 'not caring'. Young people feel compelled to conform to whatever woke social media decides has to be said, thought or done. I've always encouraged the boys to have their own opinions, and to not be afraid to express them. But it's hard when you have a few thousand people out there ready to pounce on any 'unacceptable' view. Not that I think the black square is a bad idea; it's undeniably a powerful visual to support a very important cause. Like taking the knee, though, it shouldn't be compulsory to do it. Freedom of speech and expression should allow people to decide if they want to or not, without fear of being vilified for choosing not to follow the crowd.

WEDNESDAY 3 JUNE

The front page of today's *Daily Telegraph* carries the following headline: 'Johnson takes control in shake-up at No 10.'

I was intrigued, so read the intro. 'Boris Johnson is to take direct control of the Government's handling of the coronavirus crisis ...'

Words rarely fail me. This, however, rendered me speechless. Who the f*ck has been in 'direct control' until now? At Prime Minister's Questions, Boris said of the crisis, 'I'm very proud of our record.' Proud of what, exactly? He failed to protect health and care workers with PPE, he failed on testing, he sent elderly Covid patients back into care homes, sparking a secondary epidemic, he was woefully late to lockdown, he pursued a disastrous herd immunity strategy for weeks and he's performed endless U-turns on everything from face masks to quarantine for visitors. The result of all this is the UK has the worst death rate in the world and the second-worst death toll behind the USA, which has handled the pandemic equally badly. We're becoming just as fractured as the USA by it all, too.

Meanwhile, ratings for *GMB* yesterday were the highest ever. It seems that the longer the government boycotts us, the more people are tuning in. It also suggests there is massive interest in the George Floyd story, given how much of the show we devoted to it.

A huge protest took place in London's Hyde Park this afternoon, with thousands in attendance. This is such a complex situation. Mass gatherings remain banned, for very good reason as we know they help spread the virus. But I've heard protestors saying on TV that they view racial injustice as just as big a crisis as Covid-19, and they want their voices heard. I totally get that, and I agree with them. The right to protest is as fundamental and important as the right to freedom of speech.

Beaches and parks are packed with people having picnics and sunbathing, so how can anyone legitimately stop protestors campaigning for racial equality in the wake of a brutal racial murder? But they should do so as safely as possible, and what was clear from the overhead TV news footage is that most of them aren't.

'I fully support the peaceful #GeorgeFloyd protest in Hyde Park right now,' I tweeted. 'But the total absence of any social distancing by the thousands of people protesting is insane.'

A few minutes later, Labour MP Barry Gardiner tweeted, 'Been social distancing since March. Today I broke it to join the #BlackLivesMatter demo outside Parliament and take a knee with thousands of brave young people calling for Justice.'

This seems a ridiculous thing for any MP to say and do. It's one thing for a lawmaker to support the protests, it's quite another for one to actively boast of breaking social distancing rules.

'Reckless & irresponsible,' I tweeted back to him.

Three hours later, Stanley tweeted a photo from the protest. He wasn't in the photo himself – but it was of a packed crowd of people. I called him immediately.

'Were you there?'

'I was,' he replied.

'Did you socially distance?'

'I tried, Dad, but it was very hard because a lot of people weren't. I wore a mask and gloves, though.'

'OK, just be careful what you post on social media because there will be people who will use you to have a pop at me if they can and I don't want you being caught in the crossfire.'

'Yes, I know. But I'm 22, and I'm allowed my own opinions and to make my own decisions. This was important to me. Racism is just as much a virus as Covid-19.'

He's right. And the lockdown is breaking apart anyway. A new YouGov poll says one in five of those surveyed have followed lockdown guidance less strictly in the last week than previously, with 32 per cent of those people citing the Dominic Cummings story as a reason for that.

Tonight, sensational news broke that police have identified a new suspect in the case of British girl Madeleine McCann, who was snatched 13 years ago from her family's holiday resort villa in Portugal.

The story gathered huge notoriety because her parents, Gerry and Kate McCann, both doctors, left their three young kids under five, including three-year-old Madeleine, alone as they dined with friends in a nearby restaurant within the complex.

Like most people I felt very uneasy about their parental negligence – I would never have done that with any of my children. But when I interviewed them years later, and saw the horrific grief still etched on their faces for myself, I felt a surge of intense sympathy. Their misery has been compounded by a relentless and vicious accusatory campaign on social media by large numbers of mindless keyboard warrior idiots that has been truly disgusting to witness. The McCanns have become a global punching bag for nasty, self-righteous trolls intent on making their lives even worse. It's unconscionable, and they get no protection from it.

But this development tonight seems a huge breakthrough. The suspect is a convicted German paedophile who was in the area at the time, and police clearly believe they may finally have their guy.

THURSDAY 4 JUNE

The newspaper front pages are dominated by the Madeleine McCann news. Most devoted many pages to it, relegating the Hyde Park protests much further back. I understand the excitement over the bombshell revelation and would have doubtless done much the same if I had still been an editor. But would there have been anything like this level of sustained interest if Madeleine had been a little black girl? I think not.

This is just the kind of subliminal, subconscious decision-making that goes to the heart of what black people call 'microaggressions'. Newspapers, like most of the media, are still largely run by white people who make decisions based on their own life experiences. As I said on *GMB*, 'This is the kind of thing that if I was black, I would look at and go, "Why is it one rule for white girls that go missing and another rule for black girls who also go missing but don't get this attention?"'

Obviously, I promptly got accused of being a 'race-baiting imbecile' on Twitter by people who can't accept that there is any racism anywhere and resent any suggestion to the contrary. How anyone can watch the George Floyd video and not understand that racism, overt and subliminal, is a very real thing is unfathomable to me. But once again, social media is elevating the debate from helpful conversation and eagerness to educate, to vicious tribal toxicity.

Interestingly, Meghan Markle offered some genuinely insightful comments about George Floyd today, which Trump would do well to listen to. She told students in a video message about her own painful memories of witnessing the 1992 riots in Los Angeles after the brutal beating of Rodney King, and quoted her old teacher Ms Pollia, who would tell her, 'Always remember to put others' needs above your own fears.'

Meghan told the students, 'You're going to have to have empathy for those who don't see the world through the same lens that you do.' That's what Trump either doesn't get – or doesn't want to get. She added, 'I wasn't sure what I could say to you. I wanted to say the right thing and I was really nervous that it would get picked apart. And I realised the only wrong thing to say is to say nothing.'

She raises an important point. One of the very worst consequences of illiberal wokery is that it stops people speaking out for fear they will be torn to pieces by the intolerant lynch mob on social media. Yet, how do we ever progress if we don't foster a healthier atmosphere of free speech and democratic debate? These should be the very cornerstones of any civilised society, yet we're trashing them bit by Twitter pile-on bit. I don't care what Meghan has to say about many things, especially when she is being hypocritical or whining about hardship as a princess. But she's perfectly entitled to have her own opinions, and on the issue of racism, as she showed today, she has an interesting and valuable perspective and it's important that critics like me acknowledge that.

My approving remarks about her didn't go unnoticed.

'Yes, it's time to play Things-You-Thought-Piers-Would-Never-Say Bingo!' tweeted comedian David Baddiel.

This afternoon, the conservative blogger Guido Fawkes 'exposed' Stan for attending the Black Lives Matter demo. I could have ignored it or left it to Stan to fight his own battles, but Guido has a big following and the story soon began flying around Twitter, with everyone screaming at me that I was a 'disgusting hypocrite'.

So eventually I replied, 'Proud of my son for attending the #BlackLivesMatter protest which he found profoundly inspiring. He told me he maintained social distancing as best he could in the large crowd. Not easy given many others weren't, but I'm glad he tried.'

Of course, the screams of 'disgusting hypocrite' intensified, and my comments about Barry Gardiner were soon used to support that theory. But there was no actual hypocrisy. I had tweeted my support for the protestors before I criticised Gardiner for recklessly boasting about breaking social distancing rules, and before I knew Stan had gone.

None of this mattered, though. I'm now a disgusting hypocrite, and no amount of truth will correct that. Though it's amusing to see all the same people I saw furiously defending Dominic Cummings now howling abuse about the George Floyd protestors 'risking lives'. As *Financial Times* writer Sathnam Sanghera tweeted, 'Things that are OK: driving to Durham, visiting Barnard Castle to check your eyesight, forcing hundreds of MPs into a confined space when it's clearly not necessary, the frigging Cheltenham Festival. Not OK: protesting about racial injustice.'

'You should have just said you didn't approve of me going to a mass gathering,' Stan told me tonight.

'But I do approve of you going,' I said. 'I admire you for standing up for what you believe in.'

'Thanks, Dad. That's what you always told us to do. I also think if people are flocking to parks and beaches, I should be able to protest about what happened to George Floyd. Especially after what Dominic Cummings did.'

SATURDAY 6 JUNE

Churchill's statue in Parliament Square was defaced by Black Lives Matter protestors today and daubed with the words 'WAS A RACIST'. The Cenotaph was also attacked, with one protestor trying to set fire to a flag on it. Both these things will inflame many Britons who might otherwise be sympathetic to the BLM protests, which will be an absolute tragedy.

Once again, the things we should be focusing on – racial injustice and inequality – are being eclipsed by inflammatory, intolerant and self-defeating behaviour that will damage the debate and likelihood of real change.

Later in the afternoon, things got even worse as rioting broke out between protestors and the police, including one awful moment where a female officer was thrown off her horse and badly hurt when she hit a traffic light as the poor animal bolted from rioters.

'Can someone out there please edit down just the guy hitting the traffic light over and over again to the opening bar of Gwen Stefani's "Hollaback Girl",' tweeted *Guardian* journalist Hannah Jane Parkinson, who astonishingly is the paper's mental health expert. It's this kind of staggering and vile hypocrisy that illustrates the real problem I have with the woke brigade. So many of them bang on about mental health, and the need to be kind and tolerant, yet then display such appalling savagery towards someone they don't know who was just trying to do her job.

In similar vein, the mood to 'cancel' everyone and everything has gathered momentum in the wake of George Floyd's murder, as fury over the way he was killed has spilled over into wider woke-fuelled outrage about the state of the world. J.K. Rowling has found herself the latest target after she mocked a newspaper op-ed about health-care inequality that used the phrase 'people who menstruate' to be more inclusive. 'People who menstruate,' Rowling tweeted. 'I'm sure there used to be a word for those people. Someone help me out. Wumben? Wimpund? Woomud?'

There was an immediate backlash, but Rowling – who has been rattling the transgender activist cage for quite a while – doubled down, stating: 'If sex isn't real, there's no same-sex attraction. If sex isn't real, the lived reality of women globally is erased. I know and love trans people, but erasing the concept of sex removes the ability of many to meaningfully discuss their lives. It isn't hate to speak the truth. I respect every trans person's right to live any way that feels authentic and comfortable to them. I'd march with you if you were discriminated against on the basis of being trans. At the same time, my life has been shaped by being female. I do not believe it's hateful to say so.'

Of course, this merely intensified the outrage. The LGBTQ rights organisation GLAAD said Rowling 'continues to align herself with an ideology which wilfully distorts facts about gender identity and people who are trans. In 2020, there is no excuse for targeting trans people.'

As inevitable calls grew for J.K. Rowling to be 'cancelled' – on a technical point, how do you 'cancel' a billionaire author? – another high-profile woman was cancelled in America when Ivanka Trump was no-platformed after plans for her to give a virtual commencement speech to students at Wichita State University Tech in Kansas were scrapped amid criticism of her father's response to the George Floyd protests. The university dumped Ivanka in a panic just hours after announcing she would be speaking to WSU Tech graduates.

The announcement drew immediate criticism, led by one of the university's professors Jennifer Ray, who sent a letter asking administrators to cancel it. That letter then circulated on social media and got 488 signatures from faculty, students and alumni before the speech was cancelled.

Ivanka, a top adviser in the White House, was furious, tweeting, 'Our nation's campuses should be bastions of free speech. Cancel culture and viewpoint discrimination are antithetical to academia. Listening to one another is important now more than ever!'

She's right, obviously.

All the woke crap I hoped might get cured by the pandemic seems to now be intensifying again and has never felt more disproportionate.

SUNDAY 7 JUNE

Tim Adams, the *Observer* journalist who had to watch every *GMB* show that I presented in January for an in-depth feature on me, has updated his opinion in today's paper.

'At the end of January, I wrote a story about the ways Piers Morgan shaped the nation's angry divisions,' he wrote. 'It involved a month of watching *Good Morning Britain* and reporting on how the personal obsessions of the nation's most visible anchor – with Meghan Markle and the "snowflake" generation – also became the nation's obsessions.

'I now feel duty bound to add a postscript to that report. One of the more outlandish side-effects of Covid-19 has been the transformation of Morgan into a formidable voice of righteous anger against the failures of "populist" government. Who knows what prompted this change? Perhaps the fortitude of Captain Tom or a midnight visit from Marley's ghost? It began when Morgan finally admitted that the US president he had claimed as "cool, calm and collected" was clearly "batshit" crazy. Since then Morgan has been moved to acknowledge he went "too far" in his obsession with Markle, and even recognised his eternal nemesis Ian Hislop as a fellow traveller. Last week, Anna Soubry, who received her share of Morgan vitriol, noted "Piers is on a journey". Long may it continue.'

I'm not sure I'm 'on a journey' so much as going back to my core journalistic principles when I campaigned against the Iraq War or guns in America. But there's no doubt this crisis has made me sharply aware of where society's been going wrong in recent years, and what we need to do to fix it, and of the potential that someone like me with a big platform has to help with that process rather than fuel the problem of tribalism, which is more palpable than ever.

Those who opposed the BLM protests (mostly right-wing Brexiters or pro-Trumpers) are furiously defending people's right to pack out beaches. Those who supported the protests (mostly liberal Remainers and anti-Trumpers) say the beach-goers are reckless and irresponsible. It would be so much better if we all just agreed with the bleedingly obvious and scientifically incontrovertible point that any mass gathering where people don't socially distance is dangerous during a pandemic. But partisan politics doesn't allow for such common sense or agreement.

This afternoon, a large group of BLM protestors in Bristol tore down a statue of Sir Edward Colston – a former slave trader who then invested large sums of money in the city from his ill-gotten gains – and dumped it into the river. It was an undeniably ugly mob-rule scene, reminiscent of when Iraqi civilians ripped down Saddam Hussein's statue in Baghdad. But I can't pretend I was overly dismayed to see it happen.

I'm not going to lose any sleep over an infamous slave trader, who cost the lives of 20,000 African men, women and children during boat transits, finally getting his statue comeuppance. What's more shocking to me is that there was still a statue of him lording it over black Bristolians in the first place.

I can easily understand why black people in Britain take exception to slave owners and traders lording it over them in the form of large statues in city and town centres.

I get the argument that you can't just delete bad people or events in history – but you can definitely delete edifices that celebrate them.

Sometimes, a ban is entirely appropriate. It is right, for example, that Nazi memorabilia, including Hitler statues and artefacts displaying the swastika, were outlawed in Germany. Just as I felt it was right when the Confederate flag was pulled down from state capitol grounds in South Carolina in 2015 after a 21-year-old white supremacist named Dylann Roof used it to justify trying to re-start the Civil War by murdering black people in their church. It was quite clear that he saw this flag as some kind of stirring emblem of white supremacist power and made people ask why this hated flag was still a protected species when all it does is remind people of America's darkest, most evil past and motivate racists like Roof.

Lindsey Graham, a 2016 presidential candidate and a man for whom I have a lot of time, had previously defended keeping the Confederate flag flying, telling CNN, 'It represents to some people a civil war, and that was the symbol of one side. To others, it's a racist symbol and it's been used by people in a racist way. The problems we're having in South Carolina and around the world aren't because of a symbol, but because of what's in the heart.'

But even he, a proud and staunch old-school Republican, recognised the wind was turning so fast after the dreadful massacre that to continue defying it was to make the world perceive *you* as a racist. So, Lindsey Graham did a dramatic U-turn.

'After the tragic hate-fuelled shooting in Charleston,' he said, 'it is only appropriate that we deal once and for all with the issue of the flag. I hope that by removing it, we can take another step towards healing and recognition and a sign that South Carolina is moving forward.'

He was instantly mocked and abused on social media for his change of heart. But I applaud it. A politician who listens to debate and public opinion, realises he is wrong and switches his own position shows great strength of character, not weakness.

The same cannot be said for sports network ESPN, who, in the wake of a racist attack in Charlottesville in 2017, pulled one of its announcers – an experienced Asian-American sportscaster – from commentating on a University of Virginia football game because his name was Robert Lee, the same as Confederate general Robert E. Lee.

'We collectively made the decision with Robert to switch games as the tragic events in Charlottesville were unfolding,' ESPN said, 'simply because of the coincidence of his name. In that moment it felt right to all parties. It's a shame that this is even a topic of conversation and we regret that who calls play-by-play for a football game has become an issue.' This is precisely the kind of virtue-signalling claptrap that makes a mockery of the very real issues surrounding what happened in Charlottesville.

And yet there are still incredibly offensive things that should be banned that remain untouchable because nobody dares suggest it for fear of offending someone. Take, for example, the most disgusting racial slur of all: 'n****r'. It's a six-letter noun in the English language that the dictionary defines as 'a contemptuous term for a black or dark-skinned person'. It's such an inflammatory and offensive word that for any high-profile white person like me to publicly use it in full, without abbreviating to 'N-word', is rightly tantamount to professional suicide and personal opprobrium. I don't use it; and would never use it. But it has become astonishingly ubiquitous in modern American society. According to a survey several years ago by analytics firm Topsy.com, it is used, either as 'n****r' or 'n***a', at least 500,000 times on Twitter every single day. By comparison, the words 'bro' and 'dude' are only used 300,000 and 200,000 times per day.

These shocking statistics formed part of a powerful study in 2014 in the *Washington Post*. Headlined 'THE N-WORD' – even the *Post* shied away from actually saying it – it concluded, 'The slur has become more prevalent in American life but remains as divisive and complicated as ever.'

The reason it is so ingrained in pop culture is that many black people, especially young black people reared to the soundtrack of N-word-splattered rap music, use it as a form of reappropriation. They're aware of its history; they know from their parents and grandparents that arrogant, dumb, racist whites used it as a wicked, derogatory insult against their black slave forebears. And they enjoy the freedom of being able to say it now in the knowledge that it's become taboo for whites to do so. I understand this, and I empathise. It's the same ironic reason many gays call each other 'f****ts', why supporters of Tottenham Hotspur, which has a large Jewish following, call each other 'Y*ds' and why some ardent feminists like to use the word 'c*nt' with impunity.

I get it. But I don't like it. And this is why: it doesn't work. It has the complete opposite effect to the one that I imagine everyone who does this imagines it will have. Far from 'owning' these words, seizing back control with the use of them, I believe it merely serves to empower those who wish to deploy them abusively – and encourage them to continue doing so.

Your average dim-witted, foul-mouthed bigot – and there are plenty of them, as Twitter can attest – thinks, 'If they use it, why can't I?' They hear African-Americans say the N-word to each other and claim victory. 'See, that's what they even call themselves!' It's the twisted, horrible mindset of the wretchedly ignorant.

I debated this issue many times during my tenure at CNN. Mike Tyson, who uses the N-word a lot in his excellent autobiographical stage show, insisted, 'We have to think about how this word originated, where it came from. Just because we stop saying it won't stop them [white racists] from saying it. They're mad because they say it's a double-standard if they can't say what we say amongst each other? I don't plan on stopping saying it anytime soon.' I don't think it's a double-standard at all.

The N-word is a grotesque, odious, evil stain on the English language. It symbolises everything America has fought so hard to move on from – white, imperialist, violent, sexually malevolent barbarism. Yet far from receding in society, it's spreading, out of the once clearly defined confines of private usage in the black community, into the public hallways of every school in America.

This is wrong, isn't it? Better, surely, to have it expunged completely. But this will only happen when America's black community applies the same level of tolerance to its own use of the word as that now applied in the National Football League: zero.

Teach the youth of today the N-word is so heinous that even to repeat it ironically is to perpetuate its poison. As a white man, I understand that I have no right to demand that any black person gives up using the N-word. This is a decision that can only be made by black people. But as someone who believes passionately in civil rights, I just think it's the right thing to do.

In 2016, black comedian Larry Wilmore called Barack Obama a 'n***a' while hosting the White House Correspondents' Dinner. 'All jokes aside,' he said, 'let me just say how much it means for me to be here tonight. When I was a kid, I lived in a country where people couldn't accept a black quarter-back. And now, to live in your time, Mr President, when a black man can lead the free world. Words alone do me no justice. So, Mr President, if I'm going to keep it 100: Yo, Barry, you did it my n***a!'

Obama laughed, because what else could he do? As black *New York Daily News* columnist Leonard Greene put it, 'Besides unfairly putting Obama on the spot about the most loaded word in the English language, Wilmore gave white people, many of whom have for nearly eight years been besides themselves over a black man in the White House, license to use the N-word against the leader of the free world.'

Reverend Al Sharpton was equally furious. 'Many of us are against using the N-word, period,' he said. 'To say it in front of the President of the United States in front of the top people in the media was at best in poor taste.'

I heard about the furore when I woke in London to find a tweet from the singer John Legend saying, 'Piers Morgan's next troll piece just wrote itself.' Now, I'm instinctively wary of someone who changes their surname from 'Stephens' to 'Legend'. (It's usually best if someone else gives you that title ...) And I take exception to his general belief that a white man shouldn't comment on what he sees as exclusively 'black' issues. As Annie Lennox said to me about feminism, that women have to bring men with them to effect change, so true racial equality will only come about if black and white people work together to achieve it. This was a point that tennis star Venus Williams reiterated when she said the solidarity she has seen in recent protests over the death of George Floyd, with so many white people marching alongside black people, 'brought me to tears', and that 'just as sexism is not only a "women's issue", racism is not only a "black issue".' She explained, 'In the past, I had the honor of fighting for equal prize money for all women's players at the grand slams in tennis. When we fought for and won equal prize money, everyone pitched in, men and women, all colors and races.'

When I called for the N-word to be expunged from modern discourse, Legend tweeted, 'Y'all better thank Piers Morgan for that simple straightforward solution to racism. Why didn't we think of this?'

Obviously, I don't think this alone would solve racism. As Obama himself said on a podcast in 2015, 'Racism, we are not cured of it. And it's not just a matter of it not being polite to say n****r in public. That's not the measure of whether racism still exists or not. It's not just a matter of overt discrimination. Societies don't, overnight, completely erase everything that happened 200 to 300 years prior.'

Legend is right when he says that white people like me shouldn't tell black people they can't use the N-word. But perhaps on that subject he should listen to one of the most famous black entertainers in history. Comedian Richard Pryor made his name in the 1970s and 1980s with albums entitled 'That N****r's Crazy' and 'Bicentennial N****r'. He seized on the N-word as a powerful tool to ram racism back down the throats of white people who used it to denigrate blacks. He argued that it was about 'owning' the term, the same argument used by those black Americans today who deploy it.

But Pryor dramatically changed his view of the N-word after a visit to Africa. In fact, he abandoned it completely. He explained to *Ebony* magazine, 'While I was there, something inside of me said, "Look around you Richard. What do you see?" I saw people. African people. I saw people from other countries, too, and they were all kinds of colours, but I didn't see any "n****rs". I didn't see any there because there are no "n****rs" in Africa. Can you imagine going out into the bush and walking up to a Masai and saying, "Hey n****r! Come here!"? You couldn't do that. There are no "n****rs" here in America either. We black people are not "n****rs", and I will forever refuse to be one. I'm free of that, it's out of my head. I realised that terms like "n****r" and the word "b*tch" that so many black men call our women, are tricks, like genocide on the brain.'

He was right. Why try to 'own' a word so destructive, so vile? Far better to destroy it, to remove it from popular parlance, to render it a wicked piece of linguistic history.

MONDAY 8 JUNE

The UK government, according to a new YouGov poll, now has the joint-lowest approval rating worldwide for how they have managed coronavirus. It would appear the public's blinkers have finally come off.

There is real change in the air about racism too. Yorkshire Tea's now legendary Twitter account, which was so shamefully abused when Rishi Sunak was pictured drinking their product, banned someone today from ever drinking its tea again after the follower tweeted them to say, 'I'm dead chuffed that Yorkshire Tea hasn't supported BLM.'

Someone else named Pamela then tweeted rival tea firm PG Tips to say, 'So now I've got to buy PG Tips. Well f me. This sucks. And Yorkshire Tea is done. Good luck with this bs stance.'

To which PG Tips Twitter account responded, 'Yeah, it does suck, Pamela. If you are boycotting teas that stand against racism, you're going to have to find two new tea brands now.' They added the hashtag #solidaritea.

As someone who coincidentally only ever drinks these two teas, I'm delighted to see such proactive anti-racism. And what's most delicious about it is that the racists will be too thick to know they can obviously still drink the tea if they want to.

TUESDAY 9 JUNE

Nigel Farage, former leader of UKIP and one of the main architects of Brexit, appeared on *GMB* today to attack the Black Lives Matter organisation, comparing it to the Taliban. There are perfectly legitimate concerns about the political aims of the BLM activist group, which include de-funding the police and abolishing capitalism – as distinct from the #blacklivesmatter hashtag movement, which most people take to mean a more general desire for racial equality and justice – but comparing them to the Taliban is outrageously inflammatory and he was howled down by two other guests, black civil rights activist Dr Shola Mos-Shogbamimu and white historian Professor Kate Williams. It culminated in Dr Shola exclaiming, 'The only thing Nigel Farage is an expert on is his backside because every word out of his mouth stinks.'

Twitter blew up with fury at Farage. It felt like a significant moment. The George Floyd murder has galvanised the world about racism in a way that I haven't seen for a very long time.

The subject of discrimination reared its head again today, when Harry Potter star Daniel Radcliffe launched an extraordinary attack on J.K. Rowling. 'While Jo is unquestionably responsible for the course my life has taken [...] I feel compelled to say something at this moment,' he said in a statement. 'Transgender women are women. Any statement to the contrary erases the identity and dignity of transgender people and goes against all advice given by professional health care associations who have far more expertise on this subject matter than either Jo or I. [...] Seventy-eight per cent of transgender and nonbinary youth reported being the subject of discrimination due to their gender identity. [...] It's clear that we need to do more to support transgender and nonbinary people, not invalidate their identities, and not cause further harm. To all the people who now feel that their experience of the books has been tarnished or diminished, I am deeply sorry for the pain these comments have caused you. I really hope that you don't entirely lose what was valuable in these stories to you.'

Wow. Talk about torching the hand that fed you. What's fascinating about this is that Radcliffe is preaching tolerance and acceptance while refusing to be either tolerant or accepting of Rowling's right to have a different opinion. He doesn't think he's right – he *knows* he's right. And the woman who made him a superstar must now be destroyed for daring to deviate from his opinion. This is virtue-signalling at its most virulent. Of course, it's also exactly how Rowling has herself behaved to others, including me, for many years. She's revelled in the cancel culture and taken a furiously intransigent stance on anyone who deviates from the woke world view.

It will be fascinating to see how she responds to the tidal wave of fury now cascading on her saintly head from fellow wokies. Perhaps Rowling will realise just how nasty wokedom can get when you dare to stand up to it. I hope so.

WEDNESDAY 10 JUNE

Rowling came out fighting again today, posting a 3,600-word essay explaining her position. She said she wanted to address the 'toxicity' she's experienced since voicing her opinion on transgender issues 'without any desire to add to that toxicity'. The essay, naturally, massively added to the toxicity.

She played the victim card heavily from the top, recounting the 'harassment' she's faced since first making her views known about transgenderism, and mentioning 'threats of violence', being told she 'was literally killing trans people with my hate', and receiving misogynist abuse like 'c*nt' and 'b*tch'. She said people like her often get branded 'TERF' (trans-exclusionary radical feminist) and protested that the term is used 'to intimidate many people, institutions and organisations I once admired, who are cowering before the tactics of the playground. They'll call us transphobic! They'll say I hate trans people! What next, they'll say you've got fleas? Speaking as a biological woman, a lot of people in positions of power really need to grow a pair.'

Rowling then cited five reasons for speaking out. The first was the charitable trust she set up in Scotland that works with female prisoners and survivors of domestic and sexual abuse. 'It's been clear to me for a while,' she said, 'that the new trans activism is having (or is likely to have, if all its demands are met) a significant impact on many of the causes I support, because it's pushing to erode the legal definition of sex and replace it with gender.'

The second was her 'deep concerns about the effect the trans rights movement is having on children and education'. Third was her belief in freedom of speech, which she says she's 'publicly defended ... even unto Donald Trump'. (This made me laugh – is this the same woman who revelled in me being told to 'f*ck off' on Bill Maher's TV show for saying Trump isn't the new Hitler?)

Fourth was her concern that many of those who transition end up regretting it.

And the fifth was that she herself was a victim and a survivor of domestic abuse and sexual assault. 'I'm mentioning these things now not in an attempt to garner sympathy,' she said, trying to garner sympathy, 'but out of solidarity with the huge numbers of women who have histories like mine, who've been slurred as bigots for having concerns around single-sex spaces.'

The essay prompted another avalanche of horrible abuse. Rowling made some perfectly reasonable points, many of which I happen to agree with. But none of that matters; she's been convicted of being transphobic and the court of woke public opinion is in no mood to allow any appeal.

Of course, it's heavily ironic to see such a self-righteous wokie being eaten alive by her own like this. Yet it's also incredibly disheartening to see such an important issue reduced yet again to a slanging match where nobody will back down and no consensus will ever be reached. If you don't accept every single thing the transgender lobby says about transgenderism, however much some of it may damage women's rights, you must be shamed, vilified and cancelled. Even if you're J.K. Rowling, who's devoted her life to being the wokest human being imaginable.

It's also so depressing to see so much bloody energy being expended on gender wars in the middle of a global pandemic.

This afternoon, Professor Neil Ferguson, the chief government modeller who had to resign from the Scientific Advisory Group for Emergencies (SAGE) after breaking lockdown to bed his lover, told a Commons committee, 'The epidemic was doubling every three to four days before lockdown interventions were introduced. So, had we introduced lockdown measures a week earlier, we would have then reduced the death toll by at least a half.'

This is a stunning admission. He's saying at least 25,000 people have died unnecessarily, possibly a lot more once all the estimated 68,000 'excess deaths' during the pandemic so far are properly analysed. All because Boris Johnson failed to lock down the country when people like me were screaming at him to do so.

The prime minister appeared at the daily briefing a few hours later looking like a petrified rabbit in the headlights but *still* refused to admit to *any* mistakes, and insisted we have to wait until this is all over before we can make any accurate verdicts about the UK's handling of the pandemic. We don't have to wait, though. The death rate speaks for itself; we're the worst in the world. Boris knows his dithering was a disaster and one day soon he will be held accountable for it.

THURSDAY 11 JUNE

The fallout from the Colston statue has turned utterly insane, with calls for statues of great historical figures like Queen Victoria, Lord Nelson and Robert the Bruce to go too. And after various TV personalities like Keith Lemon and Ant and Dec issued grovelling apologies in the past week for doing blackface earlier in their careers, a new puritanical purge has erupted over numerous 'problematic' movies and TV shows, even leading to episodes of *Fawlty Towers* being pulled by terrified TV execs. As I feared, far from expunging illiberal liberalism, this pandemic now seems to be fomenting it – and an inevitable backlash is building.

Yet again, the woke mob are wrecking their own cause by

misdirecting their focus and anger onto absurd targets that will only put people off supporting them. *Fawlty Towers*, one of Britain's greatest and most beloved comedies, is not the enemy here, wokies. But if you make it the enemy, you will lose the war.

This evening, it was revealed Nigel Farage has suddenly quit LBC after they told him they wouldn't be renewing his contract. Sources at the station said that black staff members were enraged by his comments on *GMB* and demanded management do something. I've always got on well personally with Nigel but, like our mutual friend Donald Trump, he has proved incapable of responding to the George Floyd murder with anything but inflammatory race-baiting antics.

Cancelling him won't resolve anything, though. If anything, it will just make him more popular.

Before I went to bed, I tweeted an urgent appeal. 'Memo to the world: don't let insane political correctness & absurd celebrity virtue-signalling destroy the very real & very powerful movement for an end to racial inequality & injustice since George Floyd's murder. Or nothing will change.'

FRIDAY 12 JUNE

Sir Winston Churchill's statue has had to be boarded up to stop people vandalising it, as have the statues near him of Gandhi and Mandela, and the Cenotaph too. This is what the world has come to: three of the greatest figures in history, and a memorial to hundreds of thousands of people who gave their lives to defend our freedom, needing to be hidden from view in case they offend people or become targets for attack. It will be an absolute tragedy if the extraordinary power and impact of the largely peaceful Black Lives Matter protests are tarnished by a small minority of fools intent on defacing or destroying iconic monuments of people who weren't perfect by any means, but whose actions changed the world for the better. For the love of God, make it stop.

SATURDAY 13 JUNE

As I feared, the attacks on Churchill's statue have given the far right the excuse they've been looking for to take on the Black Lives Matter movement. Thousands of drunken shaven-headed white yobs descended on London to 'defend Winston!' They fought with police, chanted patriotic songs and spat abuse at journalists. One idiot was even caught on camera urinating next to the memorial to hero cop PC Keith Palmer, who was murdered several years ago while protecting the public from a terrorist who attacked Westminster. He later claimed he didn't know that it was a memorial because he'd drunk 16 pints of beer. I doubt he even knew what day it was; all he knew was that he had to 'defend Winston!' from black people. Britain is teetering on the brink of a race war. It's a scary moment.

MONDAY 15 JUNE

A stunning picture, taken by Reuters photographer Dylan Martinez, has emerged of a Black Lives Matter protester carrying an injured white counter-protestor to safety yesterday as he was being badly beaten up by a furious mob.

The hero, personal trainer Patrick Hutchinson, had gone to the protest with four black security guard friends to help quell violence because they didn't want young black people to end up in jail. When he spotted the white man being set upon, he scooped him up over his shoulder and marched him away to safety as his friends formed a protective shield around them. Their collective actions almost certainly saved the man's life.

Hutchinson explained, 'I was thinking to myself – if the other three police officers, who were standing around when George Floyd was murdered, had thought about intervening and stopping their colleague from doing what he was doing, like what we did, George Floyd would be alive today still.' He added, 'I just want equality for all of us. At the moment the scales are unfairly balanced and I just want things to be fair, for my children and my grandchildren.'

They say actions speak louder than words, but Patrick Hutchinson's actions are matched by the power of his words. By saving a man completely opposed to everything he represents, and explaining so eloquently why he did it, he has sent an extraordinary message of unity to the world at a time when we most need it. For the first time in many weeks, I feel a surge of hope.

TUESDAY 16 JUNE

Another day, another hero. Marcus Rashford, the young black England and Manchester United football star, has forced the government into a U-turn over providing free £15-a-week meal vouchers for impoverished kids over the summer, given they won't be at school to be properly fed. Rashford, 22, posted a lengthy letter yesterday in which he politely but firmly articulated why this was so essential. He spoke from personal experience, having regularly gone hungry as a kid growing up in a large poor family in Manchester.

Initially, the government rebuffed his request. But we spent all morning hammering them about it on *GMB*, and social media also rose up to support Rashford – another example of where it can be a very powerful force for good when used appropriately – and the government eventually climbed down from its indefensible 'we won't feed hungry children' stance and agreed to fund the meals for 1.3 million young people.

'I don't even know what to say,' Rashford tweeted. 'Just look at what we can do when we come together, THIS is England in 2020.'

What was so impressive about his achievement is that he did it by staying calm, respectful and laser-focused on the issue, thus avoiding any of the angry, noisy and partisan political point-scoring currently deafening most debate. Footballers have been useful kicking-balls for the government during this pandemic. Matt Hancock lambasted them for not 'doing their bit' and demanded they take pay cuts – though he refused to take one himself. But ironically, Rashford has 'done his bit' by exposing the government for being heartless, and he's also shown us what can be done when we come together to right a wrong that should never be subject to partisan tribalism.

WEDNESDAY 17 JUNE

Marcus Rashford called in to *GMB* to thank us for our support – he'd been watching the show yesterday morning and felt our passionate demands for the government to listen to him had made a real difference. He revealed Boris Johnson had rung to congratulate him.

'It was a nice conversation,' he said. 'I wanted to have the opportunity to just thank him for understanding and changing his decision. He didn't have to, so it's definitely good. We've shown when we do work together we can change things.'

This is where we need to get back to as a society. Rashford's incredibly impressive civility and quiet determination, much like Captain Tom's, are in such marked contrast to all the shrieking culture-war noise, which is why his campaign resonated so strongly, and meant he got what he wanted in just 24 hours, surely the fastest government policy U-turn in history. There's a lesson for everyone who wants to effect real change: less noise and abuse, more thoughtfulness and respect. And, yes, I can learn from it too. I believe that getting angry towards obfuscating government ministers at the height of a pandemic is justified when their chronic ineptitude leads to people dying in droves, but Marcus Rashford has shown that agreement and compromise can be best achieved through civil discourse.

We also need less woke absurdity. A new report at Harvard University has discovered that 'trigger' warnings which alert over-sensitive snowflakes to potentially harmful content at the start of books and films may cause greater problems than no trigger warnings.

'We found that trigger warnings did not help trauma survivors brace themselves to face potentially upsetting content,' said Harvard University's Payton Jones, a doctoral candidate in clinical psychology and lead researcher in the study. 'In some cases, they made things worse.'

The obvious solution to this is to have trigger warnings for all trigger warnings.

FRIDAY 19 JUNE

Foreign Secretary Dominic Raab said in a radio interview today that taking the knee is a form of 'subjugation' that came from *Game of Thrones*. This was a spectacularly ignorant comment. Taking the knee has nothing to do with either subjugation or *Game of Thrones*. It was started by NFL star Colin Kaepernick, who protested against police brutality in America during the 2016 season by sitting while the national anthem was being played. After a conversation with former

Green Beret Nate Boyer, Kaepernick took the knee instead, which Boyer explained was done as a mark of respect for fallen heroes in the military.

The fact Raab doesn't know this, four years later, and after weeks of people talking about it since George Floyd's death led to people all over the world taking the knee, is unbelievable and shameful. But sadly, it confirms what I have suspected throughout this pandemic: we are currently being governed by the worst collection of shockingly inept ministers I can ever remember. Yes, they were hit with an unprecedented situation. But the reason they've failed so woefully to rise to the challenge is because they're basically, with one or two exceptions like Rishi Sunak, utterly useless.

SATURDAY 20 JUNE

A Facebook post purporting to be from tennis star Serena Williams has gone viral. In fact, it was posted by another, unknown, Serena Williams in America and she herself was re-posting the words of a friend named Gina Torres, who wrote, 'I'm sick of Covid-19, I'm sick of black vs. white, I'm sick of Democrats vs. Republican, I'm sick of gay vs. straight. I'm sick of Christian vs atheist. I'm REALLY sick of the media. I'm sick of no one being allowed to think what they want & feel what they feel without offending someone. I am sick of the nosey ass people who call the cops when anyone does anything they don't approve of. We're one race – the human race. You want to support President Trump. You do you [sic]? Your choice! You want to support Biden, fine, also your choice! You want to believe in God. Okay, believe in God. You want to believe in magical creatures that fly around and sprinkle fairy dust to make life better? Awesome, you do you. BUT stop thrusting your beliefs on others & not being able to deal with the fact that they don't have the same exact mind-set as you. [...] If you can't handle the fact that you may have a friend that has opposing views as you, then you are not any better than the bigots and the racists. I don't have to agree with everything you believe in to be a decent human being & your friend.'

I think this resonated with people so much because it's exactly what the vast majority of people actually feel. They're sick of the toxic tribalism and partisan hatred. Aren't we all, outside of the shrieking radical left and right extremists?

MONDAY 22 JUNE

A man named Alan Hawkes, from Saffron Walden in Essex, had a letter published in *The Times* today that read: 'Sir, there were several articles in Saturday's comment section with which I profoundly disagreed. Keep up the good work.' Halle-bloody-lujah.

Newspapers MUST be a fulcrum for disparate views, particularly during very controversial times with emotions running high.

When I was editor of the *Daily Mirror* during the Iraq War crisis, I regularly published pro-war pieces by Christopher Hitchens to counterbalance the paper's aggressive anti-war stance – because I knew many readers would agree with him, even if his words often enraged me.

TUESDAY 23 JUNE

Donald Trump should be preparing to pack his bags at the White House. It's hard to imagine a worse scenario for any incumbent president trying to secure re-election than his terrible handling of a global pandemic resulting in America suffering the world's worst coronavirus death toll and the US economy crashing to its worst levels since the Great Depression with 40 million job losses. Trump made things even worse when the country was engulfed by the worst race riots for 50 years, and he shamefully fuelled the fires with his shockingly tone-deaf and incendiary response to the country's rage at George Floyd's murder at the knee of a callous cop.

Any one of these fiascos would normally signal ballot box slaughter in election year. Yet somehow, unbelievably, Trump's opponents are once again doing everything in their power to wrestle another defeat from the jaws of seemingly inevitable victory. If you were scripting an escape route for Trump, it would involve exactly what is now happening: liberal protestors tearing down statues of America's greatest icons, liberal leaders allowing virtual anarchy on the streets to go unpunished and a dramatic intensifying of the absurdly self-defeating culture war nonsense that makes many Americans fear the very soul of their nation is being dismantled.

From a position of unprecedented weakness, Trump is now fighting back with his clunky but undeniably effective triple whammy 'America first' fist of patriotism, toughness and common sense. Or rather, he's being hauled off the ropes by his opponents losing their minds. This insanity has reached its peak over the past few days as protestors set about destroying monuments to some of America's most beloved historical figures.

In Portland, Oregon, they draped an American flag around a 100-year-old statue of the first US president, George Washington, set it on fire, pulled the statue down and then urinated on it. They said they did it because Washington owned slaves. That's true, he did. But he was also one of the Founding Fathers who established the United States of America with a determination to eradicate slavery, which then happened.

In San Francisco, protestors vandalised a statue of another former president, Ulysses S. Grant, the man who led the Union Army in defeating the Confederates in the Civil War. Again, they argued he was a slave owner. And again, that's true. But Grant was gifted one slave, despised the whole concept of having one and let him free within a year. He then wiped out the Ku Klux Klan by pushing legislation through Congress to prosecute them. And he appointed African-Americans to prominent government roles.

In another part of the same Golden Gate Park, hundreds more protestors tore down statues of Francis Scott Key, who wrote the lyrics to 'The Star-Spangled Banner', because he too owned slaves. This, again, is true. But he also represented a young black man suing Georgetown College for his freedom in the 1830s. And he wrote America's national anthem!

In Philadelphia, the statue of abolitionist Matthias Baldwin was attacked and sprayed with words like 'colonizer' and 'murderer'. Yet Baldwin was a very outspoken critic of slavery, fought for African-Americans to have the right to vote and founded a school in the city for black children.

The craziness has got so demented that author and activist Shaun King has even called for statues of Jesus Christ to be removed. 'I think the statues of the white European they claim is Jesus should also come down,' he tweeted. 'They are a form of white supremacy. Always have been.'

All of this, set against the backdrop of widespread looting and rioting during otherwise predominantly peaceful George Floyd protests, will have the opposite effect to the one the protestors claim to want. It won't persuade people to join their movement; it will turn them against it.

That's not to say all their arguments are wrong. I have no problem with statues of Confederacy leaders being removed. As *Washington Post* columnist Henry Olsen wrote yesterday,

'The Confederacy's vice president, Alexander Stephens, said in his "cornerstone speech", the Confederacy rested on "the great truth, that the negro is not equal to the white man; that slavery – subordination to the superior race – is his natural and normal condition". Monuments to this revolting sentiment have no place in a United States that is dedicated to the opposite principle – that all men are created equal.'

I think most Americans would support that. But to destroy monuments of great presidents, as with the defacing of Sir Winston Churchill's statue in London recently, actively alienates people from supporting the Black Lives Matter cause.

So, it will hinder, not help, the battle for racial equality and justice. The way for Democrats to win in November is simple: keep reminding the American people how badly Trump has handled the pandemic, how horrifically the economy has tanked and how atrociously he responded to George Floyd's murder. It's not difficult to paint a pretty accurate picture of a president who completely lost control of his country during its darkest hour, through his ineptitude, complacency, narcissism and chronic lack of empathy.

But nobody's talking about any of that right now. Instead, the news agenda is dominated by images of statues of beloved American icons being destroyed, and by lawless rioting and looting in cities all over the country. Trump said this week, 'The choice in 2020 is very simple. Do you want to bow before the left-wing mob or do you want to stand up tall and proud as Americans?' Whatever you think of him, this is a very effective campaign message.

In the run-up to the 2016 election, I regularly warned liberals that their strategy to beat Trump, based around constant self-righteous and often rankly hypocritical rage, wouldn't work. They ignored me, carried on screaming and lost. My message to liberals today remains the same: stop shrieking, stop indiscriminate self-harming statue toppling, stop virtue-signalling, stop pandering to ridiculous political correctness and provide America with a vision for the future that resonates better than Trump's increasingly dystopian ideal. It shouldn't be difficult to do this given the state of the country. But all I'm seeing is liberals committing political suicide.

As Anthony Scaramucci, Trump's former short-lived communications chief who's now become his biggest critic, told me on *Good Morning Britain* today, 'If they continue to tear down statues in the United States and continue to riot, that will play into the president's hands. As he searches for a campaign narrative right now, that narrative will be that people are trying to take away your cultural heritage. And he'll pit people against each other in a big culture war.'

Yes, he will. And it might work.

Wake up, liberals, before it's too late.

WEDNESDAY 24 JUNE

Is chess racist? Even as I write these words, my heart sinks. But an Australian radio show has become a global target for mockery after airing a segment asking that very question because a father tweeted that his child had asked him why the white pieces always move first in the game. The father apparently paused, 'aware of current cultural context', and wondered exactly how to answer. He didn't know if there was any racial background to the rule.

Of course there isn't. It was an entirely arbitrary decision made in the 1880s to standardise competition and had absolutely nothing to do with anyone's skin colour. But this is where wokery inevitably takes us – to ridiculous extremes where people feel compelled to see racism, or any other -ism, in absolutely everything. And all that does is annoy everyone, and prevent change happening. We have to stop this nonsense because all it does is fire up the racists.

Last night, a plane flew over the Manchester City v Burnley Premier League game, where the players wore the same #blacklivesmatter names on their shirts, with a banner saying, 'WHITE LIVES MATTER BURNLEY!'. As I tweeted, 'Let me try & help all the idiots foaming at the mouth today. 1) Black lives matter ... too. 2) Black lives matter ... as much. 3) Black lives matter ... so why are black people still treated as 2nd class citizens in many areas of society? Educate yourselves & demand equality.'

It got a huge response, mostly from people agreeing but also from a large number of people hurling abuse at me for being racist and 'anti-whites'. This debate is getting nastier.

MONDAY 29 JUNE

Shocking video footage has emerged of groups of elderly residents of Florida's retirement complex The Villages all screaming abuse at each other over Trump and Black Lives Matter. One of the pro-Trumpers, a white man in a golf cart, eventually shouts out, 'WHITE POWER! WHITE POWER!' Trump then retweeted this clip, saying: 'Thank you to the great people of The Villages. The Radical Left Do Nothing. Democrats will Fall in the Fall. Corrupt Joe is shot. See you soon!!'

Three hours later, his retweet was deleted but in that three hours, the world saw the president of the United States endorse a racist shrieking 'WHITE POWER!' I've no idea if Trump heard that part of the clip, but I don't care. He's the most powerful man in the world, and his retweets carry huge influence. As America continues to be split apart by racial tension since the George Floyd murder, the president continues to make things ten times worse.

The country desperately needs proper leadership, of the type that heals not divides. Like Dr Martin Luther King Jr, who said, 'Let us be dissatisfied until that day when nobody will shout "White Power!", when nobody will shout "Black Power!", but everybody will talk about God's power and human power.'

JULY

It's Not Black or White

WEDNESDAY 1 JULY

Twitter has announced it is replacing coding terms for more 'inclusive' terminology. The company explained, 'Inclusive language plays a critical role in fostering an environment where everyone belongs. At Twitter, the language we have been using in our code does not reflect our values as a company or represent the people we serve. We want to change that. #WordsMatter.'

Racism sensitivities will apparently be addressed by changing words like 'whitelist' to 'allowlist', 'blacklist' to 'denylist' and 'master/slave' to 'leader/follower'. Gender issues will be dealt with by changing 'guys' to 'folks', 'you all' or 'y'all' and 'man hours' to 'person hours' or 'engineer hours'. And mental health will be handled by changing 'sanity check' to 'quick check', 'confidence check' or 'coherence check', and 'dummy value' to 'placeholder value', just in case any dummies get upset.

It's great to see Twitter finally getting to grips with the appalling cesspit of vile, threatening, abusive crap that is pumped over its platform all day every day – by focusing on such comparatively trivial virtue-signalling nonsense. Yet again, the PC language cops get priority over censoring how we speak while a major social media platform does nothing to curb the appalling filth infecting its own site. As so often, it fell to Ricky Gervais to ask the obvious question. 'Why isn't this in Braille?' he tweeted.

THURSDAY 2 JULY

Facebook is facing a growing boycott from advertisers 'concerned' about its failure to deal with hateful material posted on its site. Coincidentally, I quit Facebook a few weeks ago. Not because I wanted to join the boycott, but because I've just got fed up of reading friends banging on about politics or spewing their bonkers corona conspiracy theories. I spend too much of my time immersed in that kind of noise at work and on Twitter to want even more of it on a platform that used to be a nice bit of friendly, sociable escapism from everyone shouting at each other.

I've also become increasingly concerned by the company's ongoing data security issues, and the creepy way adverts pop up on my Facebook page for stuff I've recently searched for on the internet, or even after I've been talking about something. None of this is what I signed up for all those innocent years ago. All I ever wanted from Facebook was a daily diet of happy smiling photos and posts of people whom I like enjoying themselves, to distract me from covering the often unrelentingly grim and toxic news cycle.

But the sad truth is that as Facebook has grown increasingly aggressive in the way it commercialises itself, so its users have become increasingly aggressive too, especially since two incredibly polarising events: Donald Trump's election win and the Brexit saga. And the coronavirus pandemic has sent this dynamic off the charts – turning almost everyone I know into angry amateur scientific and medical experts, all espousing their often woefully ill-informed opinions with the same intransigent certainty that they've applied to other issues in recent years, and all framing their arguments about the virus directly from the views they have about Trump or Brexit. It's been utterly exhausting to watch, and also very dispiriting.

But not as dispiriting as the renewed wokie-driven cancel culture that's returned with a vengeance since the despicable murder of George Floyd, with illiberal liberals unleashing a global wrecking ball on everything from monuments of beloved presidents to 'inappropriate' movies and TV shows – cancelling anyone and anything, dead or alive, that they can shame for perceived crimes against their woke world view. Now they've set their cancelling sights on Facebook, the world's biggest social media platform.

The 'Stop Hate for Profit' campaign – led by powerful liberal activist groups including the Anti-Defamation League, the National Association for the Advancement of Colored People (NAACP), Sleeping Giants, Color of Change, Free Press and Common Sense – asked 'large Facebook advertisers to show they will not support a company that puts profit over safety'. Their clarion call was swiftly met, with more than 160 companies agreeing to not buy ads on Facebook during the month of July. The firms include Unilever, Verizon, Honda, Magnolia Pictures, Levi's, Coca-Cola, Pepsi and Starbucks. Organisers are now working on getting European companies to join the boycott and have also urged regulators to take a hard stand on Facebook. The boycott has already cratered Facebook's stock price and the financial damage may get a lot worse very quickly. But what is it really about?

Coca-Cola made it clear why they were pulling their ads: 'There is no place for racism in the world and there is no place for racism on social media.' A laudable statement, we can all agree. There is undeniably some reprehensible material on Facebook, horrible, hateful stuff that should be removed the moment it's posted. But you should see some of the disgusting, hateful, threatening filth I get sent on Twitter, and, since George Floyd's killing, the blatant racism spewing into my feed from people seething about the notion of black lives mattering.

Twitter is spared a boycott by most of these firms because founder Jack Dorsey has started censoring President Trump's tweets and kicking infamous right-wing commentators like Katie Hopkins off the platform. Yet I don't see many hateful left-wing people, of which there are many, being censored or suspended on Twitter. It appears to be undeniably one rule for conservatives, another for liberals. Dorsey thus meets the 'woke' criteria for acceptable leadership and is spared cancellation. Whereas Facebook chief Mark Zuckerberg has tried to resist similar demands to clamp down on this kind of material, whichever side of the political divide it comes from – but will now apply warnings to some posts.

Explaining his position, Zuckerberg said in a live stream last week, 'We'll allow people to share this content to condemn it, just like we do with other problematic content, because this is an important part of how we discuss what's acceptable in our society – but we'll add a prompt to tell people that the content they're sharing may violate our policies.'

You can agree or disagree with Zuckerberg about this strategy, but one thing it's not is an attack on freedom of speech. In fact, it's the opposite; he believes so passionately in the principle of freedom of speech that he wants to allow views he personally despises to appear on his platform. And it's not like he does nothing about the problem of hateful material. Facebook removes around three million items of hate speech content around the world each month, 90 per cent of which is taken down even before being reported.

Frankly, I find Zuckerberg's position more honest than his critics give him credit for, especially with a crucial US election looming in November. Conservatives should not be unfairly targeted or silenced in the months leading up to it, not least because the left can be just as hateful, if not more so, than the right – just ask J.K. Rowling.

Much of the energy for this boycott comes from Facebook not censoring Trump. And some of his outbursts are clumsy and vile, as we saw yesterday when he tweeted then deleted a video depicting a man screaming 'WHITE POWER!' But Trump was elected by half the US population and 40 per cent still support him. Are we saying that their views just don't count – and their leader should be gagged? The way to stop Trump is through the ballot box in November, not through denying him his First Amendment rights.

And when it comes to incendiary acts, why do famous liberals invariably get a pass? Was Madonna suspended from any social media when she said she'd thought of blowing up the White House? No. Was Kathy Griffin suspended when she appeared with an image of Trump's bloodied severed head? No. But if a right-wing celebrity or media figure had done either of these things to Barack Obama, they'd have been gone in a flash, incinerated at the self-righteous altar of liberal outrage.

There's also an inherent deceit at heart of this boycott; these firms all want to massively cut back on their advertising spend anyway due to the crisis. This way, they can claim it is all being done for virtuous reasons, not financial necessity. Yet their newfound virtuous corporate halos come with large cracks. You can bet every dollar they're currently saving that they'll all come crawling back to Facebook once this temporary boycott ends, because they'll desperately need the gargantuan number of customers that Facebook brings them.

So this is a phoney war, not based on principle but fear. There's a growing terror circulating around every business and business leader that they'll be next for the ruthless woke chopping board. It doesn't take much to light the fire of public outrage in these intemperate times, but once it starts it's almost impossible to extinguish. What these firms are really doing, ironically, is bowing to a hate mob intent on destroying Facebook. And if this campaign succeeds, the campaigners will feel empowered to go after anyone else they fancy tossing on the woke bonfire.

This strikes me as a very dangerous moment in these pandemic-fuelled culture wars. What's at stake is basic freedom of speech. I don't personally want to be on Facebook anymore, but I will loudly defend its right to exist and not be subjected to this kind of bullying, hypocritical, cancel culture bullshit. Amid all this indignant rage at Mark Zuckerberg, ask yourself one question: how did we all get to see the horrific George Floyd murder that sparked this new global revolutionary zeal? It was posted on Facebook.

FRIDAY 3 JULY

Young people in the city of Tuscaloosa, Alabama are throwing Covid-19 parties featuring a competition where people who have coronavirus attend and the first person to get infected, and has the infection certified by a doctor, receives a payout from ticket sales. It sounds like a spoof – but local officials have confirmed it is tragically true. Nothing better illustrates the ignorance and arrogance of so many youngsters about the virus. They just don't care.

SATURDAY 4 JULY

Rachel Dolezal, the race-faker and former NAACP leader who was discovered to actually be white, says she feels 'vindicated' by the BLM movement. Dolezal, 42, who has now changed her name to Nkechi Diallo, still sees herself as black and wants to get involved once again in the push for social equality.

'Racially, I identify as human,' she told the *New York Post*, 'but culturally I identify as black. I do hope that we can rework the vocabulary. That's part of challenging the race world view. Overwhelmingly, most people I hear from are black or mixed or non-white in some way and a lot of people have said this is your moment, you're vindicated.'

This is classic wokie syndrome: even when it's obvious to everyone that you're wrong, just continue insisting you're right. In that respect, they are just like their nemesis, Donald Trump.

For those wondering how dangerous limitless self-identification can get, Rachel Dolezal is a perfect illustration. She was branch president of the NAACP chapter in Spokane, Washington from 2014 until June 2015, when she was forced to resign amid a scandal involving her racial identity. Ms Dolezal identified as a black woman and was lauded for it. There was just one problem with this: she's a white woman, born to two white parents. She's as black as me. Her gigantic lie was exposed when a local TV news crew turned up and asked her a simple question.

'Are you African-American?'

Dolezal froze in horror. 'I don't understand the question,' she replied, despite the question being one of the simplest ever posed to a human being.

The reporter put it another way: 'Are your parents white?'

Dolezal, knowing her game was up, ran away. As her story unravelled, it grew ever more outrageous. Her parents released pictures of their daughter as a blonde white girl and condemned her as a fraud. She was forced to quit the NAACP, was fired by a university where she lectured, lost her newspaper column and had to leave a police ombudsman commission. But the icing on her fibbing cake came when it emerged that she had once sued a university for racially discriminating against her BECAUSE SHE WAS WHITE!

Rather than simply apologise and disappear for a bit, as any normal person would do, Dolezal went on the attack, portraying herself as a victim of racism and sexism. She went on NBC's *Today* show, and was asked, 'When did you start deceiving people?'

'I do take exception to that,' she retorted, indignantly, 'because it's a little more complex than me answering a question of, "Are you black or white?"'

Well, it's not really that complex, is it? She's white, as her whole biological family confirms. It would be understandable for her to be confused if either of her parents were black, but they're not. They are resolutely, incontrovertibly white. The black man she claimed for years in interviews was her father is not actually her father. Her real father, as she well knew, is a white man named Larry. Her mother's also white. And her siblings are white. Therefore: SHE. IS. WHITE.

'It's more complex than it being true or false,' she blabbed on.

No, it's not, Rachel. It's really as simple as it being true or false, and your claim to be black is 100 per cent FALSE.

'I have a huge issue with blackface, this is not some freak "Birth of a Nation" mockery blackface performance,' she told *Today*, seemingly oblivious to the fact that this is the single greatest example of a mockery blackface performance in the history of Planet Earth: a perfectly white woman pretending to be black for decades, and using her fake skin colour to be a race campaigner.

Tendering her resignation, Ms Dolezal expressed the hope that she 'can drive at the core of definitions of race, ethnicity, culture, self-determination, personal agency and ultimately, empowerment'.

This was nonsense. The only thing she'd driven at is the core of contemptible falsehood, albeit in a very self-determined, personal way. Sitting in the audience for this farcical *Today* interview were her two sons: one, an adopted black boy called Izaiah, the other, another black boy called Franklin, conceived with her ex-husband, an African-American. 'Izaiah said, "You're my real mom," and for that to be something that is plausible, I certainly can't be seen as white and be Izaiah's mom,' Dolezal said.

So, every white person in the world who adopts a black child now has to identify themselves as black? This is the stuff of madness. Only, I don't think Rachel Dolezal is mad. I think she knew exactly what she was doing. She's a cold, calculating woman who thought she could make a good living for herself as a race activist. But only if she pretended to be black.

The deceit ran so deep and for so long that even close friends had no idea. Asked by the *Today* show to explain her skin colour, which has darkened considerably from when she was a lily-white young blonde teenager, she replied, 'I certainly don't stay out of the sun.'

In another interview, Dolezal claimed her non-existent black father had to flee the Deep South after he assaulted a police officer who was attacking him. She explained, 'My dad's exodus [was in] the great migration to the North from the Deep South, where they left on the midnight train because a white officer harassed and threatened and was about to beat my dad with a billy club, and he whipped round and slapped the officer to his knees.'

Warming to her great, whopping, brazen lie, she added, 'They got out of town because as a black family in the Deep South, if you had any kind of negative altercation with a white cop where you stood up for yourself, it was gonna go badly for you.'

Wow. A white woman pretending to be black, claiming her fake black dad had to escape the clutches of a white policeman who was going to kill him. What could be a more incendiary, inflammatory thing to say in race-torn America? And this from someone who when she was exposed was the leader of the local branch of the National Association for the Advancement of Colored People. The LEADER!

The NAACP said in a statement, 'One's racial identity is not a qualifying criteria nor disqualifying standard for NAACP leadership.' No, and it shouldn't be either. That would be racist. But what should be is *lying* about one's racial identity.

Rachel Dolezal's appalling act of deception deserved every heap of abuse that rained down on her head. But there was one positive thing to come out of her absurd, forked-tongue antics: I've rarely seen black and white Americans more united on any race issue. Everyone seemed to agree that the only statement this pathetically disingenuous wastrel should now release contains the following ten words: 'I'm Rachel Dolezal and I identify as a complete idiot.'

Yet to this day, she refuses to accept she's done anything wrong. 'There's no protected class for me,' she wailed to the *Guardian* newspaper. 'I'm this generic, ambiguous scapegoat for white people to call me a race traitor and take out their hostility on. And I'm a target for anger and pain about white people from the black community. It's like I'm the worst of all these worlds.' Well yes, she is. By pretending to be black, Rachel Dolezal betrayed everyone. Yet she remains totally unrepentant, insisting it's her right to identify as black if she so chooses, and saying she just wants to 'encourage people to be exactly who they are'. She even says that if people are allowed to identify as non-binary, gender-fluid, the same rules – or lack of them – should apply to race. 'It's very similar,' she said, 'in so far as: this is a category I'm born into, but this is really how I feel.'

In a sense, she's right. Self-identification means exactly what it says; you can identify as whatever the hell you like. But that doesn't mean the rest of us in the real world have to go along with it and we shouldn't be silenced by the woke brigade when we engage in debate about it. I don't respect Rachel Dolezal's right to be black because it's absolutely bloody ridiculous. If I suddenly said I was black, I would rightly be laughed out of town. Dolezal's woeful tale perfectly highlights why self-identification is such a dangerous thing.

WEDNESDAY 8 JULY

More than 150 writers, including J.K. Rowling, Salman Rushdie, Malcolm Gladwell, Martin Amis and Margaret Atwood, have signed an extraordinary letter published in *Harper's Magazine* pleading for an end to cancel culture. 'The forces of illiberalism are gaining strength throughout the world,' it read, 'and have a powerful ally in Donald Trump, who represents a real threat to democracy. But resistance must not be allowed to harden into its own brand of dogma or coercion – which right-wing demagogues are already exploiting. The democratic inclusion we want can be achieved only if we speak out against the intolerant climate that has set in on all sides.

'The free exchange of information and ideas, the lifeblood of a liberal society, is daily becoming more constricted. While we have come to expect this on the radical right, censoriousness is also spreading more widely in our culture: an intolerance of opposing views, a vogue for public shaming and ostracism, and the tendency to dissolve complex policy issues in a blinding moral certainty. We uphold the value of robust and even caustic counter-speech from all quarters. But it is now all too common to hear calls for swift and severe retribution in response to perceived transgressions of speech and thought. More troubling still, institutional leaders, in a spirit of panicked damage control, are delivering hasty and disproportionate punishments instead of considered reforms. Editors are fired for running controversial pieces; books are withdrawn for alleged inauthenticity; journalists are barred from writing on certain topics; professors are investigated for quoting works of literature in class; a researcher is fired for circulating a peer-reviewed academic study; and the heads of organisations are ousted for what are sometimes just clumsy mistakes. Whatever the arguments around each particular incident, the result has been to steadily narrow the boundaries of what can be said without the threat of reprisal. We are already paying the price in greater risk aversion among writers, artists, and journalists who fear for their livelihoods if they depart from the consensus, or even lack sufficient zeal in agreement.

'This stifling atmosphere will ultimately harm the most vital causes of our time. The restriction of debate, whether by a repressive government or an intolerant society, invariably hurts those who lack power and makes everyone less capable of democratic participation. The way to defeat bad ideas is by exposure, argument, and persuasion, not by trying to silence or wish them away. We refuse any false choice between justice and freedom, which cannot exist without each other. As writers we need a culture that leaves us room for experimentation, risk taking, and even mistakes. We need to preserve the possibility of good-faith disagreement without dire professional consequences. If we won't defend the very thing on which our work depends, we shouldn't expect the public or the state to defend it for us.'

I couldn't agree more. The letter writer, Thomas Chatterton Williams, explained to the *New York Times*: 'Donald Trump is the Canceller in Chief. But the correction of Trump's abuses cannot become an overcorrection that stifles the principles we believe in.'

Exactly.

Williams added, 'We're not just a bunch of old white guys sitting around writing this letter. It includes plenty of Black thinkers, Muslim thinkers, Jewish thinkers, people who are trans and gay, old and young, right-wing and left-wing. We believe these are values that are widespread and shared, and we wanted the list to reflect that.'

Rowling said she was 'very proud to sign this letter in defence of a foundational principle of a liberal society: open debate and freedom of thought and speech' and she compared the cancel culture epidemic as akin to the McCarthy years in America, saying, 'To quote the inimitable Lillian Hellman: "I cannot and will not cut my conscience to fit this year's fashions."'

Of course, there is an irony that some of the signatories, including Rowling, have been keen members of the Cancel Club for many years. But everyone should be allowed to repent their sins. I feel very encouraged by this letter.

It's always been clear to me that illiberal liberalism will only end when liberals themselves bring an end to it, and this seems a significant intervention by a large number of high-profile figures in the liberal world to say: ENOUGH. Is this the beginning of the end for wokery?

THURSDAY 9 JULY

I should have known better. All hell has broken loose over the letter. One of its signatories, transgender activist author Jennifer Finney Boylan, has now publicly recanted her support, saying she wasn't aware of who else was involved. She tweeted, 'I did not know who else had signed that letter. I thought I was endorsing a well-meaning, if vague, message against internet shaming. I did know Chomsky, Steinem, and Atwood were in, and I thought, good company. The consequences are mine to bear. I am so sorry.'

It quickly emerged that she was objecting to J.K. Rowling, for her views on transgenderism. Rowling hit back, tweeting Boylan to say, 'You're still following me, Jennifer. Be sure to publicly repent of your association with Goody Rowling before unfollowing and volunteer to operate the ducking stool next time, as penance.'

Another signatory demanded her name be removed. 'I do not endorse this @Harpersletter,' raged historian Kerri Greenidge. 'I am in contact with *Harper's* about a retraction.'

A third signatory, *Vox* journalist Matthew Yglesias, was publicly shamed by one of his colleagues for signing the letter. Emily VanDerWerff, a trans woman, said she was 'saddened' by Yglesias's involvement because the letter had been signed by 'several prominent anti-trans voices' – and it made her feel 'less safe' in their workplace.

So, a letter signed by liberals that was designed to end liberal cancel culture and censorship has exploded into a blazing firestorm that will probably lead to more people being censored and cancelled. The woke farce is complete.

TUESDAY 14 JULY

Extraordinary scenes at the *New York Times*, where top opinion writer Bari Weiss has abruptly resigned, claiming the paper has been consumed by intolerant wokies. 'Twitter is not on the masthead of the *New York Times*,' she wrote in a thunderous resignation letter, 'But Twitter has become its ultimate editor. As the ethics and mores of that platform have become those of the paper, the paper itself has increasingly become a kind of performance space. Stories are chosen and told in a way to satisfy the narrowest of audiences, rather than to allow a curious public to read about the world and then draw their own conclusions.'

Weiss, whom the *Washington Post* said cast herself 'as a centrist liberal concerned that far-left critiques stifled free speech', joined the paper in 2017 as part of editorial page editor James Bennet's desire to show the 'many shades of conservatism and many shades of liberalism'.

Ironically, Weiss's decision to leave came a few weeks after Bennet himself was forced to quit after publishing an op-ed by Senator Tom Cotton that called for troops to be used on the streets to quell rioting during protests over George Floyd's murder.

It was a very inflammatory view, but Cotton is an elected member of the US Senate and that is what he thinks. As such, his opinion is newsworthy, and I say that as someone who thinks his opinion is completely wrong. What followed next, though, was astonishing.

New York Times journalists rose up in outrage and demanded an explanation for why the op-ed had been allowed to run. Bennet posted his reasoning: 'The *Times* editorial board has forcefully defended the protests as patriotic and criticised the use of force, saying earlier today that police too often have responded with more violence – against protesters, journalists and bystanders. As part of our explorations of these issues, *Times Opinion* has published powerful arguments supporting protests, advocating fundamental change and criticizing police abuses. *Times Opinion* owes it to our readers to show them counter arguments, particularly those made by people in a position to set policy. We understand that many readers find Senator Cotton's argument painful, even dangerous. We believe that is one reason it requires public scrutiny and debate.'

This cut no ice with the paper's wokies.

'No and no and no – you've made one too many bad decisions and clearly should not have run this,' answered the *New York Times* film critic Manohla Dargis.

As the furore grew, Bennet was eventually fired, for publishing an opinion by a US senator that *New York Times* journalists didn't like. This was a shameful moment ... for the *New York Times*. A newsroom full of woke liberals rose up to silence an elected official's right to freedom of speech – and the paper's spineless editors and owners let them win. Freedom of speech has to mean just that: freedom to speak freely. By reacting the way it did, the *New York Times* behaved just like the Twitter cancel culture mob, and showed it only believes in free speech up to the point where its liberal journalists agree with it.

Bari Weiss, who had previously enraged colleagues by challenging aspects of the #MeToo movement and the Women's March, claimed 'my forays into Wrongthink have made me the subject of constant bullying by colleagues who disagree with my views'. She said some of them had called her 'a Nazi and a racist'.

Weiss added, 'What rules that remain at the *New York Times* are applied with extreme selectivity. If a person's ideology is in keeping with the new orthodoxy, they and their work remain unscrutinised. Everyone else lives in fear of the digital thunderdome. Online venom is excused so long as it is directed at the proper targets.'

Perhaps her most damning allegation came when she described a 'civil war inside the *New York Times* between the (mostly young) wokes and the (mostly 40+) liberals'.

In other words, this battle isn't even left v right.

It's liberals v wokies, a fight that is destroying liberalism.

Later today, another high-profile writer, Andrew Sullivan, announced he is leaving *New York Magazine* after many years. Sullivan, who describes himself as an 'anti-Trump conservative', said some staff and management believed that a writer who doesn't conform to critical theory (a Marxist-inspired movement that divides the world into two categories, the oppressed and the oppressors, and is now seen as the bedrock of wokeism) was harming co-workers 'merely by existing in the same virtual space'.

In his final column, he wrote, 'They seem to believe, and this is increasingly the orthodoxy in mainstream media, that any writer not actively committed to critical theory in questions of race, gender, sexual orientation, and gender identity is actively, physically harming co-workers merely by existing in the same virtual space. Actually *attacking*, and even mocking, critical theory's ideas and methods, as I have done continually in this space, is therefore out of sync with the values of Vox Media. That, to the best of my understanding, is why I'm out of here.'

Sullivan, who said he intended to vote for Joe Biden in the election, added, 'It seems to me that if this conservatism is so foul that many of my peers are embarrassed to be working at the same magazine, then I have no idea what version of conservatism could ever be tolerated. And that's fine. We have freedom of association in this country, and if the mainstream media want to cut ties with even moderate anti-Trump conservatives, because they won't bend the knee to critical theory's version of reality, that's their prerogative.'

It may be their prerogative but it's also preposterous.

As MSNBC host Joe Scarborough, a former Republican congressman who has become a leading anti-Trump voice, put it in a tweet response to the two resignations, 'I've told liberals for three decades that they're easier to beat in elections because of academia's left-wing bubble that protects liberal students from having to aggressively defend their views. Today, @ nytimes and @NYMag provided the same disservice to their readership. Grow up or be prepared to get routed by moderates and conservatives of all parties for years to come. The defeat of Donald Trump will no more be the "end of history" than was the election of Barack Obama. If you are too fragile to read one opinion column a week that unsettles you, then you are too weak to run a country.'

THURSDAY 16 JULY

I've announced the publication of this book and, exactly as I predicted when I started writing it, the instant hysterical reaction perfectly exemplifies why I needed to write it.

My launch tweet read simply, 'BREAKING: I'm delighted to announce my new book: WAKE UP – Why the "liberal" war on free speech is even more dangerous than Covid-19.'

'Oh good,' came the first sarcastic response, 'we don't have enough of these hysterical right-wing "we're under attack" books yet.'

The presumption I must be right wing to write a book about illiberal liberalism was further promoted by a musician with the Twitter name @BungleSharkfart, who calls himself 'a Centralist with no tolerance for self-serving ignorance' and raged, 'Yay just what the world wanted, more angry right-wing white man books about how their privilege has been taken away because they're ever so slightly put out ...'

One lonely voice of Twitter reason named Micky Dean politely explained, 'People can be critical of woke culture without being right-wing. Especially when woke culture attacks freedom of speech and limits open debate.' But he was drowned out by a cacophony of wokie outrage, much of it focusing on my skin colour.

Jade Azim, a self-acclaimed 'leftie-type writer' who apparently represents MPs' staff in Westminster, sniped, 'I want to know what's in the head of very wealthy famous white men when they think they're being silenced and get a book contract to talk about it.'

Of course, I've never thought I've been silenced – though many wokies have tried, often using allegations of non-existent bigotry to do so.

Some of the reaction to my book announcement followed a similar path. Natasha Roth-Rowland, a Middle East magazine editor, sneered, 'Being asked not to be racist is "a fate worse than death" is becoming its own book genre.'

Gay activist Benjamin Button, who wanted me sacked for challenging the BBC's decision to promote 100 genders to kids, said, 'Wake Up is exactly what so many minorities and oppressed people have done. They woke up to the bigotry and discrimination and smears that are peddled about and started calling for action to end them.'

If only it were that simple.

Some of my new post-Covid left-wing fans felt personally let down. 'Lazy politics Piers and you were doing so well,' said @MarkWelshyeds, 'There is no war on "free speech" but there is a war on "hate speech". The word liberals also means, in this sense, people of decency.'

Another, @mz_jnr, said, 'So basically why people should let bigoted people say and do whatever they want no matter how harmful or against the stand-point of the platforms which they stand on without accountability ... gotcha, nice one.'

A few people were bemused by the apparent hypocrisy of my argument, which they haven't actually read yet. 'To be clear,' said @stevieegg1978, 'you're taking time out from tweeting to 7.6 million followers, hosting a moderately successful TV show, and your *Daily Mail* columns, to complain you're [sic] free speech is being infringed, in the book you've just had published. Got it.'

And of course, Hitler made an appearance. 'Jesus,' tweeted @jigje1, 'this grift again. It's not a real problem Piers. Hitler was a great advocate for free speech when he was in opposition, most of the people supporting it now would have voted for him in.'

This message, in particular, said so much about the absurd way the debate on free speech has gone. The 'everyone who doesn't agree with me is a Nazi' attitude of so many wokies is not just outrageously offensive, it also ironically illustrates why this new illiberal liberalism is so fascist in its attitude.

Thankfully, there are some liberals other than me who get the dangers of all this, though. A man named Jeremy Tarling posted, 'As Christopher Hitchens said, "My own opinion is a very simple one: the right of others to free expression is part of my own. If someone's voice is silenced, then I am deprived of the right to hear."'

And the #BeKind brigade was well represented by @tetjerry who tweeted, 'Hope you won't get Covid in the meantime, 15 October is quite far away, and it could easily ruin the title.'

Ultimately, though, it was someone named @theiandemon who posed the most interesting question about the book. 'So, is this aimed at your pre-Covid Brexit right-wing Boris fans that you lost during Covid, or the left-leaning fans that backed your stance taking the government to task? Not sure there will be much centre ground in your fanbase for sales on this.'

There lies the problem.

There cannot be any centre ground.

Everything has to be tribal, based on partisan politics and a shocking erosion of free speech.

I gained right-wing Boris fans before the pandemic because I was a Remain-voting liberal who wanted the democratic vote to Brexit honoured and even voted Conservative to ensure it happened. This made me an enemy to extreme left-wingers, the Remoaner wokies, who refused to accept the result.

Then I harshly criticised Boris Johnson and his government for their dreadful handling of the coronavirus crisis and lost many of my newfound right-wing fans who were incapable of separating Brexit from Covid-19. In the process, I gained and regained new left-wing fans delighted by my apparent conversion back to the cause.

Yet the truth is, I'm just a reasonably liberal person who believes in democracy, freedom of speech and holding governments (of any persuasion) to account.

This book is therefore 'aimed' at anyone who thinks those things are a problem, and in particular people who call themselves liberals but behave in a very illiberal way.

CONCLUSION

Time to Wake Up

So, where are we? And more to the point, where are we headed? As I write, it's mid-July. Yet 2020 has already become one of the most dramatic, traumatic, life-changing years in modern history. I feel utterly exhausted, and all I've had to do is sit at a desk and harangue incompetent ministers. God knows how our health and care workers must feel, having worked so hard for so long in such unbelievably difficult and dangerous circumstances to stop people from dying – as colleagues died around them.

It's been such a weird, turbulent time. One that's left us all feeling very discombobulated. And the only certainty is that nothing seems certain anymore. All the things we took for granted before Covid-19 came along, all the freedoms we enjoyed, have been ripped away from us in a way that most of us have never experienced.

Coronavirus has been the ultimate test for us, the public, and for our leaders. Some, such as intensive care unit doctors and nurses, Captain Tom, Marcus Rashford and Jacinda Ardern, have covered themselves in glory. Others, like Madonna, the Beckhams, Boris Johnson and Donald Trump, have exposed themselves as woefully incapable of rising to this unprecedented challenge. But we are where we are now, and nobody's quite sure where that is, what it all means or how the hell it will all play out.

Tom Hanks summed it up well when he was asked by the *Guardian* how he thought America had handled the pandemic. 'Oh dear!' the actor sighed. 'I have nothing but question marks about the official position as well as the individual choice. There's really only three things everyone needs to do: wear a mask, social distance, wash your hands. I know societally it's been politicised, but I don't get it, man. I don't understand how anyone can put their foot down and say: "I don't have to do my part." That's all we have as human beings and that's all we have in the midst of the 19 different crises that we're facing right now, between Covid-19, worldwide economic disaster, what happened to George Floyd – the great reckoning that we're all going through. What do we have that we can have faith in? Well, we can have an understanding of yesterday, we can have a plan for today and we can have hope for forever, and that's it. That's my wisdom. It ain't much ... but is there anything else?'

I'm not sure there is. Though as another Tom, the great Captain, has shown, hope can take us a long way.

I started this year full of angst-ridden exasperation at the way the world seemed to be going completely nuts. The brutal tribal wars being waged over Brexit and the Trump presidency, combined with the often absurdly trivial but equally viciously fought culture war over political correctness, had turned us into a snarling beast of a society that preferred screaming abuse at each other to actually resolving our differences. Virtue-signalling, that ghastly, fraudulent curse of the modern age, enveloped every issue and rendered any genuinely democratic debate impossible.

Driving all this was wokery, the ferociously illiberal liberalism fuelled by social media that aims to shame, vilify, cancel and silence anyone who dares voice contrary opinions to the tightly controlled narrow woke world view. I found it all so infuriating. This was not liberalism as I knew it, or anything like it. It was a new form of fascism. And I strongly believed it was empowered by the fact the world had actually never been a better place to live – safer, healthier and more prosperous than at any time in recorded history. The lack of anything to really worry about had led a whole cosseted generation to create endless fake firestorms. Fuelled by social media echo chambers, we were eating ourselves alive.

But then came Covid-19, a deadly virus that swept across the entire world with a terrifying virulence causing panic, death and economic destruction. For a few brief weeks, as the world collectively reeled from this uniquely all-encompassing new threat to our very existence, everything changed. It seemed to give us all the short, sharp shock we perhaps needed to develop a proper perspective on life. Locked down in our homes like prisoners, we fell back on family and friends and local communities – and shunned spoilt, rich celebrities at the same speed we seemed to abandon the pointless culture wars.

Nobody, least of all me, cared about gender self-identity or vegan sausage rolls as our hospitals got overrun and our loved ones began to die. The pollution-devoid air got cleaner and nature bloomed, we walked and cycled where once we drove and crammed onto tin-can trains, and we learned to work from home without the hell of the daily commute and all the tensions of office politics.

I've never worked harder, yet nor have I enjoyed my downtime more. Yes, I missed pubs and restaurants. But I didn't miss flying all over the place, or the endless round of annoying meetings and social events I didn't really want to attend, or, if I'm honest, shaking hands with endless strangers or, worse, being hugged and over-enthusiastically kissed by them! By losing our freedoms, we gained other freedoms – the right to just stay at home and relax. And on Thursday nights, we began coming together to clap and cheer our health and care heroes on the frontline in a joyous, unifying display of heart-warming solidarity. By staying apart, we actually grew closer together than I can ever remember. We really were all in this together.

But then it all went horribly wrong.

I don't know when exactly, or why. Perhaps lockdown sent us all slightly mad, or perhaps the George Floyd murder sent many of us into a blind fury. But by the time summer arrived, the world seemed to regress into an even worse state of tribalism and nasty, intransigent partisanship. The new, kinder, more caring and united atmosphere was replaced by anger and division again. And wokery returned too, only more absurd and even more self-righteous than before.

Illiberal liberalism roared back with a vengeance, smashing down 'problematic' statues, cancelling movies and TV shows, launching witch-hunts at authors like J.K. Rowling for deviating from the woke view on gender, and igniting ridiculous debates like 'Is chess racist?' It's been so depressing. Far from the virus turning us into a better world, it seems to have had the complete opposite effect. We've regressed to screaming at each other again, agreeing about nothing, and cancelling everyone and everything.

And the more the wokies have shrieked and wrecked, the more they have given their right-wing opponents the excuse they needed to wage their own kind of culture war: the one that relies on liberals being so woefully intolerant that they play right into the hands of populists like Donald Trump. 'Look at these maniacs destroying everything you hold dear!' they cry, sadly with good reason.

So, it's not just been absurd to watch, it's also been nonsensically self-harming. The coronavirus and murder of George Floyd should have been two cataclysmic events that brought us all together to fight a deadly disease and the ongoing horror of racism. Instead, they've been hijacked by wokies and populists to inflame, polarise and destroy. The world now feels like an incendiary tinderbox ready to blow. And at the heart of it lies freedom of speech.

When I look back through my diary of this extraordinary period, I see it return again and again as the one burning issue that is causing so much of the controversy and division. In a nutshell, we've reached a point in history where to merely express an unpopular opinion, or tell an 'inappropriate' joke, can be enough to wipe out a lengthy, successful career and destroy a life. We've became a timid, mute, fearful society in which everyone must walk on constant eggshells for fear that they will be next for the social media pile-on and politically correct execution. And though there's no doubt that right-wing activists delight in creating merry tribal hell, there's also no doubt they absolutely love exploiting wokery for their own benefit.

That's why I've written this book from the point of view of a frustrated liberal and targeted my own side for attention and criticism, not the opposition. I've done so in the hope that liberals will finally wake up and understand why their pattern of behaviour in recent years has grown so utterly ridiculous and achieved the precise opposite of what they intended. The endless screaming, shaming and cancelling just doesn't work. It led to Brexit happening, against all the apparent odds, and it led to President Trump happening – again, against all apparent odds. And it has fuelled populism around the world as the 'silent majority' rebel against the 'noisy minority' that spends its entire time trying to tell everyone what to say, think and do – on pain of instant destruction.

What's most extraordinary is that many of the loudest wokies have zero self-awareness about their own culpability in all this. Actress Phillipa Soo tweeted, 'Cancel culture: If you are "cancelled" but do not wish to be, you must WORK to EARN back people's respect by owning up to the thing that cancelled you in the first place, LISTENING to others, EDUCATING yourself, and ADVOCATING on behalf of the people that you have offended/harmed.'

The arrogance of this statement is stupefying. What she means is that to avoid being cancelled, you have to agree with her and her woke friends about how to think and behave. Soo's self-righteous delusion is shared by James O'Brien, a popular and successful radio presenter, who wrote a book entitled *How to Be Right*. It was well named; it never crosses O'Brien's mind that he might not be right, or that anyone who disagrees with him might not automatically be a vile bigot. As cancel culture exploded in June/July, he tweeted, 'There's no actual "culture war", is there? It's just a new way of describing disagreements between people who hate racism & discrimination & people who love it. Meanwhile, "woke" has just replaced "politically correct" as the most pretentious way of saying "not a massive bigot".'

I chuckled when I read this, because of course it was the absolutely perfect illustration of woke illiberal liberalism. He just didn't understand that, or perhaps didn't want to understand it. In fact, he was so proud of his thought process that he made it his new pinned tweet.

I like James and think he's an excellent broadcaster, but he is part of the problem. He has no interest in doing anything but double and treble down on his own entrenched opinions and accuse anyone who doesn't blindly agree with him of being not only wrong but stupid, which is why they don't understand they're wrong. In that sense, he's like J.K. Rowling, who loved leading the woke cancel culture mob right to the point it turned on her for expressing opinions about transgenderism that the woke brigade didn't like. And, ironically, O'Brien's tweet about there being no cancel culture led to calls for *him* to be cancelled. It was fascinating to watch.

Dr Emma Hilton, a developmental biologist, replied to him, 'Someone tried to have me sacked for talking about "male" and "female" anatomy. No actual culture war?'

'I trust they failed,' O'Brien replied. 'People call for me to be sacked every day for saying words. Am I at war without realising it?'

Well, yes, James, you are. One of his fans named Cynthia then got involved, tweeting, 'James, I love you, I listen every day, but please don't trivialise this. Women professors like Emma are under constant attack for just stating facts.'

'I don't mean to trivialise anything,' he replied. 'I was thinking mostly of statues and racists when I wrote my tweet & am a bit surprised by the direction of some replies. Presumably, nobody would argue that Emma and her colleagues are on the same side as Donald Trump in this so-called "war"?'

To which a critical thinker blog writer named Andy Lewis answered, 'That is precisely what people do argue. If you stick up for the sex-based rights of women, or even defend the material & objective existence of women (as JKR did) you will be seen as being a Trump-supporting, less-than human, morally awful sub-human – & they will get you sacked.'

Lewis added, 'I would love to be in the position to say to him ... "You know what I am going to do here, don't you? I am going to ask you what the word 'woman' means."'

'You are in that position Andy!' exclaimed O'Brien. 'I'm incredibly confused and acutely conscious of the pain caused by holding any strong public position on this issue. But I don't believe that people with penises should be allowed into women only spaces. That's as far as I've got.'

Oh-oh … O'Brien had just pulled a J.K. Rowling, and that could only mean one thing. As Jonathan Pie tweeted, 'I have this weird feeling that James might start to believe in a culture war very soon.'

Within seconds, the transgender lobby came for O'Brien, and came for him hard. Transgender activist Paris Lees raged, 'Do you think I should be discriminated against? I've never discussed my privates publicly as it's no one else's business. Maybe I've had an operation, maybe I haven't. Should I be free to continue using the ladies as I have my entire adult life? Because I'll be honest, the fact we're even having this conversation is making me feel like I don't want to live in this country anymore. Who would police it? Are we gonna have people checking people's underwear before you're allowed in public loos? ID cards? How would a ban work?'

O'Brien was done for. He was now a TERF, and would therefore have to be shamed, vilified and cancelled as he was all day by other transgender activists. And irony of all ironies, many of those attacking him accused him of being too stupid to understand why he was wrong!

What O'Brien discovered the hard way is that cancel culture is a very real thing and it has little to do with the narrow prism of racism. I think most right-minded people would share the view that overt racists should be 'cancelled' in the way that historian David Starkey was cancelled in July for saying slavery wasn't genocide because 'so many damn blacks' survived.

Or when the grime artist Wylie went on a disgusting anti-Semitic tweet storm several weeks later. People like that should not be given platforms to air their repugnant views on social media, or on TV or through books and positions of authority at universities. But O'Brien is a not a racist, and I know he comes at the world from a good place, not a place of malevolence. It's just that he can't see why he is in any way to blame for the cancel culture mentality or the rise of illiberal liberalism.

Owen Jones, another left-wing firebrand, supported O'Brien's general view by saying, 'The "culture war" actually means minorities fighting for their rights on one side, and those fearful of the consequences of them succeeding on the other. "Being cancelled" all too often means "public figures being criticised on Twitter for things they've said". It's ill defined. Too often people seem to think freedom of speech means "saying things without being challenged by others who are also using their own freedom of speech".

But nobody's said that. What people like me say is that freedom of speech must be fiercely protected from attempts to shut it down, and that most of the attacks on freedom of speech now come from people claiming to be tolerant liberals.

I replied to him, 'Challenging opinions is perfectly fine & indeed essential in any democracy. But being "cancelled" for having an opinion is the very opposite of freedom of speech, it's suppression of free speech of the kind enforced by fascist dictators.'

'But that's exactly the point,' retorted Owen. 'Fascist dictators actually cancel people: they torture, imprison and murder people for having different opinions. That's not the same as people passionately expressing disagreement with things said by public figures.'

'Destroying people's careers & wrecking their lives,' I replied, 'for expressing opinions that the "woke" brigade don't like, is a form of fascism & it has to stop or it will destroy democracy.'

Owen then reminded me I had called for David Starkey to be banned from TV, after a previous racist outrage back in 2011, as evidence I am a hypocrite. But cancel culture is not about whether obvious racists should be given platforms. It's about potentially seeing your life and career turned upside down for expressing opinions that the woke brigade don't like, about anything. I'm lucky in that although there have been repeated attempts to 'cancel' me, including petitions to have me sacked, I've survived because I have strong-minded employers who refuse to bow to the mob, and I have a powerful TV, newspaper column and social media platform to fight fire with fire. That's why James O'Brien will survive his TERF war too.

But I've seen so many others go down with a whimper, trampled by furious wokies intent on destroying their careers and lives for having objectionable opinions.

This has to stop.

Cancel culture has to be cancelled.

It's not tolerant, or liberal.

It's intolerant and illiberal.

It's also poisonous.

People must be free to express honestly held opinions without the fear of losing everything, or democracy will die. Freedom of speech is a vital cornerstone of any strong democracy. It is the enemy of dictators, which is why it must be protected. But to protect it, liberals have to go back to being liberals, and that means listening to alternative voices and views, and respecting others' right to have a different opinion. As George Orwell said, 'If liberty means anything at all, it means the right to tell people what they do not want to hear.'

To illustrate just how bad this has all got, consider that a British MP, Labour's Nadia Whittome, actually wrote a column for the *Independent* in July about the transgender issue in which she said, 'We must not fetishise "debate" as though debate is itself an innocuous, neutral act. The very act of debate in these cases is an effective rollback of assumed equality and a foot in the door for doubt and hatred.'

In other words, we must all agree with her, or we're hateful.

I challenged Whittome by tweeting, 'Good grief. How can a democratically elected MP have such a dreadful view of debating? Even by woke standards this is absurd.'

To which she replied, 'In the past there were "debates" on allowing openly gay and bisexual people in the military. I clearly mention debate in this context: creating a debate about people's fundamental rights or equal status is a hostile act. Don't spin it to stoke a right-wing feeding frenzy.'

This was an extraordinary response on so many levels.

I replied to her, 'How were those rules changed without debate? How is *anything* ever changed without debate? What do you think goes on in Parliament all day every day? (Clue: debates.) Why do you assume only right-wing people find this kind of illiberal woke nonsense insane?'

But Ms Whittome didn't want to hear any of this. Her opinion on trans rights is the only acceptable one, and if anyone dares to debate it, they are automatically right-wing hate-mongers.

And this is a democratically elected member of Parliament!

Life, as we've discovered during the coronavirus crisis, is a precious thing. Our freedoms can be suddenly taken away from us in the flash of a global pandemic. But one freedom the virus couldn't take from us was the right to free speech. I was able to rant away at government ministers on *GMB* because I live in a democracy that enables journalists to do that. In countries like China, Russia or North Korea, I'd be dead by now. That's why Donald Trump is so wrong with his 'fake news' tirades and branding of the media as the 'enemy of the people'.

A free press, for all its flaws, is a vitally important cog in the wheel of proper democratic society.

I don't like being criticised, or being told my opinions suck, any more than anyone else. But I don't want people who disagree with me to be cancelled. I want to argue with them and try to change their minds. As Oscar Wilde said, 'I may not agree with you, but I will defend to the death your right to make an ass of yourself.'

The media, which should be fighting ferociously to defend the same right, doesn't help itself when it bows to the mob over freedom of speech. Watching a newspaper as prestigious and supposedly impartial as the *New York Times* surrender all pretence at objectivity, as it did over the Senator Cotton affair, made it clear that the threat to freedom of speech is very real and very dangerous.

Fortunately, some other media bosses are made of tougher stuff. When 280 members of staff at the *Wall Street Journal*, a rival of the *NYT*, signed a letter to their publisher several weeks later claiming it pushed 'misinformation' in the opinion pages, the paper's editorial board hit back saying it wouldn't 'wilt under cancel culture pressure' or yield to 'conformity and intolerance'. The board also reassured *WSJ* readers that it would continue to fight back against 'a culture of growing progressive conformity and intolerance'.

This is what needs to happen more: those who control the ability to actually enforce cancel culture refusing to surrender to woke mob rule.

I don't think freedom of speech has ever been more important, or under more threat. There seems to be a concerted effort to suppress any dissenting opinion that hasn't been signed off by the woke brigade. It's destroying democracy, and we have to understand that before it's too late. We also have to understand that the world can emerge from this crisis in a far better state if we WAKE UP and realise where we've been going so wrong. University students need to grow a pair and stop no-platforming people they don't like or agree with. Schools need to stop giving everyone participation prizes and explain to kids that, in life, you win and lose, so it's better to be prepared for both eventualities. The mental health debate needs to stop suggesting that teaching mental strength and resilience to kids is somehow wrong, and should in fact encourage ways to develop both. The PC language cops need to stop telling us how to speak or what words they find acceptable. The celebration of morbid obesity isn't going to help win the war on obesity – one which is so vital now given how much more vulnerable obese people are to the coronavirus – so let's stop celebrating morbidly obese models and thin-shaming stars who get themselves fit and healthy. Transgender activists need to stop screaming and cancelling everyone trying to protect women's rights, and work with those people to reach sensible compromises, especially over things like sport, prisons and toilets. Radical vegans need to stop taking out their 'hanger' on carnivores like me. I might even be persuaded to eat a little less meat if you make the vegan food tastier and stop shaming me all the time. Radical feminists need to stop berating men 24/7. We're not all diabolical, and most of us really do believe in gender equality. And let's cut all the damn hypocrisy. Those who scream loudest about 'respect' and 'tolerance' and 'kindness' tend to be the least respectful, tolerant and kind.

If you can't practise what you preach, then don't preach at all.

I don't absolve myself from blame for the place we've found ourselves in. I've got a massive platform through a daily TV show, widely read columns on one of the biggest newspaper websites in the world and 7.6 million Twitter followers – and I haven't always used it wisely. I've learned through this pandemic that there is a far greater pleasure to be derived from helping Captain Tom Moore raise millions or shining a light on migrant workers in the NHS than there is in waging war over vegan sausage rolls. There's also a far greater purpose in holding government ministers to account for their life-and-death decisions than there is in constantly sniping at the likes of Meghan Markle.

I've also learned that when we come together, we are demonstrably stronger than if we stand in our partisan tribes hurling abuse at each other. The key to unlocking all this tribal warfare is tolerance. For an example of what I mean, look no further than the England cricket team that won the World Cup in 2019.

The side contained two Muslim players, Moeen Ali and Adil Rashid, both of whom shun alcohol as part of their faith. This could have caused serious conflict had they chosen to enforce their beliefs onto the rest of the team and forbidden any alcohol to be used in their presence. But instead, they reached a sensible compromise. After all, English cricket and alcohol have been happy bedfellows for several centuries. When England won, and the jubilant non-Muslim players began spraying bottles of champagne around as they were handed the trophy, an equally jubilant Ali and Rashid ran off – away from the champagne and out of the picture.

Twitter promptly blew up in its usual faux outrage at this scene, with ignorant trolls appalled by what they perceived to be a 'lack of respect' from the Muslim stars. In fact, it was the complete opposite. As Man of the Match Ben Stokes explained in his book *On Fire*, 'It really grinded my gears when some keyboard warriors on social media made a thing of Moeen and Adil dashing out of the team line-up for the champagne spray moment. As a group, we know all about the religious beliefs of Mo and Rash, and the non-Muslims in the squad have the deepest respect for them, just as they respect us and our behaviours. We know they do not want to be around alcohol or come into contact with it. They never ask us to refrain from popping the champagne. And they never would. All they do ask is that we have a team picture first. They then rush stage left to avoid the spray. We have no problems, they have no problems. The only problem, I would say, belongs to the people that make a big deal of this.' Stokes added, 'We ask Mo and Rash all the time about certain aspects of their religion that we might be ignorant about and they happily inform us. We are proud to have Muslim players in our team and have a genuine curiosity about their lifestyles and routines. To suggest a lack of respect could not have been further from the truth. There is full respect going both ways.' To emphasise this, England's Dublin-born captain Eoin Morgan, when asked if England had enjoyed the 'luck of the Irish', replied, 'We also had Allah on our side.' This seemed such a sensible, mutually tolerant way to deal with a potentially sensitive issue. Ultimately, it all comes down, again, to basic common sense.

Finally, and most importantly, the woke brigade need to calm the f*ck down. I'm all for people waking up; in fact there's never been a more vital time to do it. But that doesn't need to be done via constant self-righteous hysteria, because apart from how annoying that approach is, it also rarely works. Look at the way a Syrian refugee hospital cleaner and a professional footballer got major government policies overturned through un-hysterical, non-self-righteous pleas for fairness that resonated with the public in such a powerful, effective way. The woke brigade need to stop finding absolutely everything offensive, focus on what actually matters, listen to alternative views and start bloody laughing again. They're all so damn serious about absolutely everything that they're sucking every vestige of fun out of life. I would put them all to this simple test: if you can't go to a British seaside resort and laugh at the saucy postcards, then you need to lighten up.

Laughter is always a better medicine than indignation. *The Times* columnist Janice Turner perfectly summed up the essential problem with wokery: 'This is a generation in which activism has become a lifestyle choice, an approved Halloween costume, a facet of fashion; behold how companies like *Vogue* to Dove rush to monetise "wokeness". It sets down rules – on what to eat, wear, say or behave – as detailed as a religious doctrine. Any infraction is treated as a heresy, while self-appointed Twitter purity tsars, like the actress Jameela Jamil, punish wrong-thinkers with the zeal of Iranian religious police attacking women who refuse to wear the hijab. Now a sinner or a non-believer can be cancelled. This bleak, dehumanising term hovers over any celebrity, it keeps them silent, watchful, effortlessly "woke".'

Surely the coronavirus has shown us that life can be very fragile, and snuffed away from us in a second? So, we may as well make the best of it, not behave like intolerant, humourless imbeciles.

The crisis has also shown us the power of real leadership. German Chancellor Angela Merkel, much derided during her lengthy tenure for being 'boring', rose brilliantly to the challenge of the pandemic precisely because she had the requisite 'boring' skills to keep the virus under control: she was a trained physicist who instantly recognised the danger and took it very seriously from the start. As a result, Germany has had massively fewer deaths than either the USA or UK, both run by populist bullshitters whose weaknesses got horribly exposed when it really mattered. 'We are seeing that the pandemic can't be fought with lies and disinformation,' Merkel said in a speech in July, 'and neither can it be with hatred and agitation. Fact-denying populism is being shown its limits. In a democracy, facts and transparency are needed.'

Yes, they are.

And empathy too.

Jacinda Ardern, the prime minister of New Zealand, is another leader who has rightly earned praise for the way she has handled the pandemic – combining firmness and decision-making authority with a real emotional feel for her people. Asked by the *Guardian* to summarise the most important qualities that have underpinned her leadership, she replied, 'Kindness and not being afraid to be kind, or to focus on, or be really driven by empathy. I think one of the sad things that I've seen in political leadership is – because we've placed over time so much emphasis on notions of assertiveness and strength – that we probably have assumed that it means you can't have those other qualities of kindness and empathy. And yet, when you think about all the big challenges that we face in the world, that's probably the quality we need the most. We need our leaders to be able to empathise with the circumstances of others; to empathise with the next generation that we're making decisions on behalf of. And if we focus only on being seen to be the strongest, most powerful person in the room, then I think we lose what we're meant to be here for. So I'm proudly focused on empathy, because you can be both empathetic and strong. [...] The world doesn't need a whole lot of massively thick-skinned politicians; they do need people who care.'

Another wise verdict came from a more surprising source, former British Prime Minister Theresa May – a lady not noted for the power of her rhetoric. 'Nationalism is no ally in this battle without borders,' she said in a piece for *The Times*. 'Against a backdrop of populist politics in many countries, the search for political solutions to economic and social challenges has become a competition of absolutes. A polarised politics has taken hold. It views the world through a prism of winners and losers and sees compromise and cooperation as signs of weakness. Lost is the idea that countries do better by working together to solve common problems, even if doing so sometimes means an apparent sacrifice of short-term benefit for the greater good. In its place is a cynical calculus: "I'm right and you're either with me or against me." This is the world which the pandemic hit.'

Coronavirus should have changed the world but it didn't. Not yet anyway. But it's not too late. As Neil deGrasse Tyson, the acclaimed astrophysicist, said, 'If a predatory enemy to our species can't unite everyone on Earth to fight it, I'm left wondering what hope remains for Civilisation.'

Unity is the biggest casualty of the wokery epidemic. We've forgotten how to argue without rancour, to reach compromise, and to forgive. Liberals need to go back to being liberals again. Then people really might wake up.

ACKNOWLEDGEMENTS

Writing a book is stressful enough in normal times, let alone during a global pandemic.

So, I feel a particularly heartfelt debt of gratitude to all those who have helped me get *Wake Up* produced in these unprecedented circumstances, led by the brilliant team at HarperCollins UK. From the moment I met with CEO Charlie Redmayne and Executive Publisher Oliver Malcolm in my local café last autumn to first discuss the idea for this book, I knew I was in perfect hands. Oli deserves particular praise for coming up with the concept for *Wake Up* and driving the writing process with such creative, challenging and perceptive oversight.

I'd also like to thank the following:

Zoe Berville, for her very thoughtful and skilful editing. It's never easy to edit a former editor's words but she and Oli did such a good job, I ended up applauding their barbaric cuts to my far longer first draft!

Tom Whiting, for his excellent copy-editing, and 'Professor' Mark Bolland, for his astute fact-checking.

Sales Director Tom Dunstan, Publicity Director Isabel Prodger, Marketing Communications Director Julie

MacBrayne, Publishing Operations Director Simon Gerratt, Production Director Monica Green, Senior Production Controller Alan Cracknell, Editorial Director (Audio) Fionnuala Barrett, Audio Assistant Charlotte Brown and Senior Legal Advisor Arthur Heard, for all their much-appreciated contributions.

My literary agent Eugenie Furniss at 42, for her peerless negotiating skills and, thanks to her expert proofreading eye, for saving me from myself.

Rob McGibbon, my oldest friend in journalism, for his ever-valuable advice and vital ideas for the text.

Martin Clarke, Publisher of DMG Media, for his wise counsel and expert stewardship of my dailymail.com columns, where many of my opinions in this book were first aired.

Mail on Sunday editor Ted Verity and the paper's *Event* magazine editor Andrew Davies, for their support with my weekly 'Insider' diary, which also provided me with much inspiration for *Wake Up*.

ITV's Director of Television Kevin Lygo and *Daytime* supremo Emma Gormley, for letting me be me on air, even when the inevitable flak flies!

Susanna Reid, my long-suffering TV wife, for providing the eloquent counter-arguments to everything I say.

All my other colleagues at *Good Morning Britain*, who have worked so hard in very testing conditions during the pandemic – especially Dr Hilary Jones, our ever-present voice of medical reason.

My exceptional PA, Tracey Chapman, for making sure everything in my life happens, on time.

Alan Goldman and Lisa Robinson, for managing my business affairs with such care and professionalism.

My parents, for their ongoing unequivocal love and support in all that I do.

My actual wife Celia, for her extraordinary patience, serenity and unexpectedly splendid lockdown cooking, which sustained me through many a long writing session.

And my four children, Spencer, Stanley, Bertie and Elise, for their frequent, passionate and often very damning critiques of my opinions! I wouldn't have it any other way.